KYOTO

KYOTO

A CULTURAL HISTORY

John Dougill

OXFORD
UNIVERSITY PRESS

2006

OXFORD
UNIVERSITY PRESS

Oxford University Press, Inc., publishes works that further
Oxford University's objective of excellence
in research, scholarship, and education.

Oxford   New York
Auckland   Cape Town   Dar es Salaam   Hong Kong   Karachi
Kuala Lumpur   Madrid   Melbourne   Mexico City   Nairobi
New Delhi   Shanghai   Taipei   Toronto

With offices in
Argentina   Austria   Brazil   Chile   Czech Republic   France   Greece
Guatemala   Hungary   Italy   Japan   Poland   Portugal   Singapore
South Korea   Switzerland   Thailand   Turkey   Ukraine   Vietnam

Published by Oxford University Press, Inc.
198 Madison Avenue, New York, New York 10016

www.oup.com

Oxford is a registered trademark of Oxford University Press

Co-published in Great Britain by Signal Books

Library of Congress Cataloging-in-Publication Data
Dougill, John.
Kyoto : a cultural history / John Dougill.
   p. cm. — (Cityscapes)
Includes bibliographical references and index.
ISBN-13 978-0-19-530137-3; 978-0-19-530138-0 (pbk.)
[etc.]
1. Kyoto (Japan)—History.   I. Title.   II. Series.
DS897.K857D68 2005
952'.1864—dc22   2005049875

9 8 7 6 5

Printed in the United States of America
on acid-free paper

Foreword

Benjamin Disraeli once wrote: "London—a nation, not a city." If this is true of England's major metropolis, it is equally true of Japan's old capital—Kyoto. A dominant municipality in its own right, this city at the same time reflects all of Japan, its history, its politics, its art. To understand Kyoto is to understand the land itself.

But how best to present this complicated, history-layered, intricate and complex place? John Dougill's way is both lucid and intelligible. Rather than creating a straightforward history, he has (following the idea of "imagination" suggested in the series title) provided a thematic approach, with chapters ordered chronologically about such topics as "City of Genji", "City of Zen," etc. The varied aspects of the city are explored within a sequential narrative that avoids both the topographically orientated guide-book approach, and the political narration of the straightforward history. I know of only one other volume that has similarly preserved the varied narrative of Kyoto. This is Gouveneur Mosher's estimable *Kyoto: A Contemplative Guide*, now long out of print.

The approaches of the two authors are otherwise quite different. Dougill is the more inclusive; he incorporates everything that the reader might expect and then goes on to include more. Thus we learn that the great period for court ladies writing their journals lasted for just three hundred years and that the last (Lady Nijo's) was completed "long before Geoffrey Chaucer had even got started." We also learn that haiku is abetted in its certain elusiveness "by the tendency of Japanese sentences to dispense with subjects." Indeed, "according to linguists, some seventy percent of spoken Japanese and fifty percent of the written language does without subjects." Japanese decorative dragons, we read, are distinguished by having three claws, while those of Chinese origin have five. We even learn which Kyoto temple served as set for the derring-do of Tom Cruise in *The Last Samurai*—it was the Chion-in.

It is through such information that not merely the fact itself but also its context is revealed. All of the famous places (Golden Pavilion, Silver Pavilion, Rock Garden) are there as well as many others less-known, such as Enryaku-ji on Mount Hiei. Here, the place and its history are discussed and illustrated by extracts from various early chronicles before Dougill goes on to give the fullest account I know of the *ajari*. This term is usually translated as "living saint" and refers to those adepts who endure the extreme of Tendai's asceticism. Ninety days of chanting with just two hours of sleep a night (only in lotus position), with only two toilet breaks a day. At the same time, continual chanting of the names of the three thousand Buddhas with a full prostration for each. And that's the easy part—it is all uphill from there.

By mixing past and present, Dougill gives us Kyoto's historical particularities and at the same time can suggest their resonances. The result is a true cultural history—and one which is unusually well balanced.

The Edo period is frankly described as "the world's most successful example of totalitarianism." The tea-culture of medieval Japan is found to be unusually important; in fact, a whole chapter is devoted to it because "a study of Kyoto without it would be like leaving the jazz out of New Orleans."

Supporting this mass of information are quotations from ancient texts, from the *Genji*, from Kawabata and Tanizaki, and from the movies. At the same time, insight is given into certain Kyoto attitudes. One is the assumed exclusivity of the place (the Boston of Japan?). The author writes "Go for the weekend to Osaka, or worse Tokyo, and you feel like a country bumpkin out among the bright lights." Behind the diffident pose stands the assumed elitist, the exclusive and insular inhabitant, a social role which, when exercised, afflicts both the native and the temporary Kyotoite. I know some foreign residents who profess to loathe Tokyo and, in fact, never visit.

Of course, counter to such traditional assumptions, is the fact that—like everywhere else—Kyoto is rapidly changing. It is true that much has been lost. Alan Booth wrote that "when you view Kyoto from any point of vantage . . . its ugliness can make you weep." Alex Kerr called the callous Kyoto Tower "a stake through the heart," and proclaimed that "Kyoto hates Kyoto."

True as this may be, Kyoto culture is still centuries deep and is only slowly being eroded. Besides (and this is Dougill's perspective) such change is not only inevitable, but also "good." The spectacle of change supports the Buddhist notion that life is in eternal flux and, in any event (as Edward Seidensticker has sagely observed): "The relationship between tradition and change in Japan has always been complicated by the fact that change is in itself a tradition."

In this book John Dougill gives us a living city that is, at the same time, an exemplar for its country, a gorgeous historical chronicle, and a container for culture as utilitarian and form-follows-function as any of the arts described.

Donald Richie
Tokyo, Summer 2005

Preface and Acknowledgments

"Kyoto's elusiveness might be its very essence."
Sen Souoku, head of Mushanokoji tea school

I first came to Kyoto when travelling round the world in 1975. I was entranced by white-faced elevator girls and the bird-sounds broadcast in underground shopping malls. The highlight of my stay was the Daimonji festival, at which spirits of the dead returned by firelight to otherworldly abodes. Shortly afterwards I had an epiphany while walking uphill to a temple, and realized that what I was seeking on my travels lay not without but within. Cherishing this insight, I journeyed on to complete the circle and return to the beginning from which I had set out. "The end is where we start from," noted T. S. Eliot:

> *We shall not cease from exploration*
> *And the end of our exploring*
> *Will be to arrive where we started*
> *And know the place for the first time.*

The next time I came to Kyoto was twelve years later. In the meantime I had set up home in Oxford, a city I had grown to love, but a combination of teacher burn-out and a Sagittarian lust for adventure took me off to a university job in Kanazawa on the Japan Sea. At weekends I would visit Kyoto and revel in the cultural opportunities it afforded. I walked the length of its hills, went to *gaijin* talent shows, and visited some of the famous sights. During the week I would lie on the floor of my Kanazawa flat, where I felt cut off from the mainstream, and dreamed of getting a job there.

In 1994, the 1200th anniversary of Kyoto, my dream came true. Now I feel as if I am living a charmed life. My apartment looks over the length of the Eastern Hills, and the rays of the rising sun come seeking me out each morning. On the other side there are views over the ancient woods of Shimogamo Shrine, here before the city was ever conceived, and beyond that to the sunsets over the Western Hills.

Few cities can compare with the wealth of Kyoto's treasures. The city's tourist office lists 17 World Heritage Sites, 90 gardens, 140 museums and galleries, 177 festivals, 471 notable temples and shrines, as well as 263 other tourist sights—and let us not forget the 82 special trees and the rolling schedule of seasonal flowers, for nature-appreciation is also part of Kyoto's rich heritage.

It is not the quantity, however, but the stunning quality that puts the city up there with the greatest in the world. In preparation for writing this book, I have been going out every weekend and ticking off one breath-taking item after another. There seems little danger of exhausting the list. Take the large temples, for example, each of whose many sub-temples may contain a treasured object or an exquisite garden. It seems that there are always special showings—once a year, once every three years, or even, as with a garden I visited only the other day, once in a hundred years.

It has been said that if Japan were a human being, then Tokyo would be its brain, Osaka its stomach, and Kyoto the heart. Where better to live than in the "heart" of the culture? It has been my good fortune to spend my working life in such a city, while continuing to return in the summer vacations to Oxford. To divide one's time in this way between these two great cradles of creativity is a pleasure. To write of one while being published in the other is nothing less than a privilege.

✳ ✳ ✳

This book could not have been completed without the input of several people to whom I would like to express gratitude, particularly those who were kind enough to read through parts or all of my manuscript. Risa Kotera gave me the benefit of her shrewd insights, and Katsura Miyahara provided expertise in art matters. For the chapter on Buddhism I was helped by Martin Repp of the NCC Centre for the Study of Religions, for that on Zen by Norman Waddell of Otani University, and for the section on Amidism by Galen Amstutz of Ryukoku University. In meeting the ajari, I was helped by Yuko Yuasa and Matsuura san. In tea matters I had valuable feedback from the "chajin" Brad Croft and the tea master, Jack Convery. For the chapter on geisha the Gion connoisseur

Peter Macintosh was of great help: see www.kyotosightsandnights.com. Christopher Herron accompanied me on several outings, and taught me much about Japanese gardens. Ian Roepke generously allowed me to look through back copies of the monthly *Kyoto Visitors Guide*, an excellent publication by a true lover of Kyoto. I should also like to thank my colleagues at Ryukoku University, acknowledged experts in their fields, whom I have bombarded with annoying questions. They include Professors Itoi, Takeda, Higashinaka, Kojima, Kusaka, Kida, Tsuzuki, Asada, and Miyama, as well as Michael Lazarin, Stephen Wolfe, and Tom Wright. Last but certainly not least, I would like to thank those with whom I have spent many happy hours exploring Kyoto's backways and discussing cultural oddities. These include Masayo Repp, Kazuko Ogura, the Kyoto tourguide Paul Satoh, and Yuki Hamamura. Finally, a special word of appreciation to my "personal assistant" Yuriko Suzuki. To all of the above, and to the many other Kyoto citizens who have helped in various ways, my very best thanks.

Like others who have written on Japan, I owe an enormous debt to the writings of Donald Keene, in particular the magisterial series published by Columbia University Press, which includes *Seeds in the Heart*, *World Within Walls*, and *Dawn to the West*. Quotations I have drawn from these include the passage by Ki no Tsurayuki, poems by Komachi, the passage by Norinaga, the extract from *Hojoki* by Kamo no Chomei, the translation from Asai Ryoi about the floating world, and extracts from Basho's essay on *The Unreal Hut*. The passage from Kukai is taken from Kosei Publishing's *Shapers of Japanese Buddhism*, ed. Yusen Kashiwahara and Koyu Sonoda. Michinaga's poem is from a translation by H. Paul Varley in *Japanese Culture*, University of Hawaii Press. Quotations from Shonagon's *Pillow Book* are from the Ivan Morris translation published by Penguin. The Izumi Shikibu poems about hair and dying are translated by Thomas Fitzsimmons; the poem about the dewdrop not staying long is taken from Jane Hirschfield and Mariko Artani in *The Ink Dark Moon*. Saigyo's poem about remaining in the capital too long is translated by Burton Watson, and that about learning to manage loneliness is by W. R. LaFleur. The quotations from Kamo no Chomei's *Hojoki* are taken from A. L. Sadler's translation, *Ten Foot Square Hut*, published by Tuttle, as is the passage from *The Tale of Heike*. Lines from the Noh play *Sotoba Komachi* are translated by Sam Huston Brock, while the lines from Inaba-do are from Don Kenny's *The Kyogen Book* published by *The Japan Times*. The quotations from *Gossamer Years* are from a translation by Edward Seidensticker. Passages from Saikaku are taken from the translation by Kenji Hamada in Tuttle's *The Life of an Amorous Man*. The haiku by Buson is taken from *Haiku Master Buson* by Yuki Sawa and Edith Shiffert, published by Heian International. Passages from Tanizaki's *The Key* are from the Tuttle translation by Howard Hibbet, and that from *In Praise of Shadows* is translated by Thomas J. Harper and Edward Seidensticker in Leete's Island Books. Quotations from Mishima's *The Temple of the Golden Pavilion* are translated by Ivan Morris in the Tuttle edition; and those from Kawabata's *The Old Capital* are from J. Martin Holman's translation in a North Point Press publication. The Pico Iyer passage comes from *The Lady and the Monk*, published by Bodley Head in London.

Notes

Names are written in the Japanese way, with the family name first followed by the given name. A glossary of Japanese terms can be found as an appendix.

The word "shrine" is used for Shinto, and "temple" for Buddhist places of worship. Temple names are written with a hyphen to help identify them: To-ji, Nanzen-ji, Myoshin-ji, etc. (-ji means "temple").

The book covers the following historical periods:

1) **Heian (794–1186)** An aristocratic age with rule by the emperor from Heian-kyo, the original name for Kyoto.

2) **Kamakura (1186–1333)** Rule by military rulers, or shogun, from Kamakura (near present-day Tokyo). It marks the coming to power of the samurai.

3) **Muromachi (1333–1573)** Rule from Kyoto by the Ashikaga dynasty. For the final hundred years, central power collapsed in a Period of Warring States, or Sengoku (1467–1568).

4) **Azuchi-Momoyama (1573–1603)** Unification of the country by the warlords Nobunaga Oda and Hideyoshi Toyotomi. Foreigners arrive in Japan, and Hideyoshi attacks Korea.

5) **Edo (1603–1867)** An age of isolationism with rule by the Tokugawa dynasty from Edo (now Tokyo). Perry's "Black ships" arrive from the US in 1853 to demand the opening of the country.

6) **Meiji (1868–1912)** Restoration of the emperor and end of samurai rule. Removal of the capital to Tokyo, and a period of rapid modernization with many Western influences.

7) **Taisho** (**1912–1926**) Industrial growth, reinforcement of imperialism, and the Great Tokyo Earthquake of 1923.

8) **Showa** (**1926–1989**) Expansionism in China and Korea; militarism at home; American occupation following the Second World War; and a post-war "economic miracle".

Contents

Foreword by Donald Richie   v

Preface and Acknowledgments   ix

Notes   xiii

Maps   xvii

Chapter One: City of Kammu (Heian)   1

A New Beginning   1
Spirit of Place   5
Spirit of the Age   9
Court Verse   12

The Poet Beauty   14
The Courtly Lover   15
The Grand Wizard   17

Chapter Two: City of Genji (Heian)   20

The Cult of Beauty   20
The Pursuit of Love   23
Pillow Talk   26;

Poet of Passion   28
The Shining Prince   30
Postscript   36

Chapter Three: City of Buddhism (Heian-Kamakura)   37

Religious Syncretism   37
Tendai Eclecticism   40
Living Saints   43
Shingon Esotericism   46

Amidism   48
Pure Land Devotion   54
True Pure Land Devotion   57

Chapter Four: City of Heike (Heian-Kamakura)   60

Epic Origins   60
The Tyrant   61
The Hero   63
The Tragic
Female   66

The Poet Wanderer   67
Court Verse Revisited   70
Chomei's Hut   71
Kenko's Idleness   73

Chapter Five: City of Zen (Kamakura-Muromachi)   76

The Wordless Way   76
Constructs   81
The Wild Man   85

The Art of Zen   88
Dry Landscapes   91

Chapter Six: City of Noh (Muromachi)   96

Torchlight Drama   96
Noh Genius   97
The Repertory   100
The Art of Noh   101

Past and Future   104
Comic Interlude   105
Moral Skits   107

Chapter Seven: City of Unification (Azuchi-Momoyama)   109

The Strong Man   109
The Second Founder   112
Decorative Art   117

Art Schools   119
Picturing Kyoto   122

Chapter Eight: City of Tea (Momoyama)   124

Tea Spirit   124
Tea Master   128
Tea Garden   133

Tea Room   135
Tea Art   139

Chapter Nine: City of Tradition (Edo)   143

A Military Touch   143
Heian Revival   148
Art Sublime   150
The Floating World   153

Haiku Master   156
The Literati   159
Capital Crafts   161
Edo Ends   166

Chapter Ten: City of Geisha (Edo)   173

City of Geisha   173
A Work of Art   173
Pleasure Quarters   176
A New Profession   180

The Flower Districts   182
Gion Walking   186
Fact and Fiction   190

Chapter Eleven: City of Japaneseness (Meiji and after)   197

Reinvention   197
The Janus City   200
War Survivor   202
The Japanese Hollywood   204
Kurosawa's Gate   206
Mizoguchi's City   208

Tanizaki's Key   210
Mishima's Golden Pavilion   214
Kawabata's Old Capital   216
The Modern Metropolis   219
Culinary Capital   223

Further Reading   227

Glossary   229

Key Historical Dates   233

Index of Literary & Historical Names   237

Index of Places   241

Key to Main Map of Kyoto

● PLACES OF INTEREST	GRID REF
Fushimi-Momoyama Castle	E-7
Gion	E-4
Gojo Bridge	E-4
Gosho (Former Imperial Palace)	D-3
Katsura Imperial Villa	C-5
Kyoto National Museum	E-4
Mushanokoji (Tea School)	D-3
Nijo Castle	D-3
Omotesenke (Tea School)	D-3
Pontocho	D-2
Ryoan-ji (Dry Landscape Garden)	E-3/4
Sanjusangedo	C-2
Saiho-ji (Moss Garden)	E-4
Sanjo Bridge	B-5
Shijo Bridge	E-3
Shimabara	E-4
Shisendo	D-4
Shugakuin Imperial Villa	F-2
Urasenke (Tea School)	D-2

■ TEMPLES	GRID REF
Chion-in	E-4
Chiskaku-in	E-4
Daigo-ji	G-6
Daikaku-ji	A-3
Daitoku-ji	D-2
Eikan-do	F-3
Ginkaku-ji (Silver Temple)	E-4
Higashi-Hongan-ji	D-3
Hokyo-ji	D-2
Honen-in	F-3
Jurin-ji (Narihira Temple)	A-6
Kinkaku-ji (Golden Temple)	C-2
Kiyomizu	E-4
Kodai-ji	E-4
Koryu-ji	B-3
Mibudera	D-4
Myoshin-ji	C-3
Nanzen-ji	F-3
Ninna-ji	C-2
Nishi-Hongan-ji	D-4
Ryoan-ji	C-2
Saiho-ji (Koke-dera) (Moss Garden)	B-4
Seiryo-ji	A-3
Senbon Emma-do	D-2
Sennyu-ji	E-5
Shokoku-ji	D-2
Shoren-in	E-3
Tennyu-ji	A-3
Tofuku-ji	E-5
To-ji	D-5
Zuishin-in	F-6

□ SHRINES	GRID REF
Fushimi-Inari	E-5
Heian	E-3
Imamiya	D-2
Kamigamo	D-1
Kenkun	D-2
Kitano-Tenmangu	C-2
Shimogamo	E-2
Yasaka	E-4

● OUTSIDE KYOTO	GRID REF
Biwa, Lake	H-3
Ishiyama	H-4
Kameoka	A-3
Kurama	E-1
Nagoya	H-4
Nara	E-7
Ohara	F-1
Osaka	C-7
Otsu	H-3
Takao	A-2
Tokyo	H-4
Uji	G-7

Original Plan of Heian-kyo

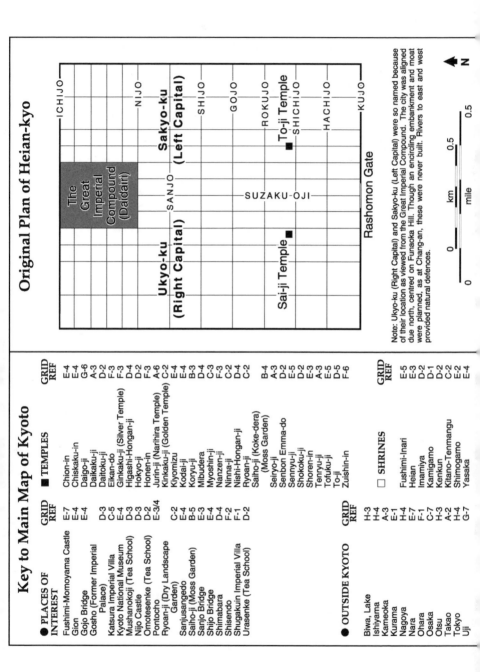

Note: Ukyo-ku (Right Capital) and Sakyo-ku (Left Capital) were so named because of their location as viewed from the Great Imperial Compound. The city was aligned due north, centred on Funaoka Hill. Though an encircling embankment and moat were planned, as at Chang-an, these were never built. Rivers to east and west provided natural defences.

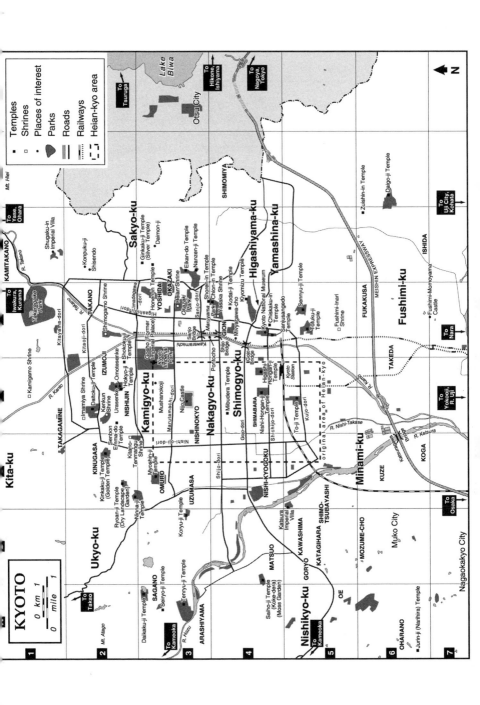

KYOTO

Chapter One
CITY OF KAMMU

A New Beginning

Great cities are often endowed with creation myths. Kyoto has no need of such glorifying fiction, for the facts of its founding are extraordinary enough. It was born of a desire to escape the curse of a former capital, and the site was chosen on a hunting expedition. The positioning was aligned by geomancy, and the layout modelled after the fabled capital of China. Along the central axis ran a massive boulevard thought to have been the widest in the world. The new capital was named Heian-kyo in a poetry contest and the meaning, "City of Peace and Tranquillity," proved apt. For three centuries there was virtually no violence, not even capital punishment. It remained the capital for over a thousand years.

In earlier times, the custom had been of the periodic moving of the capital. Disasters were ascribed to the presence of evil, the remedy for which was removal. The death of an emperor would initiate relocation, as might floods, disease, earthquakes and failed harvests. It not only provided escape from defilement, but enabled a fresh start by a new administration.

By the eighth century the expenses involved in such mobility had become prohibitive, and in 710 Japan's first permanent capital was set up in Nara, some thirty miles south of Kyoto. Such was the situation when Emperor Kammu (737-806) came to the throne in 781. According to tradition, he was the fiftieth emperor in direct succession from the sun-goddess. He had not expected to come to power, for he had Korean ancestry on his mother's side, thereby polluting the "purity" of the imperial line.

Kammu proved himself a vigorous leader and is numbered among "the three greatest emperors" of Japanese history. His reign of twenty-six years was one of the longest of the age, and among his achievements were reform of the administrative system, auditing of the tax registers and control of the north. A pamphlet issued by Heian Shrine sums up his achievements this way:

During the 25 years of his reign, Emperor Kammu reformed the legal system, provided help for the needy, encouraged culture and learning, reorganized the provincial administrative system and promoted trade with other countries. He thus contributed immeasurably to the development of the nation. Thereafter, Kyoto flourished for more than 1000 years.

One of Kammu's preoccupations was the straitjacket of Nara Buddhism. Like the cardinals of medieval Europe, the monks were steeped in political intrigue, and one of them, named Dokyo (d. 772), had even attempted a coup. In an attempt to free himself, Kammu set up a new capital at Nagaoka, to the south-west of modern Kyoto. However, a series of deaths there convinced the court that there was an avenging spirit at large. So, just ten years, the emperor decided to move again. It cannot have been an easy decision, for work on the new capital had not been completed. On the other hand, it was relatively easy to dismantle and move the wooden buildings.

This time the emperor determined to find a place that would be secure once and for all. Royal diviners were set to work, and under the guise of hunting expeditions Kammu set off in search of suitable land. He soon found just the place, in a nearby river basin. "The mountains and rivers are the collar and belt of this area and make it a natural fortress," he declared contentedly. The local landowners were the powerful Hata family, who were allies and also of immigrant stock. Their offer to make the land available clinched the matter.

The influential clan had arrived from the Korean kingdom of Paekche in the fifth century and settled in the Kyoto basin known at the time as Yamashiro. They brought with them new techniques, such as silkworm culture and weaving. They were also skilled at land management, having carried out flood control of the Katsura river, and their abilities proved an asset for Kammu. Already by the early seventh century they had set up Koryu-ji to house a beautiful statue of Miroku, and at the start of the eighth century they had built the shrines of Matsuo Taisha and Fushimi Inari.

The Hata dominated the west of the river basin, living in what is now Uzumasa, while over on the east lived another powerful clan, the Kamo. They had migrated from the Yamato area near Nara and were based around the large Kamigamo and Shimogamo shrines. It was in the land between the two large clans that Kammu chose to build his new capital, adopting the ancient shrines as spiritual guardians for his city.

The location fitted all the geomantic requirements (derived from *feng-shui*). It was shielded on three sides by mountains to the north, west and east. There were south-flowing rivers to the east and west, as well as a large body of water to the south (Lake Ogura, near Uji, has since been reclaimed). In the vulnerable north-eastern corner, thought to be a weak spot through which demons could enter, stood the formidable Mount Hiei. The site also had important strategic benefits. Rivers provided passage to the Inland Sea, while to the north nearby Lake Biwa enabled water transport to reach within thirteen miles of the Japan Sea. At the same time, land routes facilitated access to the eastern provinces.

An ambitious building scheme was set up, which took fifty years to complete. The layout was based on the grid system of Chang-an (modern day Xian), capital of Tang China and the most magnificent city of the age. In a curious parallel, on the other side of the world Charlemagne was at this time building his capital at Aachen in imitation of Ravenna. In both cases the intention was to dignify a city through the prism of reflected glory.

As a Confucian, Kammu believed in a rational and hierarchical society, presided over by an enlightened leadership. The new capital was intended to embody this belief in physical form. The parallel streets ran three miles from east to west, and three and a half miles from north to south. The symmetrical layout provided order at the centre of the realm; in the straight and orderly lines lay the framework of a visionary city. The central boulevard, Suzaku-oji, was a massive ninety-two yards wide and meant to act as a fire break. Even the narrowest streets of this grand capital were seventy-eight feet wide.

To protect the city, a network of protective shrines was set up at key geomantic points, and the whole site circumscribed by the directional animals of Chinese mythology. To the north, the black serpent-turtle haunted the mountains; in the east, the blue-green dragon sipped on the waters at Kiyomizu; the red sparrow-phoenix soared in the southern sunshine; and the white tiger lurked in the mists of the Western Hills.

The imperial compound was sited in the north, from where Suzaku-oji led directly south to the city's main entrance, the mighty Rashomon (made famous in the film of the same name by Kurosawa). This eight-pillared, two-storey gate was built to impress. Boarded by a short moat, it was painted in white and red with green roofing. Steep steps led up to it, meaning that those who entered the city had to dismount and struggle up in humble manner. Only two temples were allowed in the city, and these were placed down in the south away from the court. To the east of Rashomon stood To-ji (East Temple), and to the west Sai-ji (West Temple, no longer in existence). In a further move to undermine the Nara priesthood, the emperor encouraged new forms of Buddhism (see Chapter Three).

Heian-kyo was built for an aristocracy enjoying the height of its power, and the imperial compound took up fifteen per cent of the total area. It was a city-within-a-city into which ordinary mortals were forbidden to enter. The nobility was split into eighteen categories, the top three ranks of which were reserved for the immediate family of the emperor. Because of the reverence in which aristocrats were held, they were never referred to by name but by rank or place of residence. For ordinary citizens, they were "cloud-dwellers". By contrast, common folk were herded into small city blocks, surrounded by walls. The rectangular grid meant that there were 1,200 such blocks, all of uniform size and carefully monitored. "The inhabitants of the capital were not citizens, but simply encaged subjects," writes urban historian Gunter Nitschke. Many were brought to work in the city as forced labour, for compulsory service in lieu of tax payment was written into the law of the land.

If you climb one of Kyoto's surrounding hills, you can still make out something of the original layout in the grid-like streets. Kammu's city lay somewhat to the west of the modern city centre, a shift that took place in the Middle Ages. Of Heian-kyo, sadly, not a thing now remains—except for a small patch of garden called Shinsen-en that formed part of the imperial park. The reason is simple: fire. The wooden buildings were vulnerable, and the imperial enclosure itself burned down fourteen times in 400 years. Earthquakes added to the destruction, and floods too: by mid-Heian times, the western half of the capital had partly become water-meadows. As a result, the city shifted eastwards, and in so doing it metamorphosed into Kyoto.

Spirit of Place

Kammu's choice of location had historic ramifications. River basins have their own microclimate, and mention of Kyoto inevitably provokes comments about the weather. "You poor thing," I was told by Japanese friends when first moving here. There is a special expression—*sokobie*—for the bitter-cold at the bottom of the basin in winter. But it is summer which attracts most of the adverse comments, being uncomfortably hot and humid. There is a noticeable difference even from neighbouring cities like Osaka and Kobe, and fifteen minutes by car suffice to take one out of the muggy river basin to wooded inclines where the air feels fresher. The writer Tanizaki Junichiro, who loved everything about Kyoto, chose to live elsewhere for just this reason:

> *The trouble is the climate. Kyoto is a Pygmalion creature. She grew to her present glory from a vast, ancient marshland in a basin surrounded by mountains far from the sea. Like a model still troubled by schoolgirl acne, Kyoto suffers from her topography which produces extreme humidity, savagely cold winters, and blisteringly hot summers. The locals—being used to it—don't seem to mind at all.*

The drawbacks in terms of climate are outweighed in the minds of most by the benefits. The nineteenth-century historian and poet, Rai Sanyo, named his riverside study "Purple Hills and Crystal Streams", and the phrase has been taken up as an epithet for the city, for it aptly describes the blessings of nature. Considering its position, the city is wonderfully green. Rome and San Francisco lie close to the same latitude, yet despite the similarity of temperature there is a striking difference in rainfall. It helps account for the lush vegetation in this "Flowering Capital" and how Kyoto was able to give birth to *ikebana*, the Japanese style of flower arranging.

Throughout the year successive waves of colour break upon the city. Plum and peach blossom heralds the more famous cherry, after which follow azalea and iris. In summer come hydrangea, water lily and lotus, while in autumn there are the "seven famous grasses" followed by the changing maple leaves. Winter sees the camellia as well as the rich red berries of the nandin. The annual round has won much admiration, for each season has endearing traits: the white-and-pink blossoms of spring; the glistening moss in the summer rains; the brilliant colours of the autumn leaves; and the sprinkling of snow on the winter mountains. The changes have inspired many a lyrical passage, none more famous than the opening of Shonagon's *The Pillow Book* (c. 1000):

> *In spring, it is the dawn that is most beautiful. As the light creeps over the hills, their outlines are dyed a faint red and wisps of purplish cloud trail over them.*
>
> *In summer the nights. Not only when the moon shines, but on dark nights too, as the fireflies flit to and fro, and even when it rains, how beautiful it is.*
>
> *In autumn the evenings, when the flittering sun sinks close to the edge of the hills and the crows fly back to their nests in threes and fours...*
>
> *In winter the early mornings. It is beautiful indeed when snow has fallen during the night, but splendid too when the ground is white with frost; or even when there is no snow or frost, but it is simply very cold and the attendants hurry from room to room stirring up the fires and bringing charcoal, how well this fits the season's mood.*

For a landlocked city, Kyoto is notable for the abundance of its water. As well as being surrounded by rivers, Heian-kyo had six canalized streams passing through the city, which were channelled to gardens. Aristocratic villas had streams passing under their walkways and feeding into a pond. Even today the sound of running water is never far away. When Truman Capote came to visit in 1955, he described Kyoto as "a water city, crisscrossed with shallow rivers and cascading canals, dotted with pools as still as coiled snakes and mirthful little waterfalls that sound like Japanese girls giggling."

The flow of water is supplemented by some 3,000 wells. No garden worthy of respect is without one, and many a temple houses an ancient shaft. They draw on an underground supply thought by experts to be equal in quantity to Lake Biwa, Japan's massive inland sea. In ancient times the wells had a mystic aura, and nowadays many are still known for their special qualities. The Turtle Well at Matsuo Taisha is said to prolong life, while at Kiyomizu Temple a sacred spring gushes out of the side of the hill. Making trips to collect spring water has long been a Kyoto custom, and tea masters journey many miles to obtain just the right taste for their guests.

The city's "purple mountains" have been no less crucial to Kyoto's sense of identity. The enfolding hills, which ring three-quarters of the city, leave only the southern plain exposed. For the writer Kawabata Yasunari (1899-1972), they were "small gentle mountains" which give the city a cosy feel. The "twin peaks" are Mount Atago in the west at 3,030 feet, just outreaching its eastern counterpart of Mount Hiei at 2,779 feet. But it is not these solitary giants that characterize the setting so much as the long encircling ranges. Locals like to talk of the "thirty-six peaks of the eastern hills", for example, though I know of no one who can distinguish them.

The mountain slopes, undeveloped and thickly-forested, are constantly changing in appearance. Sometimes they stand close and intimate, as if one could reach out and touch them; sometimes they appear dark and distant with mist swirling round their tops, as in an ink-painting. From verdant green, they can suddenly turn dark and menacing when storm clouds threaten. They can even seem purple, in keeping with the imperial colour used to denote the city.

Vantage spots are not hard to find. The most popular is that of Daimonji, where a large Chinese character ("Dai") has been scoured into the hill to represent the "Great" Wheel of Buddhism. From its midpoint, one can gaze over the city below. To the south, the plain stretches away towards Osaka and the Pacific Sea. Sunsets viewed from here can be spectacular, and the crimson bands across the far horizon douse the city in a mellow glow. It was from here that the hero of *The Tale of Genji* (c. 1005) took his farewell when he went into exile:

> *Genji climbed the hill behind the temple and looked off towards the city. The forests receded into a spring haze. "Like a painting," he said. "People who live in such a place can hardly want to be anywhere else."*

Reluctance to build on inclines in a land of earthquakes means that Kyoto lies like a lake at the bottom of the basin, lapping at the edge of the foothills. Despite the concrete sprawl of modern times, there remains plenty of green. Not only are the surrounding hills free of development, but there are large pockets of nature dotted around the city. The biggest is that of the former imperial palace, packed with 50,000 trees. The hilly confines have restricted Kyoto's growth, and it is this that makes living here such a delight. Despite being a big bustling city, it is surprisingly intimate and convenient to cycle around. Locals like to refer to it as "the biggest village in Japan" because of the close-knit feeling. Walk downtown, and you are sure to meet someone you know. Go for the weekend to Osaka, or worse Tokyo, and you feel like a country bumpkin out among the bright lights.

The existence of a *genus loci*, or spirit of place, has been recognized since ancient times, and one of those most attuned to it was the much-travelled D. H. Lawrence: "Different places on the face of the earth have different vital effluence, different vibration, different chemical exhalation, different polarity with different stars: call it what you like. But the spirit of place is a great reality." One wonders what Lawrence would have made of Kyoto, for all kinds of theories have been put forward about the city's inclinations. The encircling mountains are said to account for the insularity of the people, though the aristocratic heritage may be more to the point. It has been said, too, that the gentle contours of the hills shape the gentle manner of the citizens, though it is well to remember that the city has been often wracked by civil strife.

On that tenth day of that tenth month of 794, when Kammu moved to his new capital, did he have any sense of the spirit of place? Could he have ever imagined where it would lead? A portrait of him, done in Meiji times, shows an intelligent man dressed in formal Chinese fashion with drooping moustache and goatee beard. He looks every inch the good Confucian. He was also a conspicuously virile man, who not only fathered a city but six princes and nineteen princesses.

In 1895, in celebration of the city's 1100th anniversary Kammu was deified in a ceremony at the specially-built Heian Shrine. The city founder now acts as guardian spirit, not just of the ancient capital but by extension of the country as a whole. "Home for the Ancestral Deity of Kyoto and Japanese Heritage", proclaims the shrine proudly. From its palatial confines the patriarch continues to keep watch over the lush river basin where he was once inspired to build the country's capital. What, one wonders, does he think of it now?

Spirit of the Age

The Heian era (794-1185) is usually divided into two parts. The first was dominated by Chinese borrowings, while the second saw the development of native arts and customs. The dividing line comes in 894, when missions to China were abandoned. This signalled the move from adoption to adaptation, which is often seen as the salient trait of Japan. Even now, over a millennium later, the pattern of importing and reshaping foreign practices remains plainly evident.

The imported fashions of early Heian times were reflected in the architecture of the Great Hall of State, which dominated the imperial compound of Heian-kyo. Though it no longer exists, you can see a five-eighths replica at Heian Shrine which was put up for the city's 1100th anniversary. The huge central structure is fronted by eight vermilion columns beneath a blue roof and flanked by long connecting corridors leading to small halls. The bright colours, symmetry of layout, and sloping roof make it strikingly Chinese in atmosphere.

The statesman Sugawara no Micihzane (845-903) lived right at the end of the "Chinese period" of the Heian Era. In fact it was he who proposed abandoning the missions to China, which was plagued by instability. Michizane was a gifted scholar who had found favour with the emperor and had become the second most powerful figure at court. It was the first time that anyone from outside a narrow circle of aristocrats had ever risen so high, and it upset the Fujiwara family who dominated court affairs. They spread rumours that he was plotting against the new emperor, the young Emperor Daigo, and as a result Michizane was sent into exile at Dazaifu in Kyushu. It proved a miserable experience. He lived in relative poverty with two of his eighteen children, while the rest of his nearest and dearest remained in the capital. In his most famous poem, written in Chinese, he focused his feelings of longing onto his favourite plum tree:

When the east wind blows this way
Oh, blossoms in the plum tree
Send your fragrance to me!
Be ever mindful of the spring,
Though your master is no longer with you.

The plum, a relative of the apricot, had been introduced from China around the eighth century. It was a favourite of the Heian court, and its pink and reddish blossoms were much celebrated. It was only later at the end of Heian times that the cherry blossom usurped its role, because of its shorter time-span. The beauty lay in the poignancy of the ephemeral blossom.

After just two years of exile Michizane died, a broken man. Soon afterwards, a series of disasters struck the capital. There was drought, an earthquake, and lightning hit the imperial palace. His chief enemy died of a mysterious illness. Not long after these events Emperor Daigo himself died. Rumours spread that this was all due to the spirit of the wronged statesman. Then, in 942 a woman had a dream in which Michizane asked to be enshrined at Kitano Tenmangu, where the god of thunder was honoured.

Placating wrathful spirits was already established practice, and steps were put in motion. The process culminated with Michizane's deification as Tenjin (Spirit of the Sky) in recognition of his ability to direct lightning. According to the shrine brochure: "the process of divinization of Michizane was greatly assisted by sympathy with his misfortune of having died in exile, by admiration for his unchanging spirit of loyal service, by the mute judgement of the masses against their rulers, and by the social unrest caused by the ever-continuing disasters."

The enshrinement proved a popular success, and worship of Tenjin spread across the country. The deity took the attributes of the scholar and became a god of learning, literature and calligraphy. Today there are Tenmangu shrines throughout Japan, and at exam times they are packed with students praying for success. "Please help me pass my coming exams," beg the thousands of votive tablets. The shrines are busy, too, in early spring, for one thing they invariably have are plum trees. Kitano Tenmangu boasts two thousand.

A thirteenth-century scroll relates the life of Michizane in lively fashion, like a medieval *manga* in pastel colours. One scene shows a red-faced Thunder God hurling lightning at courtiers dashing desperately for cover. There is a touch of Zeus and thunderbolts about it that highlights the similarities between Japanese *kami* (spirits) and Greek gods. Like overgrown children, the deities toy with human life and are in constant need of placation.

The period after Michizane's time, when contacts with the continent ceased, was dominated by the influential Fujiwara family. They remained the "power behind the throne" for virtually three hundred years, and they managed this by the simple expedient of marriage. For generations on end, Fujiwara daughters were married off to prospective emperors. By encouraging early abdication, the fathers were then able to rule as regents or Grand Chancellors to their imperial nephews and grandsons. In effect, it was a peaceful *coup d'état* by which the emperor was reduced to a figurehead. Family politics were never managed so well for so long.

The height of Fujiwara power came in the figure of Michinaga, who "reigned" from 995 to 1028. By this time, so skilful had the family become that he managed to marry off four of his five daughters to future emperors (he was only thwarted from a "clean sweep" because, in the great lottery of life, one of the daughters married a crown prince who went insane). Given the power of his position, Michinaga could permit himself a touch of satisfaction in one of his poems:

The full moon makes me feel
That the world is mine indeed
Like the moon I shine
Unveiled by clouds.

Such was the turnover of emperors in this age that Michinaga was father-in-law to four of them, grandfather of two others, great-grandfather of another, and, astonishingly, great-great-grandfather of yet another. Such, too, was the inter-marrying that Emperor Go-ichigo was not only his son-in-law, but his grandson too. Ruling dynasties are known to be close-knit, but short of incest this must surely be one of history's prime examples of "keeping it in the family".

Court Verse
For Heian aristocrats, accomplishment in poetry was taken for granted. Rather than a decorative art, it was a vital means of expressing strong emotions. Of the many collections, the most celebrated is the tenth-century *Kokinshu* (Collection of Ancient and Modern). It was the first of twenty-one imperially sanctioned anthologies, and for over a thousand years it served as poetic model. The collection contains 1,111 poems, arranged according to season and other topics. The chief characteristic is the articulation of delicate feelings in a way that is atmospheric, rather than explicit. For the poet and critic Oono Makoto, it exemplifies the "refined animism" that runs throughout Japanese culture. This comprises a sensitivity to nature, awareness of transience, and the promotion of harmony. The notion was first expressed by the poet Ki no Tsurayuki (c.872-945) in a preface to the collection.

Japanese poetry has the human heart as seed and myriads of words as leaves. It comes into being when people use the seen and the heard to give voice to feeling aroused by the innumerable events in their lives...

*It is song that moves heaven and earth without effort, stirs emotions
in the invisible spirits and gods, brings harmony to the relations
between men and women, and calms the heart of fierce warriors.*

The passage built on the political creed of Prince Shotoku (573-621),
who had begun the country's first constitution with the following
words: "Respect above all harmony. Your first duty is to avoid discord."
Indeed, the two Chinese characters for "Japan" and "harmony", both
pronounced *wa*, had been collided into one and the same ideograph:
Japan literally was harmony. Tsurayuki's genius lay in the articulation of
an aesthetic to underlie this.

Since humans resonate in tune with nature, runs his thesis, the
poet can promote unity by capturing "good vibrations" and
communicating them to others. This was done through sound, for the
poems of the age were not lifeless lines, but meant to be chanted out
loud (which is why they are called *uta*, or songs). These *waka* or
"Japanese songs" were thus a form of harmony, in more ways than one.

The *Kokinshu* consists for the most part of short poems that are
based on a syllable pattern of 5, 7, 5, 7, 7 (*haiku* was formed later by
dropping the last two lines.) The brevity of the form leads to an
elusiveness, which is abetted by the tendency of Japanese sentences to
dispense with subjects. (According to linguists, some seventy per cent of
spoken Japanese and fifty per cent of the written language does without
subjects.) This gives scope for the fusion of outer and inner worlds, as
in this poem by Tsurayuki where poet, cuckoo and nature combine in
fellow feeling:

*In this endless rain
The very sky resounds to
The plaintive "cuckoo":
What regrets could give rise to
This crying the whole night long?*

The melancholic note sounded here is characteristic of the poetry
as a whole. Sleeves are soaked in tears, love's illusions bewailed, life's joys
bemoaned as fleeting. The sadness of impermanency is ever-present, for
to the Heian mind transience was the dominating fact of existence. Life
was fragile, and life expectancy short. This meant that nothing could be

enjoyed on its own terms, for nothing could last. Scattered blossoms, the falling of leaves, lost love: the themes reflected an aesthetic known as *mujokan*, which stemmed from Buddhism. All is change. All is flux. The only permanent thing in this world is non-permanence. Like writers in modern times who turn neuroses into novels, Heian versifiers found release in the ritualistic expression of life's sad beauty. In the poetic conventions, transience could be tamed—if only temporarily.

The Poet Beauty

Two contributors to the *Kokinshu* hold a special place in Kyoto's heart. The first is Ono no Komachi (fl. 850), famous for her beauty; the other is Ariwara no Narihira (825-80), a grandson of Emperor Kammu. They belong to the Six Great Poets of the Heian Era, and though little is known of their real lives, they are celebrated figures in folklore.

So little is known of Komachi's life that all that can be said with certainty is that she was a lady-in-waiting who is remembered in Japan as one of the ancient world's three most beautiful women (together with Cleopatra and the Chinese Youkihi). It seems she retired early to become a nun, possibly after an unhappy love affair, and she left behind some eighty poems. Most speak of longing and frustration:

> *This night of no moon*
> *There is no way to meet him.*
> *I rise in longing—*
> *My breast pounds, a leaping flame,*
> *My heart consumed in passion.*

The best-known story about Komachi concerns a suitor named Fukakusa no Shosho. Before she would give herself to him, she asked that he prove his sincerity by visiting from his distant home for a hundred successive nights. The prince completed the journey ninety-nine times, only to be caught in a snowstorm on the very last night when he died. Haunted by his memory, Komachi turned into a crazy old woman, and this is how she appears in the Noh play, *Sotoba Komachi*:

> *It was his unsatisfied spirit possessed me so*
> *His anger that turned my wits.*

In the face of this I will pray
For life in the worlds to come...

The poet appears in a handful of other plays, among which *Komachi at Sekidera* is the most celebrated. Written five hundred years after her death, it portrays her as an old woman of nearly a hundred living on a hill between Kyoto and Otsu. For the first hour of the play she barely moves, but towards the end, despite her great age, she performs a dance. "How deeply moving, how deeply moving the flowering branch of an old tree," comments the Chorus.

Many places claim association with Komachi, though none so strongly as the temple of Zuishin-in to the east of Kyoto. It was supposedly built on the site of her last residence, and houses a statue of the poet as a wrinkled old woman. This was carved at her own request, as a reminder of life's transience. It was a subject close to her heart, and forms the theme of her most famous poem:

The flowers withered
Their colour faded away
While meaninglessly
I spent my days in the world
And the long rains were falling.

The scent of Komachi still lingers in the air of Kyoto, for hers was a story that tells of the Heian heart. Love and loss; the transience of beauty; human vanity—here were the great themes of the age. She was said by later generations to be cold-hearted, but what great beauty does not learn to be wary of her suitors? Certainly, there is little of coldness in her poetry, which speaks of yearning and passion. Her life has a tragic quality, as she plummets Greta Garbo-like from pin-up to recluse. A figure of beauty in life, she left posterity with the beauty of her poems. *Ars longa vita brevis.*

The Courtly Lover

As with Komachi, almost nothing is known of the real Ariwara no Narihira. His reputation derives almost entirely from stories told about him in the tenth-century *The Tales of Ise*. This is a collection of 125 episodes framed around the verse of "a certain man". The authorship is a mystery, and there are at least ten credible theories as to how it was compiled. One of the episodes concerns the poet's love for Nijo no Kisaki, a favourite of the emperor. The affair was illicit, but the courtly lover was prepared to risk all:

> *Now Narihira was allowed free access to the palace where the ladies of the court dwelt, and he would visit the chamber of this girl and sit directly beside her. But she entreated him, "If you come to see me thus, His Majesty will hear of it, and we shall perish. Please do not come this way again." Narihira answered her:*

> *In love with you*
> *I have lost all sense*
> *Of hiding from men's eyes.*
> *In exchange for meeting you,*
> *Is death so great a price to pay?*

When the affair was discovered, Narihira was exiled and Nijo no Kisaki locked up in a windowless tower. Later, full of longing, the poet went to revisit the western wing of the palace where Kisaki used to live. The occasion inspired a poem, which later generations considered to be one of the best ever *tanka* (short poem).

> *Is this not that moon?*
> *And is this not the same spring*
> *As it was before?*
> *My body is still the same—*
> *Yet everything is different.*

Narihira was made the subject of several Noh plays, most notably the fifteenth-century *Izutsu* by Zeami. It took its theme from a pair of poems in *The Tales of Ise* exchanged by childhood sweethearts. Though the couple had not met for some time, they confirmed their affection for each other through verse (his is on the left, hers on the right).

> *Since I last saw you*   *The mid-parted hair*
> *I seem to have grown so that*   *I once measured against yours*
> *I am taller than*   *Hangs down past my waist.*

The top of the wooden well   *For whom should it be put up*
Against which you measured me.   *Unless it should be for you?*

The temple of Jurin-ji, in the south-west of Kyoto, stands on the site of Narihira's last residence. It is a pleasant place, nestling close to the Western Hills, and on a small rise at the back of the temple is a grave marked as that of the poet. Temples often make claims of association with famous figures in order to boost their prestige, and the stories have to be taken with a pinch of salt. Conveniently there is a lot of this around, for the hill on which the temple stands is known as "salt mountain", and the resident priest—an eccentric figure—is keen to explain why. One of the pastimes of Heian aristocrats, he says, was the making of salt by boiling sea water. This was used to make a "beach" around a small pond, in which were set beautiful sea-shells. Once when Nijo no Kisaki came to stay in a nearby shrine, the poet supposedly sent word to her to watch the sky and added purple dye to the boiling water as a token of his affection. Whether the story is true or not I have no idea, but it is nice to think of the solitary princess viewing the skies and seeing the steam rise emblazoned with the colour of his love.

In later years Narihira's legend became linked with that of Komachi. Who could resist matching the courtly Casanova with the famed beauty? A medieval tale tells of how he was riding one evening over the heath of Ichiharano to the north of Kyoto when he heard a disembodied voice reciting the first lines of a poem. Looking around, he could only see a skull. When he was told that it was the place where Komachi had died, he spent the night there and completed the verse. Poetry had united the two—in spirit, if not in flesh.

The Grand Wizard
More than most cities, Heian-kyo lay close to the spirit world. It is as if its low-lying mists fostered a hidden world of unseen forces. Exorcisms were common practice, and a potent mix of folk-beliefs and superstitions governed everyday life. Almanacs held sway over major decisions, dreams were analysed, and elaborate rituals were used to counteract misfortune. People sought advice before embarking on journeys, for directional taboos could affect the route of the shortest trip. A six-day calendar of auspicious and inauspicious days determined even the most mundane activities, such as nail-cutting and hair-washing.

It was in the mastery of such matters that Abe no Seimei (c.921-1005) made his name. He was a court advisor who practised Onmyodo, the Way of Yin-Yang. This had been introduced from China and affected all areas of life, including decisions of state. The divination that lay at its heart derived from complex calculations involving astronomy, geomancy and numerology. Its protective mark, said to destroy evil spirits, was a five-pointed star representing the five elements.

In Western terms, Seimei was a Merlin with the gift of second sight. He served six different emperors, and was acclaimed for the accuracy of his predictions. He had an excellent eye, and was able to see star constellations that others could not. Medieval folk collections later puffed up his reputation by giving him supernatural attributes. One story told how he had first come to prominence through identifying devils that were invisible to his seniors. It was said that he could raise the dead, conjure up human look-alikes, and that his mother had been a white fox (intermediary with the spirit world).

One of the folk tales about Seimei involved him in a mysterious case of bird droppings. These had landed directly onto the head of a nobleman, and in his examination of them the Grand Wizard determined that the courtier was about to be murdered. He was advised to spend the night in prayer, and the next morning, to his amazement, a man appeared at his door begging forgiveness for having wanted to kill him.

Another incident concerned a swordsman named Watanabe no Tsuna, who was one day walking across a bridge called Ichijo Modoribashi. Coming towards him was a beautiful woman, who suddenly turned into a demon and attacked him—a true "devil in disguise". In the ensuing struggle, Tsuna cut off the demon's arm and took it to Seimei, who sealed it with a spell. Later the wicked creature tried to reclaim its lost limb in the form of Tsuna's wife, but was thwarted by the strength of the spell. The frequency of she-devils in the Japanese tradition makes for a feminist's field-day, and the Noh play, *Kanawa*, provides another instance. It tells of a man plagued by nightmares which Seimei ascribes to a rejected wife. The Grand Wizard prepares himself to meet her in combat, and when she appears he is able to overcome her wrathful spirit. Clearly it takes a special type of man to overcome the fury of a jealous woman.

Following Seimei's death, a huge shrine was established in his honour, but sadly it was destroyed in the wars of the late fifteenth century. In its place a more modest affair was erected. Today its concrete surrounds make a sorry spectacle, for nothing is as sad as a shrine bereft of nature. Nonetheless, it hosts a constant stream of visitors, for Seimei's star has burnt bright in recent years. Novels by Baku Yumemakura and an award-winning series of *manga* by Okamo Reiko started a boom in the 1990s, which was further fuelled by television and movies. To appeal to post-modern tastes, the Grand Wizard was repackaged as a handsome Heian magician battling evil forces. Like Harry Potter, the stories fed into a New Age fascination with the occult.

Something of Seimei's world can be sensed at Daishogun-hachi Shrine, where in a three-storey building are housed all manner of astrological aids and Taoist deities. The thick ledgers reveal the complexity of the worldview. The shrine stands in what was once the north-west corner of the imperial compound, and the nearby Kitano Tenmangu Shrine was part of the same complex. Here were studied stars and heavenly spirits. In this corner of Kyoto, between the realm of Seimei and that of Tenjin, the veil that separates the present from the past is thin indeed. For those with imagination enough, the spirit—and spirits—of Heian-kyo lie strangely close to the surface.

Chapter Two
CITY OF GENJI

The Cult of Beauty
One of the striking aspects of Heian literature is the predominance of
women writers, particularly in the "golden age" of the late tenth and
early eleventh centuries. This was during the time of Emperor Ichijo
(980-1011), who had two empresses around whom developed rival
salons. In one was Sei Shonagon, author of *The Pillow Book*. In the
other was Murasaki Shikibu, author of *The Tale of Genji*, as well as the
poet Izumi Shikibu (they were unrelated, for *shikibu* was the title of the
office held by their fathers).

The women were drawn from the ranks of the middle aristocracy,
who sought an advantageous marriage for their daughters by sending
them to court. They were given a good education, for artistic
accomplishment was highly valued. The chief task for the ladies-in-
waiting was to entertain the empress, and creative writing was one such
means. There was every incentive to produce good material, for writing
that won the admiration of the court enhanced the status of the
empress. There was plenty of time, too, for the women led restricted
lives and had little to do beyond their duties.

Since it was considered unladylike to write in Chinese characters,
women used *kana*, a phonetic alphabet. This precluded them from the
formal style of literature, but ironically it gave them an advantage in
personal styles of expression since the script was closer to spoken
Japanese. Confessional genres like journals became so closely identified
with women that in *The Tosa Diary* (935) Ki no Tsurayuki even
pretended to be female.

It is through women's writings that we have such a fascinating
picture of the aristocracy. It was a small and secluded society,
somewhere between three and five thousand people. Income was
provided by distant estates, and the beneficiaries used their leisure to
cultivate the senses. The tone had been set by Kammu's son, Emperor
Saga (786-842), who offered the following advice to his successor:

"Just stroll among these hills, along these rivers, without concern for rank, take your pleasures with brush or with lute, and have no thought of what you will do next." He retired to a villa, which has since been converted into the temple of Daikaku-ji, where he was fond of boating. We can see here the kind of lifestyle to which the nobility inclined. It gave rise to an aesthetic known as *miyabi*, or courtly refinement, which affected all areas of life from clothing to pastimes. At a time when much of Europe was engaged in feudal struggle, the Heian court produced one of the world's most sophisticated cultures.

Appreciation of nature was one area in which Heian courtiers developed refined tastes. There were outings at which participants strove to capture in verse the beauty of the natural surrounds. The Heian ear was more finely attuned than our own dulled senses, and insect noises were noted for their musical qualities. Crickets were particularly treasured. These were hung in cages, and their chirping accompanied by a flute. Another popular pastime was moon-viewing. Villas had purpose-built platforms, and careful thought was given to the creation of atmosphere. The rippling waters of a pond, or the swaying tops of bamboo trees were considered most suitable. There were special gatherings for the full moon at which participants tried to capture its effect in words. The spring and autumn moons were noted for their special beauty, though it was the harvest moon that won the highest acclaim. Such was the popularity of the custom that Kyoto became known as the "Moon-Viewing Capital".

Incense mixing provides another example of how refined Heian sensibilities could be. The fragrance was held to calm thoughts and elevate the senses, "sweetening" the mind, as it were. Great care was taken in the blending to get just the right effect. It was a highly skilled art, with balance and ratio a matter of minute precision. There were contests to test ability, and at gatherings rare snippets of prized wood were passed round for appreciation. The incense was far more delicate than that to which we are used nowadays, and when I once had the opportunity to sample some Heian favourites, worth hundreds of pounds, I have to confess that I was sadly unable to even distinguish them.

Incense also played a part in the creation of personality; clothing was doused in the scent of special mixtures, which acted as an extension of the individual. In the dark of night when romantic liaisons took place, people were recognized as much by their distinctive smell as by their appearance. It was as if they were surrounded by a sweet-smelling aura. In *The Tale of Genji*, the coming-out of Genji's daughter occasions the mixing of a special scent, which develops into a competition among household members. Later, a rivalry develops between the prince's son, Kaoru (meaning "fragrance") and his grandson Niou (meaning "perfumed highness"). The former smells sweet by nature, suggesting good karma, while the latter has to resort to his own creativity.

By modern standards, the appearance of the aristocrats could be startling. Whitened faces were offset by blackened teeth (the white paste was made from dried nightingale droppings). Men shaved their temples to create a raised hairline and women shaved their eyebrows, painting replacements high on the forehead. Those who have seen the films *Rashomon* (1950) or *Ugetsu Monogatari* (1953) will be familiar with the style. Female beauty took its ideals from the Chinese. Plump rounded cheeks, small lips, slanting eyes and single eyelids were the fashion. Hair was worn long—very long—hanging down to the floor, rubbed with oil and made to glisten. Brushing was a daily ritual, though washing was something of a special occasion to be performed only on auspicious days. Verse about hair provides a sensual subset of Japanese poetry, as here in this verse by Izumi Shikibu (fl. 1000):

> *Not caring about*
> *The black disorder of my hair*
> *I lay prostrate;*
> *I ache with the loss*
> *Of he who was first to caress it.*

The care that went into grooming was matched by that taken with clothing. Women wore multi-layered kimonos, which varied according to occasion and season. The ceremonial costume, *juni hitoe*, consisted of twelve bright monochrome robes, the edges of which were visible in successive layers at the sleeves. A patterned over-robe completed the outfit. The effect could be stunning, as Murasaki Shikibu describes in her *Diary* (c. 1000):

Her majesty wore her usual unlined crimson dress, robes of crimson lined with purple, pale green lined with darker green, white lined with pale green, and yellow lined with darker yellow. Her mantle was of light purple figured silk, over which she wore an informal outer robe that was white lined with pale green.

Coordinating the colours was a major preoccupation, and incompetence was considered shocking. Murasaki writes of the mortification at court when two ladies "showed a lack of taste when it came to the colour combinations of their sleeves." It was this kind of sophistication that led the Meiji-era critic Seisetsu Sassa to write with a touch of national pride: "When in the world, where in the world, has there been a culture like that of our Heian court, so utterly ruled by sensibility? Where in the world have the moon and flowers been so admired?... The unique culture of our nation is this emotionalism, this love of beauty."

It is worth remembering that life in Heian-kyo bore very little relationship to the image we have nowadays of Japan. As Professor Ivan Morris has pointed out, there was no sushi, no samurai, no geisha, no *tatami* mats, no haiku, no Noh, no Kabuki, no Zen, tea ceremony or flower arrangement. It was a very different world, and one with very different assumptions from those with which we are familiar. Nowhere is this clearer than in the realm of relationships.

The Pursuit of Love

The aestheticism of the aristocracy, which pervaded every aspect of their lives, even extended into their love life. This has aroused much interest in modern times. By and large, men and women inhabited separate worlds, and it was thought improper for ladies to show their faces: screens, drapes and fans shielded them from view. Large veiled hats were used when travelling. It created an air of mystery, and as in Victorian times when a pretty ankle could seem erotic, the shadowy outlines and tantalizing glimpses left much to the imagination. "Bright green bamboo blinds are a delight," writes Shonagon, "especially when beneath them one can make out the many layers of a woman's clothes emerging from under brilliantly coloured curtains of state."

Love affairs tended to follow a common pattern. They were initiated after a courtier had caught a glimpse of a woman, or heard about her reputation. He would then pen her a poem, to which she was expected to respond. There was an aesthetic dimension, for it involved the ability to write pleasing verse on a suitable shade of scented paper. An appropriate blossom or sprig might be attached. Particular attention was paid to the calligraphy, since handwriting was seen as the key to the soul. Letters were scrutinized in detail for clues, and Murasaki's hero is able to discern all about his correspondents even before he meets them.

Once the woman had indicated her willingness, the man would pay her a visit. By convention this took place at night, and he would leave before dawn. These visits continued for the duration of the relationship, meaning that the whole affair was carried out under the veil of darkness. The night-time visits were the subject of much verse, as here by Izumi Shikibu:

This dewdrop
On a bamboo leaf
Stays longer
Than you, who vanish
At dawn.

On returning home, the man was expected to write a "morning after poem", to which his lover would send a suitable reply. Sei Shonagon provides a pen-sketch of such a scene:

A young bachelor of an adventurous nature comes home at dawn,
having spent the night in some amorous encounter. Though he still
looks sleepy, he immediately draws his inkstone to him and, after
carefully burring it with ink, starts to write his next-morning letter.
He does not let his brush run down the paper in a careless scrawl, but
puts himself heart and soul into the calligraphy. What a charming
figure he makes...

For all the rituals, it seems that sexual relations could be easy-going. In *The Tale of Genji*, the eponymous prince at one point steals into a room and in the darkness hits on the wrong woman. He makes love to her anyway. On another occasion he is disappointed by a woman and sleeps with her younger brother instead. Morality played second fiddle to style. Aesthetics, not ethics, were what mattered. Casual affairs were one thing, marriage altogether another. When Genji's grandson, Prince Niou, is given instruction in the ways of the world, he is told that "When you have made yourself a good solid marriage, then you can bring in anyone who strikes your fancy and set her up wherever it suits your convenience." On the other hand, "Ordinary people are expected to be satisfied with only one wife." Polygamy was a perk for the privileged, and leading figures took a number of secondary wives or mistresses. Genji, for example, is pushed into an official marriage while a young teenager, then after being widowed he marries again for love but also takes on an official wife as well. Living arrangements in such liaisons were flexible. Husbands and wives kept separate quarters in the same palace, or they lived in different residences altogether, with the wife staying in her family home.

There is an account of a Heian marriage in *Gossamer Years*, which gives the viewpoint of a second wife. It covers the years from 954 to 974, and is by an unnamed author known as "Mother of Michitsuna". She was married to a leading statesman, but was frustrated with her situation. She rails at her husband when he is absent, nags at him when he visits, and is so wracked by jealousy that she gloats over the death of her rival's baby. Here is a woman who loved too much, a monogamous soul in a polygamous set-up. The tone is surprisingly modern, as in this passage where she admits to being in a bad mood when he comes to call on her:

His playful manner I found most irritating, and before I knew it I had begun pouring out all the resentment I had stored up over the months. He said not a word, pretending to be asleep, and after I had gone on for a time he started up and exclaimed, "What's this? Have you gone to bed already?" It may not have been entirely gracious but I behaved like a stone for the rest of the night.

The restricted choices open to women meant that they were preoccupied with the emotional life, much as in Jane Austen. If Byron was right in saying "Man's love is of man's life a thing apart, 'Tis women's whole existence," then how much more so for the Heian ladies. Their writing tells of long nights of waiting and dreams of imagined meetings. It is a world of romance, relationships, and secret rendezvous. According to Sei Shonagon, nightlife in the imperial palace involved much rustling in dark corners:

> *Throughout the night, one hears the sound of footsteps in the corridor outside. Every now and then the sound will stop, and someone will tap on a door with just a single finger. It is pleasant to think that the woman inside can instantly recognize her visitor. Sometimes the tapping will continue for quite a while without the woman's responding in any way. The man finally gives up, thinking that she must be asleep; but this does not please the woman, who makes a few cautious movements, with a rustle of silk clothes, so that her visitor will know she is really there. Then she hears him fanning himself as he remains standing outside the door.*

The imperial palace where this took place was a cluster of free-standing buildings connected by covered corridors. It was built in the *shinden* style, based on Shinto structures. The buildings were raised about a foot off the ground and roofed with layered cypress bark. The long corridors which connected the buildings ran through landscaped grounds, and the whole complex was integrated into nature through its unpainted wood and natural materials.

Here is where the imperial family lived, each member housed separately with their own servants. The rooms were open and airy, containing a large interior space which was separated into sections by hanging blinds or curtain stands. Such is the setting for the great works of Heian literature. Such is the environment in which *The Pillow Book* and *The Tale of Genji* take place.

Pillow Talk

For Arthur Waley, *The Pillow Book* is "the most important document of the period" because of the way it details court life. Yet it is anything but dry; the book has a meandering nature which initiated the *zuihitsu* (follow your pen) genre. There are anecdotes, poems, musings—and lists. Lots of them: 164 in all, according to the book's translator, Ivan Morris.

The author, Sei Shonagon (b. c. 965), was taken on at the age of twenty-eight as story-teller to the nineteen-year old Empress Teishi. The pair got on well, as an anecdote indicates. The empress had been given a pile of paper, a valuable commodity, and asked her lady-in-waiting how she should use it. "Use it as a pillow," came the reply. The implication was that the pile could prop up the head like a Japanese pillow while at the same time serving for nocturnal jottings. In reward for her wit, Shonagon was presented with the precious paper.

The result is a book of witty observations which have entertained readers for generations. So sharp is the writing that it brings alive the characters of long ago. "I have never come across anyone with such keen ears as Masamitsu, Ministry of the Treasury," she writes, "I believe he could hear the sound of a mosquito's eyelash falling on the floor."

As Shonagon guides us around the Heian court, the caustic commentary provides some entertaining fare. Happiness is being able to piece together a torn letter someone else has thrown away. Priests should be good-looking so that they can hold the attention of their congregation. And disappointment is a knock at night time that turns out not to be by the person longed for—"the most depressing experience of all". Even the lists the author makes are fascinating, for insight sits alongside idiosyncrasy. Among her "Embarrassing Things" are children who repeat nasty remarks to the person concerned, and parents who coo delightedly over an ugly baby. Another list, "Things That are Near though Distant", contains just three things: paradise, the course of a boat, and relations between men and women. The remarks are not limited to court affairs, for Shonagon delights in nature. She writes of the beauty of the tapping of the beetle in the dark, and she describes a fruitless expedition to the woods in search of inspiration for a cuckoo poem. "Anything that cries out at night delights me—except babies," she notes characteristically.

Mixed in with the wit is a dash of snobbishness. She delights in the socially elevated, but despises the vulgar and ugly. On one occasion she asks rhetorically, "What could be more magnificent than to see so august a personage as His Majesty seated there in all his glory?" On another occasion she consigns the prettiness of snow on the houses of common people to her list of "Unsuitable Things".

But it is in the matter of romance that one warms to Shonagon, and many of her remarks have a Wildean wit. "One can tell if a man really loves one because he will insist on staying all night, however much one may urge him to leave," she notes. Fear of scandal meant such visits were carried out in secrecy, and she writes amusingly of one such incident:

"There was a man in the corridor early this morning who had no business to be here," I heard one of the ladies-in-waiting say... I was listening to her story with interest, when suddenly I realized that she was talking about a visitor of mine.

The reader sometimes gets the impression that Shonagon treasures refinement more than feelings. "One's attachment to a man depends largely on the elegance of his leave-taking," she writes: "It is also very pleasant to find that a flute has been left next to one's pillow by a gentleman who has been visiting one." Yet as with Oscar Wilde, one suspects the cynic's comments conceal a romantic soul:

When the moon is shining, I love to receive a visitor, even if it is someone who has not come to see me for ten days, twenty days, a month, a year, or perhaps seven or eight years, and who has been inspired by the moonlight to remember our previous meetings.

Despite its fame, *The Pillow Book* did not become known in the West until relatively recently, and it was only in 1967 that a complete translation was published. Now the book is a popular Penguin classic. Some things never date, and the woman who declared "A lover's visit is the most delightful thing in the world" is one of them. When she jotted down her observations all those years ago, could she have ever imagined they would become a "pillow" for so many readers around the world? It would surely have made her list of "Extraordinary Things".

Poet of Passion

One of Shonagon's contemporaries was the poet, Izumi Shikibu (fl.1000). Over 1,500 of her *waka* remain, from which it is evident that she led a turbulent emotional life. Like Komachi, she is known for the intensity of her feelings.

In the burning fire of my love
It seems the firefly of the river
Is my own soul
Leaping up in longing.

Izumi was brought up at court, and was married twice to middle-ranking men. She took her name from her first husband, who was a provincial official of Izumi province. It seems that she had an affair which made her husband and father repudiate her. This gave her a scandalous reputation when she returned to court, and a well-known anecdote tells of Michinaga walking past a group of courtiers, one of whom was holding her fan, when he stopped to write on it "Fan of a fickle woman".

The great love of Izumi's life, however, suggests that she was a woman of considerable passion. The story is related in *Izumi Shikibu's Diary*, which is more a literary work than a journal, containing information the "diarist" could never have known. It begins with Izumi grieving for the death of her lover, one of the sons of the emperor. At this point she was approached by the dead man's half-brother, Prince Atsumichi (980-1007). He announced his intentions by sending a poem with a sprig of orange blossom, to which she replied:

Rather than recall
In these flowers
The fragrance of the past,
I would like to hear this nightingale's voice,
To know if his song is as sweet.

The difference in status made the relationship improper, but it developed into something of a grand affair. There was even a right royal scandal when Izumi was seen in the back of Atsumichi's carriage at the Aoi Festival. Later, the prince installed her in his palace, to the displeasure of his wife who walked out on him. The *Diary* ends at this highpoint for Izumi, though not long afterwards tragedy struck when the prince died in an epidemic. It was her second bereavement in four years, and in her grief she poured out more than a hundred poems of heartache:

Yearning for you
My heart has shattered
Into a thousand pieces
But never will one particle
Of my love be lost.

Later Izumi married again and went with her husband to the provinces. As in the verse of Komachi, Buddhist themes run through her work, creating a tension between the attachments of love and a desire for non-attachment. Nothing is known of her in later life, although it seems that she died a nun in Kyoto and she lies buried in a sub-temple of Toboku-in. In the fifteenth-century Noh play, *Toboku*, she is movingly celebrated as a saved soul thanks to the power of poetry:

Poets live on for ever—
So writes Ki no Tsurayuki.
Their verse moves Heaven and Earth,
And melts the Demon's Heart.
Both Gods and Buddhas lend it their ear.
The verse inspired by the Capital,
Flower-bedecked beneath a tender sky,
Springing from a poet's heart,
Fulfils the "Way of Heaven".

It is clear from her poetry that Izumi knew the cruellest stings of life, for here was a soul who gambled all on love and paid the price. Yet her verse rings out in defiance, as if to proclaim, in Tennyson's immortal lines, "'Tis better to have loved and lost, Than never to have loved at all." Intense, emotional, heart-rending, Izumi's poetry hardly seems to have dated. She deserves greater recognition.

The Shining Prince

In 1964, Unesco selected Murasaki Shikibu (c.973-c.1031) as one of the "world's great personages". Her achievement, *The Tale of Genji*, is a work of monumental importance, and has claims to be the oldest novel ever written. It served as inspiration for centuries on end, and countless works of art and literature are indebted to it. For the Nobel Prize-winning Kawabata Yasunari, it remains the "highest pinnacle of Japanese literature".

Murasaki was born into the minor ranks of the Fujiwara family and brought up in the capital. When her father was appointed governor of Echizen (now Fukui Prefecture), she accompanied him there and married an older man, who apparently died soon after the birth of their daughter. It is thought that she began writing her novel at this time, and her reputation prompted Michinaga (a distant cousin) to invite her to serve his daughter, Empress Shoshi.

Murasaki Shikibu's *Diary* covers two years of the author's time at court. The writing lacks the brilliance of Shonagon, but is nonetheless revealing. Of Izumi Shikibu, she notes acidly that she "has a genius for tossing off letters with ease... I cannot think of her as a poet of the highest quality." Shonagon fares little better, she is described as boastful, conceited, and too clever by half. As for herself, Murasaki writes: "Pretty and coy, shrinking from sight, unsociable, proud, fond of romance, vain and poetic... Such is the opinion of those who do not know me, but once they meet me they say, 'You are wonderfully gentle to meet with.'" Such comments have led critics to contrast the quick-witted Shonagon with Murasaki's retiring observer

The Tale of Genji is a huge affair, with fifty-four chapters that revolve around the life and loves of Hikaru Genji (the Shining Prince). It covers four generations, seventy-five years, and a staggering 430 characters. Keeping charge of such a sprawling account is an accomplishment in itself, yet somehow the author manages to make each character a distinct personality. The book is traditionally divided into three parts. The first tells of the rise of the glittering young courtier, and in virtually every chapter there is a new love affair. The second part sees a mature Genji involved in court politics, exile, and the establishment of a grand palace. With his death in Chapter 42, the third part focuses on his son and grandson, who become rivals for a lady of Uji.

The descriptions of court life contrast with those in Murasaki's *Diary*. Whereas the latter describes the everyday reality of observation, the novel portrays the romanticized world of the imagination. Here is built a glittering Camelot with a hero who is a paragon of virtues. "No one could see him without pleasure," runs Arthur Waley's translation:

He was like the flowering tree under whose shade even the rude
mountain peasant delights to rest. And so great was the fascination
he exercised that those who knew him longed to offer whatever was
dearest to them.

The manly ideal of Heian times privileged such qualities as sensitivity, grace and elegance, and by modern standards Genji is extraordinarily

effeminate. He has delicate feelings, fusses about his appearance, and even looks like a woman. This prompted the casting of an actress to play him in the film, *Sennen no Koi* (A Thousand Years of Love, 2002).

The author was clearly a little in love with her hero, and the female characters are irresistibly drawn to him. This enables her to create a gallery of striking portraits, which are strung together by Genji's Oedipal Complex. His mother, a favourite of the emperor, died when he was two years old, and he embarks on an unconscious quest for replacement. An arranged marriage in his early teens provides little comfort, and he seeks consolation with older women. Prominent amongst Genji's lovers is his father's mistress, Fujitsubo, who bears a strong resemblance to his mother. An illicit night of passion results in a son, presumed by all at court to be that of the emperor. It is an act that comes back to haunt the hero in later life when his own wife has the child of another man—a classic case of karma.

Of all the women associated with Genji, the most "haunting" is Rokujo, another of his older lovers. She becomes so consumed with jealousy that her spirit takes possession of his pregnant wife, Aoi no Ue, who dies as a result. With her demonic power, Rokujo lingers in the mind of the reader, just as her spirit continues to plague Genji even after she herself has died.

But the great love of Genji's life is the devoted Murasaki no Ue (from whom the author derived her name, as courtiers used it to refer to her). As a niece of Fujitsubo, she first enters the story as a charming ten-year old. She, too, bears a resemblance to the prince's dead mother, and he is so smitten that he takes her off to his palace without even telling her father. Here he raises her Pygmalion-style to be his wife. Yet though he loves her dearly, he causes her distress not only by fathering a child with another woman, but also by taking another wife. Reading all this, one cannot help but wonder why Murasaki chose to idealize such a fickle hero. Heian thinking clearly played a part in this decision, for Genji's fleeting affections echo the changing seasons and underline the theme of evanescence. His nature is a part of the larger nature. At the same time, Murasaki is at pains to stress his sensitivity, for he treats each lover with special consideration and remains concerned for their well-being even after the flames of passion have died down. Yet there remain aspects of Genji's behaviour that beggar belief. How can a man who has a child by his father's wife be considered "shining"? And how about his affair with his half-brother's betroved? Why does he frighten the innocent young Yugao by carrying her off without revealing his identity? And what are we to make of the "kidnapping" of the young Murasaki no Ue? Though he acts as guardian to her for years, one day he suddenly forces himself on her, and it is clear that she is devastated. When he returns later the same evening, he finds her distraught, yet all he can say, astonishingly, is "What can be the trouble? I was hoping for a game of Go."

The disparity between Genji's "shining" qualities and his unshining behaviour was noted by the critic Motoori Norinaga (1730-1801). The conduct of the prince, he pointed out, was at odds with conventional morality. How could he then be championed as an ideal? The explanation he put forward has since become accepted wisdom:

> The Tale of Genji *does not dwell on his iniquitous and immoral acts, but rather recites over and over again his awareness of the sorrow of existence, and represents him as a good man who combines in himself all good things in men... The impure mind of illicit love affairs described* in The Tale of Genji *is there not for the purpose of being admired but for the purpose of nurturing the flower of the awareness of the sorrow of human existence.*

The argument centred around an aesthetic called *mono no aware*, which derives from the Buddhist view of the illusory nature of existence. The notion underpins the novel, and the option of retiring to become a monk or nun is never far from the surface. Even at thirty, Genji feels drawn to withdraw from life, and following the death of Murasaki no Ue, he is again filled with a longing to take orders. "I have often wondered," he says at one point, "whether the Blessed One was not determined to make me see more than others what a useless, insubstantial world it is."

Genji proved an immediate success, and handwritten copies were circulated at court. Not long afterwards the author of the *Sarashina Diary* (c.1070) wrote of her excitement at reading the book. As a young girl, she lived in a world of her own imagining, and when she was given a set of *Genji* volumes by an aunt, she was entranced by the romance.

The height of my aspirations was that a man of noble birth, perfect in both looks and manner, someone like the Shining Genji in the Tale, would visit me just once a year in the mountain village where he would have hidden me.

Some hundred years later came the striking illustrations of the *Genji Emaki*, or picture scrolls. These unwind horizontally and divide the story into arm-length sections containing text and illustrations. In this way the story unfolds, literally, before the eyes of the viewer. The scrolls were also the focus of small parties where the text would be read out, after which participants would gather round to admire and discuss the pictures. There were originally fifty-four Genji scrolls, one for each chapter, though only fragments survive. A much-reproduced scene shows Genji, his official wife Nyosan (the Third Princess), and her father, the retired emperor. It is a painful moment for all concerned because Nyosan has given birth to another man's son and is about to become a nun. The sense of isolation is emphasized through the heavy diagonal lines which separate them, while the "bird's eye" perspective views them from a distance and lets the observer imagine the feelings.

In later times, Noh plays feasted on *Genji* and made classics of certain episodes: Rokujo's jealousy of Genji's first wife, Aoi, for example. Two popular plays, *Nonomiya* and *Aoi no Ue*, focus on the clash between the women at a festival at Kamigamo Shrine. This occurred when Rokujo's small carriage was pushed aside by Aoi's servants. Though she had arrived first, hoping to see Genji in the parade, she went unnoticed back among the commoners. Her resentment later built up into a murderous rage.

It was not until the twentieth century that the outside world became aware of the novel, following a translation by Arthur Waley in six volumes (1925-33). This was a huge hit, and the poetic language won the book comparison with the translation of Proust's *A la recherche du temps perdu* (In Remembrance of Things Past, 1913-27). Waley was friends with the Bloomsbury set, and like them he had a Modernist agenda in seeking alternatives to the well-worn conventions of Victorian realism. His book proved influential: "In the late 1920s," wrote the novelist C. P. Snow, "most literary young people whom I knew were under the spell of *The Tale of Genji*." Virginia Woolf, who was an admirer, may even have had the prince in mind when she wrote *Orlando* (1928).

As a translator, Waley was free and easy, omitting passages and even a whole chapter. Since then other translations have appeared. Seidensticker's (1976) is considered accurate if terse, while Royall Tyler (2001) steered a middle course by retaining the rambling sentences of the original. My own preference is for Waley despite the faults, since it commands the majesty of a classic, though this can provoke heated discussions with partisans of the other versions.

Together the translations have helped spread the fame of the book, yet the city marks its association with the author in quiet terms. Unlike Moscow, with its statues of Tolstoy and Pushkin, Kyoto has no grand monument to its greatest writer. Given its heritage, perhaps it has no need to concern itself with a single author. Instead, it is left to the small town of Uji, where the final chapters of the novel are set, to house a Genji Museum. Here stand model palaces, paintings of famous scenes, and a film-narration retelling the tragic tale of Ukifune. This is the solitary figure with whom the book closes.

Following Genji's death, the court life gives way to a darker world, deprived of the prince's shining glory. From the heart of Heian-kyo, the focus switches to a settlement in the south-east where the young Ukifune is being wooed simultaneously by Genji's son and grandson. Torn between them, she attempts suicide by throwing herself in the river, but is rescued. Following this act of desperation, she retires to become a nun, forsaking the world at the tender age of twenty-one. Secluded in her temple, she refuses to meet anyone, even her brother. It completes the move away from the glittering life at court. A book that began with the glories of this world ends with thoughts of the next.

Postscript

Two hundred years after *Genji*, a lady-in-waiting known as Lady Nijo wrote an autobiographical account of court life entitled *Towazugatari* (An Unasked for Story). The book was long forgotten, but was discovered by a scholar in 1940 and translated into English in 1973 with the title *The Confessions of Lady Nijo*. The contents suggest that little had changed at court during the two centuries, despite the enormous changes in the country as a whole. The diarist tells of moon-viewing, poetry composition, and a contest between ex-emperors as to who could find the loveliest flowers.

The book has a "kiss-and-tell" fascination. It begins with the author's deflowering at thirteen by retired emperor Gofukakusa, and though she was at first mortified, by the next morning "I felt more attracted to him than ever before, and I wondered uneasily where these new feelings had come from." She became his mistress, though not exclusively his, for she had four children by three different men.

Gofukakusa had a taste for voyeurism, and on one occasion he encouraged her to make love to a man in an adjoining room, separated only by a paper partition. He also encouraged her romance with his half-brother, an eminent priest who once asked her to join him privately after evening prayers. "Even when we walk in paths of darkness, we are guided by the Lord Buddha," he told her. "My heart was not entirely possessed by love," confesses Nijo, "and yet late that night, seen by no one, I slipped out and went to him." He became the love of her life.

Lady Nijo's account marks the last of the great journals by court ladies. They cover some three hundred years, and as a genre constitute one of the treasures of world literature. It is a remarkable accomplishment, all the more so when one considers that this last great work was completed long before Geoffrey Chaucer had even got started.

Chapter Three
CITY OF BUDDHISM

Religious Syncretism

Kyoto has the greatest concentration of temples in Japan, and streams of visitors descend on the city each year to view their treasures. These can be wonderfully intriguing, for Buddhism arrived in Japan trailing a thousand years of history from its journey through India and China. It was introduced by a Korean mission in the sixth century, and by the time Heian-kyo was founded it already played a dominant role in cultural terms. Like medieval Christianity, it not only shaped people's view of the world, but also coloured the nature of their art.

Japan's native religion, Shinto, was not so much a belief system as a loose amalgam of practices rooted in the agricultural cycle. It had no holy book or unifying theology; indeed, it had no name until it was given one to distinguish it from Buddhism. It soon reached an easygoing accord with the imported religion, and mutual tolerance was promoted by Prince Shotoku. In many ways, the faiths complemented each other. Shinto was concerned with the placation of *kami* (or gods), whereas Buddhism looked to personal salvation. Shinto was thisworldly, and Buddhism other-worldly. Shinto shunned death as a defilement, whereas Buddhism saw it as central. Even nowadays, Shinto takes care of the rites of passage through life, while Buddhism is associated with funerals. "Born Shinto, die Buddhist" remains the norm for most Japanese.

In Heian times the relationship between the religions deepened as new forms of Buddhism recognized the Shinto *kami*. It led to the syncretism that characterizes the Japanese tradition—the ability to unify seemingly incompatible beliefs. For centuries there was no clear borderline between the faiths, and priests often combined both roles. Buddhism took care of the soul, while Shinto looked after the spirit of place. Still today out of a population of 125 million, some 117 million Japanese claim to be Shinto, while 90 million belong to Buddhist sects.

Picking out the vestiges of syncretism has been something of a hobby of mine on my tours around Kyoto. I like the oddity of a *torii* (Shinto's sacred gateway) in a Buddhist graveyard, or Shinto ropes decorating temple buildings. At Kitano Tenmangu there is a mandala in which the *kami* are laid out in Buddhist form, and at To-ji is a statue of the Shinto god Hachiman dressed as a Buddhist priest. Best

of all is a *torii* at Kitano Tenmangu Shrine which has a lotus petal base: a Buddhist graft on a Shinto shoot. The intertwining of the two faiths is even writ large on the surrounds of the city, for the markings of the Daimonji festival include both Buddhist characters as well as a *torii* scoured into the hillside.

There are many who shy away from Buddhist temples, and those of us who live in Kyoto are used to visitors reluctant to visit more than a couple. Perhaps it is an acquired taste: I should know, for I am one of those who have been "converted". During my first years in Japan I was reluctant to explore them, since my own sympathies inclined me more towards Shinto. It was some time before I came to appreciate the fascinating wealth of Buddhist arts.

Let me cite as an example of the "finds" one can come across a wonderful picture scroll known as *Chojugiga* (Animal Caricatures). It belongs to Kozan-ji, in the north-west of the city. Done in simple ink outline, the twelfth-century sketches parody human vanities. In one scene, a frog raises its arms in triumph after winning a sumo contest against an upended rabbit. Another scene shows a monkey in priest's robes reciting a Buddhist scripture before the figure of a cross-legged frog. The artist clearly had a strong sense of the ridiculous, and the satirical drawings could be seen as the great ancestor of modern *manga*.

For those still sceptical about the attraction of temples, a visit to Sekizan Zenin in the north-east of the city might prove persuasive. It is the city's finest example of syncretism, with a combination of Shinto and Buddhist styles in the temple buildings. There is even a mirror, one of Shinto's "three sacred regalia", next to the Buddhist statuary on the altar. Outside in the temple compound Buddhas, *kami*, and folk spirits jostle in happy proximity. The religious instinct is here expressed through Sanskrit prayers, magic rites, fire ceremonies, water purification, and Taoist fortune telling—something for everyone. Seated on the temple roof is a monkey, symbol of the mountain spirit. It faces towards the imperial palace where sits another, thus creating a "force field" preventing the ingress of evil spirits into the city. The effect is underpinned by linguistic symbolism, for the Japanese for monkey—*saru*—means "Go away!" More than just a pun, it is a monument to the magic of words and an indication of the playful side of what can appear a morbid religion.

But the undoubted glory of Kyoto's temples is the amazing statuary that stands at their heart. Many of these figures are staggering creations which possess a mysterious power, as their makers were able to imbue them with a special spiritual quality. Some are held in such awe that they are rarely if ever put on display. Appreciation is helped by a little background knowledge, though confusingly the deities vary from sect to sect. At the top of the spiritual hierarchy stand the *nyorai* (Supreme Buddhas), which in Kyoto terms means "the big four": Yakushi Nyorai with his jar of healing; Dainichi Nyorai who created all things; Amida Nyorai who lives in the Western Pure Land; and the historical Buddha, known in Japanese as Shakasama (because he was a member of the Shaka clan) or as Shakyamuni ("sage of the Shaka"). Surprisingly to many, the latter is the least common.

Beneath the *nyorai* in rank are the *bosatsu* (Boddhisattva), who have put off assuming their place in paradise in order to serve mankind. In other words, they are voluntary intermediaries between this world and the next. The most common are Jizo (protector of children and travellers) and Kannon ("goddess of mercy"). Miroku, too, enjoys local fame because of a single statue—that at Koryu-ji. Known as "the Buddha of the future", Miroku promised to be the next to manifest in this world, and the Koryu-ji statue shows him seated with elegant fingers extending towards his cheek as he contemplates the salvation of mankind. The sublime features make this one of the most celebrated artworks in Japan, though its origins are controversial. Most critics assume it was made in Korea and presented to Prince Shotoku in the early seventh century, but some maintain that only the wood was donated and that the sculpting was done in Japan.

Both *nyorai* and Bodhisattva, known collectively as Buddhas, stand on a pedestal of lotus petals to indicate their enlightenment. The plant symbolizes purity because of its ability to produce a white flower from even the dirtiest of ponds, so the open lotus indicates a divine flowering. The toga-like robes and knotted curls of the statues betray the influence of ancient Greece, improbable though this may seem. It came about through Alexander the Great's conquest of Central Asia, when the Mediterranean style was passed to Gandhara and then along the Silk Road. It is rather startling to find a touch of Hellenism in old Heian-kyo, but perhaps it is only right that there should be a connection between these two ancient cultures of "sweetness and light".

Seated within Kyoto, it is comforting to think of the many figures that offer protection to the city. High on Mount Hiei stands Yakushi Nyorai, jar in hand to dispense healing and comfort. Not far away, on Kurama's holy hill, Bishamonten, the guardian of the north, looks towards Kyoto and the city he protects, while in the temples of Esoteric Buddhism sits Dainichi Nyorai, creator of all things. The many representations of Amida speak of his Pure Land in the western realm, and his attendant comes bearing balm in the form of the thousand-armed Kannon. Complementing these are the myriad *kami* of Shinto, from Atago's fire spirit in the west to the great Susanoo no Mikoto at Yasaka in the east. Keeping an eye on them all is Kammu's presiding presence. It is a fecund universe, and one that in its pluralism offers a pleasing kind of reassurance. Few cities can claim to be so blessed.

Tendai Eclecticism

The arrival of two new sects, Tendai and Shingon, in the early days of Heian-kyo was a major development, as they maintained that enlightenment was attainable by all, not just by those following monastic rules, and they brought with them some exotic practices. There were spells, symbols, mantras, mandalas, fire ceremonies, incantations, asceticism and invocatory hand gestures. Like Catholicism in England, the "high church" finery appealed to the aesthetic tastes of the aristocracy.

When Kammu first founded Heian-kyo, his concern to "seal" the vulnerable north-east corner led him to make contact with a priest living on Mount Hiei. This was Saicho (767-822), known also by his posthumous name of Dengyo Daishi. The son of an aristocrat, he had entered orders at eighteen but grew disenchanted with the worldliness of the priesthood and dropped out to be a hermit. In 788, together with a handful of followers, he built a small temple near the top of Hiei. Kammu lent the monk his encouragement, and in 804 he sent him on a mission to China to study with the priests of Mount Tiantai (the Japanese name for which was Tendai). When Saicho returned, he set up a teaching centre on Hiei called Enryaku-ji.

Because of its location, the temple assumed protection of the capital, and by extension of the state as a whole. It took its task seriously. To prevent the entrance of evil spirits, there was almost continual chanting and ringing of bells. The new sect was a "broad church" that embraced a wide range of practices, from Zen meditation to visualizations and mantra. These were later augmented by mountain asceticism. Emphasis was put on learning, with Saicho recommending a twelve-year period for training. "Even the dullest stone becomes sharp after twelve years of daily polishing," he noted.

From a small seminary, Enryaku-ji grew to be one of the largest complexes in the world. At the height of its power, between the eleventh and fifteenth centuries, the temple spread twenty miles in all directions and had 400 sub-temples. A head of the temple called Jien (1155-1225), poet and theologian, boasted that:

> *Though mountains are innumerable,*
> *When people say "the mountain"*
> *It refers to only one—Mount Hiei.*

Such an outflow of writings poured out of Enryaku-ji that historians have called it "the well spring of medieval culture". At one time or another, nearly all the outstanding figures of Japanese Buddhism studied on the mountain. These include Honen, founder of the Pure Land Sect; Shinran, of the True Pure Land Sect; Ippen of the Ji Sect; Eisai, of Rinzai Zen; Dogen, of Soto Zen; and Nichiren, whose teachings inform Sokka Gakkai and the Nichiren sects. It is a remarkable record, which led Hiei to be dubbed the "Mother of Japanese Buddhism".

As Enryaku-ji grew in size, it acquired warrior-monks to protect its interests. By the eleventh century, these formed one of the most powerful armies in the land. The militia included some dubious types, for law enforcers were not allowed onto the mountain's sacred land. From time to time, warlike monks would descend on the city to push the demands of the temple, and even the emperor was powerless to resist them. "There are three things which I cannot control," said Emperor Shirakawa: "the waters of the Kamo River, the roll of the dice, and the monks of Mount Hiei."

One can get an impression of the warrior-monks from Mizoguchi's film *Shin Heike Monogatari* (1955), where they stream down the mountain carrying weapons, emblems and palanquins. It is an intimidating sight. At their head is a portable shrine bearing a Shinto deity called Sanno, from whom the emperor was descended. Opposition to the monks was thus cast as opposition to the imperial family. As they parade through the city, the proud and arrogant monks demand obeisance from all they pass. Even samurai are made to kneel in respect.

For centuries Enryaku-ji continued to throw its weight around in this way. Efforts were made to stamp out other sects, and early Zen followers were subjected to threats. There was armed conflict with Nara, and with a rival Tendai group at Miidera. Worst of all was the treatment of the Nichiren sect: in 1536, all twenty-one of its Kyoto temples were destroyed, and the priests slaughtered.

Thirty-five years later, Enryaku-ji's power came to a dramatic end when Oda Nobunaga, unifier of Japan, turned on the wilful monks.

> *If I do not take them away now, this great trouble will be ever-lasting. Moreover, these priests violate their vows: they eat fish and stinking vegetables, keep concubines, and never unfold the sacred books. How can they be vigilant against evil, or maintain the right? Surround their dens and burn them, and suffer none within them to live!*

Marching up the sides of the mountain, Nobunaga's troops laid waste to the temple complex. Some 25,000 people were massacred, and its 3,000 buildings set aflame. It is said the sky remained bright for three full nights, and that Kyoto was covered in ash.

Although the temple revived after Nobunaga's death, it never recovered its former power. The complex today, impressive enough, is just one-twentieth of what it once was—hard to imagine for anyone who has walked round some of the 130 buildings. The Central Main Hall stands near the top of the mountain, facing away from Kyoto towards the north-east and the devils it guards against. It has a strange atmosphere; there is a central raised section for visitors and a dramatic ten-foot drop to the floor below where priests pray before tall altars. The effect of the empty space is chilling—literally so, since cold air fills the gloomy recess. A heavy darkness hangs about the inner sanctum, and from across the empty space gold-leaf statues loom out of the darkness. *Kowai* (frightening), I once heard a woman say as she peered in.

These days a visit to Mount Hiei is a tale of two worlds. On a material level are cable-cars, an all-year ski slope, a "garden museum", and a winding roadway along which coaches shuttle between souvenir shops. D. T. Suzuki, the writer on Zen, remarked that he was "revolted" by the commercialism. On the other hand, ascent by foot along the quiet forest paths reveals the spiritual side of the mountain. Solitary temples house chanting priests, and rigorous ascetic exercises are performed in secluded places. Here one gains a sense of the self-discipline that for centuries has guided, and still guides, life on the mountain. Here too can be found the *ajari*, or living saints, whose dedication to their faith constitutes without doubt the city's most extraordinary tradition.

Living Saints

Tendai's asceticism can test the limits of endurance. Ninety days of chanting with only two hours of sleep at night. Ninety days of meditation with two toilet breaks per day and sleep in the lotus position. Continual chanting of the names of 3,000 Buddhas with a full prostration for each. And all done with only a thin covering at night time, even in the bitterly cold winters. (The temperature can be over five degrees colder than in the valley below.)

The austerities introduced by Saicho were augmented by those of the native *shugendo*, which had origins in shamanism and mountain worship. The supreme challenge, known as *sennichi kaihogyo* (1,000-day walking austerity), was established by a priest called So-o in the ninth century. It consists of 100-day blocks of arduous walking split up over a period of seven years. By the end, the candidate will have covered some 25,000 miles, equivalent to walking around the world—in straw sandals. The course is over eighteen miles long and completed in the dark of night, when, as one practitioner put it, "You come face to face with yourself." Along the way, the candidate has to stop for prayer at no fewer than 225 stations of worship. Each requires a different form of ritual, which has to be memorized beforehand. This alone takes several weeks. The night-time walking is not an exercise for the faint-hearted. There are steps, steep slopes, and sudden drops, not to mention monkeys, wild pigs, bears, and poisonous snakes. I once had the chance to ask a successful candidate, Mitsunaga Kakudo, about this and he brushed aside the question, saying that one soon became "friends with the darkness".

The practice is dedicated to Fudo Myo-o, the deity who personifies resolve, and the priests who volunteer themselves pledge to complete the austerity even at the cost of their lives. To show their commitment, they dress in white (the clothing of death) and carry a cord and knife with which to kill themselves should they fail. For the first 300 days, the candidate cannot wear *tabi* (Japanese socks), which means that the straw sandals cut into the skin. Spares have to be carried because they wear out and even disintegrate in rain. The outfit is completed by a distinctive hat which is also carried at first, as the right to wear it has to be earned. It is long and folded over on both sides, symbolizing an unfurled lotus leaf that will only open with the gaining of enlightenment.

The most stringent part of the course comes after six years, when there is a nine-day fast in which not only is no food taken, but also no liquid and no sleep. This is the supreme austerity, in which the candidate is confronted with his mortality. By way of preparation, he eats a symbolic last meal after which he bids those attending a final farewell. In the ordeal the old self will "die", giving birth to a new self that is at one with Fudo Myo-o.

During the fast, the candidate is accompanied by monks who prod him whenever he threatens to nod off. Time is taken up with prayer, sutra readings, and 100,000 repetitions of the Fudo Myo-o mantra. By day four, it is said that a bad smell as of a rotting corpse becomes evident. By day five the saliva dries up, leaving a taste of blood. To stop the gums sticking to the side of the mouth, the candidate is allowed to draw water at two o'clock every morning. However, the mouth can only be rinsed out: every precious drop of water has to be spat back into the cup. The well is 200 yards away, and by day three candidates need support. By the last day they cannot walk at all. When the 44-year old Fujinami Genshin emerged in 2001, many in the crowd of supporters burst into tears; his weight was almost half of what it had been, and, usually cheerful, he could not even raise a smile.

In the last year comes a grand encirclement of Kyoto, which is done in addition to the route around Mount Hiei. It makes for a total of some fifty-six miles, which takes sixteen hours at a brisk pace. The practice alternates between days when the candidate descends into the city, staying overnight, and days when he reverses the direction and returns up the mountain. All this is done with little over four hours sleep a night and a frugal diet of soup, rice and vegetables. As the candidate enters the city, he is joined by a small group of supporters, one of whom is armed with a T-shaped piece of wood with which to propel him along when his strength fails. It is the most public of the events, with supporters bowing by the roadside to be blessed.

Following this, there remains a final 100-day course around Mount Hiei, though the last twenty-five days are left uncompleted as a token of future endeavour. The candidate is now awarded the title of Grand Ajari, and is honoured by a ceremony at the Former Imperial Palace, where he alone of all visitors is allowed to keep on his footwear. It is as if his straw sandals have been welded to his feet by the endless walking.

Given the nature of the achievement, it is surprising how little known the *ajari* are: even some Kyotoites are unfamiliar with them. This contrasts with the fame of their Tantric cousins in Tibet, whose magical feats have a worldwide reputation. Records for the practice were burnt by Nobunaga's troops in 1571, but since then there has been an average of one candidate every nine years. Three are known to have died during the course.

There are presently seven living *ajari*. The most famous is Sakai Yusai (b. 1926), one of only three people in history known to have completed the course twice. He became a priest in his late thirties, after suffering business failure and the suicide of his wife. Now he is a friendly figure who runs a small temple on Hiei and makes himself readily available. Asked about the hardships involved, he simply smiles and expresses gratitude for "a path to understanding and true appreciation of the natural world". Holy Mount Hiei, "Mother of Japanese Buddhism", still guides her children towards salvation, now as she has done for centuries.

Shingon Esotericism

At the time that Saicho was founding Tendai, there was another remarkable priest active in Heian-kyo. This was Kukai (774-835), the founder of Shingon and a man of exceptional qualities. As well as a calligrapher, he is credited with compiling the first popular dictionary, systematizing the *kana* syllabary, and setting up the Eighty-eight Temple Pilgrimage in Shikoku. He is remembered, too, as a philanthropist, who helped villagers with bridge-building and agricultural projects. For some, he is nothing less than "the father of Japanese culture".

Kukai was born into the provincial aristocracy, and at eighteen went to Heian-kyo to study to be a statesman. He dropped out to train as a monk, and went on his own initiative on the same mission to China as Saicho. Though he expected to stay twenty years, he had mastered the esoteric teachings of Shingon after just two and returned to Japan to set up headquarters at Mount Koya in Wakayama-ken. In 823, he was given charge of To-ji in Heian-kyo. It was a rare honour, for it was one of only two temples in the capital. He developed it into a huge seminary. The present complex, which contains twenty-four acres in a moated compound, is just a quarter of its former size.

Shingon is described by the Agency for Cultural Affairs as "a blend of abstruse metaphysical teachings and rituals deeply imbued with magic". As with Tendai, the purpose is to strive towards enlightenment. But whereas Tendai encourages learning, Shingon favours mysticism. It also insists on the primacy of oral transmission, as the following tale indicates. Despite being the senior of the two, Saicho had gone to study esotericism from the gifted Kukai. One day he asked to borrow a book, but was refused on the grounds that "words are rubble; the profundities of the secret doctrines are not found in the mere sentences of a text." This led to friction between the two men, and relations later broke down altogether when Saicho's favourite disciple defected.

Shingon's view of the universe is complex, and the path to understanding is aided by visual representation in the form of mandalas. Kukai explained the purpose this way:

Since the Esoteric Buddhist teachings are so profound as to defy expression in writing, they are revealed through the medium of painting to those not yet enlightened. The various postures and hand gestures depicted in the mandalas are products of the great compassion of the Buddha; the sight of them may well enable one to attain Buddhahood.

At To-ji are two mandalas that are the oldest in Japan and date from the late ninth or early tenth century. The Womb World represents the physical sphere, and shows hundreds of deities in diminishing squares towards a central square in which is Dainichi Nyorai, the source and expression of the universe. The Diamond World, also on silk, represents the transcendental sphere. It is simpler and intended as a study guide. Devotees meditate on each Buddha in turn to internalize the symbolic nature.

The temple also houses a three-dimensional mandala in the form of statues laid out by Kukai. In a city of stunning sights, this is one of the most remarkable. Within the imposing building stand twenty-one massive statues, which represent the heart of the Shingon universe. They are dark, forbidding, and powerful. Short necks and fat cheeks give them a solid feel. Yet there is tremendous variety too, for serene Buddhas with sublime expressions are juxtaposed with ferocious, multi-headed monsters. The most eye-catching is the fearful Fudo Myo-o, said to have been the devotional image of Kukai himself. The deity's terrifying expression is directed towards the enemies of Buddhism such as ignorance and greed, through which he slices with the sword he carries. Ever vigilant, he serves as inspiration to believers to never give up.

The mysteries of Shingon are on display every year in a festival at Chishaku-in, in the east of Kyoto, which celebrates the birth of Kukai. It takes the form of a fire ceremony, which derives from ancient India where fire was treated as a magical element that transforms what it consumes and provides a connecting link between earth and heaven. The full hierarchy of Shingon, all shaven-headed, turns out for the event. Costumes range from the ordinary attire of black shawl over white robes to ceremonial outfits of yellow, purple and green. That of the head priest is a dazzling gown of gold brocade. Also in attendance are eighty *yamabushi* (mountain ascetics) in hemp robes, white leggings, and deer-skin aprons. Around their necks hang green or red pom-poms, and on the forehead is a black circular headpiece. Each item serves a symbolic as well as a practical purpose.

Following a memorial service, a square section of ground is roped off, in the middle of which stands a mound of cypress sprigs. To one side is an altar table piled high with offerings. Then to the sound of conches and the beat of a drum, the *yamabushi* march into the square chanting and ringing stick-rattles to ward off evil. There follows a series of purification rites, in which ceremonial axes and knives slice through the air. Prayers are read out, bells rung, sticks waved over incense, and from each corner of the square a symbolic arrow is fired high into the air. When the mound of cypress sprigs is set alight, a fog of thick smoke emerges, which is fanned and stimulated by the sprinkling of water. For a while the huge menacing mass of smoke hovers over the mound, then billows slowly up into the sky. This carries away the defilement of those in attendance.

From beneath the smothering dark smoke, flames splutter into life and burst into a roaring fire, around which the *yamabushi* circle like witches at Beltane. Meanwhile, the head priest blesses a pile of wooden tablets before tossing them one by one into the flames. The requests written on these float up to the gods on high. Before the final prayer, a Shinto-style stick is waved in purification over the onlookers, and their bags are bathed in smoke to ensure safety for the coming year.

Noticeable throughout are the complex hand movements of initiates. Each gesture, each finger position, has a precise function to do with cleansing or summoning. The mystique adds to a ceremony charged with symbolism, and it is difficult not to be drawn into the spell. As a spectacle, it is a piece of inspired—divinely inspired—theatre. Small wonder that the aristocrats of Heian-kyo were so drawn to the rituals. Small wonder, too, that the sect has won a cultish following in modern times.

Amidism

Anyone visiting Kyoto's temples will soon become familiar with the figure of Amida, whose name derives from the Sanskrit for Infinite Light. The popularity of the deity stems from a passage in an ancient

Buddhist scripture that tells of the vows he made to mankind. One of these was that he would not become a Buddha until he received in his Pure Land (situated in the west of the Buddhist universe) all those who called on his name.

In early Heian times the practice had been introduced from China of reciting a mantra called *nembutsu*, which runs *Namu Amida Butsu*— "I take refuge in Amida Buddha." At first this was restricted to the monks of Mount Hiei, but during the tenth century it found wider favour as preachers spread the message among common folk. This was due in part to a kind of "millennial angst" known as *mappo*. According to Buddhist lore, the death of the historical Buddha would be followed by three distinct periods. In the first, his teachings would flourish; in the second, there would be a decline; and in the third, there would be degeneration. This last stage, known as *mappo*, was calculated by theologians to begin in 1052, after which earthly enlightenment would be all but impossible.

The consciousness of *mappo* led to a sense of anxiety, and a number of *nembutsu* preachers roamed the country, spreading the good news about Amida. One of the most influential was a wandering beggar-monk called Kuya (903-72). The "Saint of the Market Place" used a unique chanting style to reach out to the marginalized. These were cruel times, and the promise of a better life must have held great appeal:

To chant the nembutsu just once
Namu Amida Butsu
That is all there really is
Chanting it, we become the Buddha
And sit upon the lotus throne.

Not long after Kuya, a Tendai monk named Genshin (a.k.a. Eshin Sozu 942-1017) produced *The Essentials of Salvation* (984), in which he argued that in an age of *mappo* Amida's mercy offered the only hope. The joy of birth in his Pure Land was compared to a blind man able to see for the first time, and the pleasures of paradise were contrasted with the horrors of hell. The book was influential among the aristocracy, affecting Murasaki Shikibu and Fujiwara Michinaga among others. The latter was particularly ardent, and once claimed to have repeated the *nembutsu* 700,000 times in a five-day retreat.

As well as being a writer, Genshin was one of the best artists of his time. His work can be seen at the temple of Sanzen-in, to the north-east of Kyoto, where there is a superb example of a "paradise garden". Mossy lawns surround a hall from out of whose confines shines a radiant Amida flanked by his kneeling attendants, Seishi (the embodiment of Amida's wisdom) and Kannon (the embodiment of Amida's compassion). Here is the Pure Land in earthly form.

There were once a hundred such Amida Halls in and around Kyoto, though only three survive. One is the Phoenix Hall of Byodo-in, which many consider the most beautiful building in Japan. It is widely known, for it is found on the back of every ten-yen coin. It stands at Uji, to the south-east of the city, and was built to coincide with the beginning of *mappo* by the son of Michinaga, Fujiwara Yorimichi (990-1074). It was once part of a huge estate, but of the thirty original buildings—miraculously—it alone survived. It is best seen from the far side of the lotus pond that stands before it. From the

central hall, two "wings" in the form of long, curving pavilions, stretch out as if simulating the phoenix in flight. They give the building an expansive charm; for the historian George Sansom, it is "a structure with such an airy grace that it seems to be rising to escape from earthly sorrows."

Inside the hall is a statue of Amida, which is an acclaimed national treasure. Gilded, lacquered, and eight feet tall, it shows the deity seated in meditation, with hands resting on his lap and looking downwards with compassionate eyes. The interior is purposely dark, and the statue was originally surrounded by candle-light reflected in mirrors to give a sense of miraculously floating in space. On the surrounding walls were bright paintings, faded now, of souls being received into the Pure Land. To devotees in the past, it must have seemed a heavenly vision.

The statue is the sole surviving creation of master-sculptor, Jocho (d. 1057), remembered as the founder of the woodblock style of production. Earlier statues were carved from a single trunk; in Jocho's system sculptures were broken into sections, which were worked on by different craftsmen under the master's supervision. The statues are markedly softer and more elegant than the chunky works of earlier times. Esoteric statues impress; those of Amidism console.

In Heian times there were formal court parties at which the doors of the hall were thrown open to reveal Amida seeming to descend out of the gloom, surrounded by fifty-two colourful Bodhisattvas attached to the walls. It is thought that the scene was accompanied by musicians seated in the long "wings" of the pavilion. The effect was so startling that Lady Nakatsukasa wrote in 1282 of understanding after this why people could believe in paradise. There was even a popular saying: "If you have doubts about the Pure Land, cure them by going to Uji."

Amida's descent to collect the souls of the dead, known as *raigo*, was a popular theme in the art of the time. Paintings were used in the rite for the dying, in the hope that the last image in this world would be the reality of the next. Holding a cord attached to a painting or statue was thought to ease the passage from impure to Pure Land; Michinaga famously died in this way. The cords were multi-coloured: red for compassion; white for purity; orange for passion; yellow for wisdom; and green for the return to Buddhahood.

Early pictures of the descent are dominated by the figure of Amida, who is placed in the centre of the picture on a large purple cloud. There is an example at Sanzen-in, where a golden Amida is accompanied by twenty-five attendants dancing and playing music. Later pictures place greater emphasis on speed, as if artists were concerned to dispel anxiety about hanging around after death. At Chion-in there is an example from the late Kamakura period (1186-1333), showing a diagonal descent as Amida and his attendants "surf" clouds over steep mountains. The rapidity of movement suggests they will arrive at the moment of death—a comforting notion.

Representations of Amida's descent also occur in three-dimensional form, and the garden at Sanzen-in offers a fine example. Rocks represent Amida and his attendants, while azalea bushes symbolize the clouds on which they speed. These are set on a hilly slope, down which spills a narrow stream to a small pond that contains a flat viewing rock. Standing on this in the heat of a summer's day gives a sense of being bathed in Amida's mercy.

There is an enactment of Amida's *raigo* each year in a charming festival held in a sub-temple of Sennyu-ji. The compound contains an Amida Hall from which children acting as Amida's attendants parade to the hall below. From there they return with the "dead soul", which is placed on the altar before Amida. Coloured ribbons run off from the statue to provide devotees with a link to the saviour. There is a feeling of intimacy as participants and audience crowd into the hall—children and mothers, mountain-ascetics and priests, the faithful and the sightseers. It is a delightful occasion, which brings to mind children's staging of the Nativity.

During the eleventh century, with the onset of *mappo*, Amidism grew in strength. It was at this time that a priest named Eikan (1033-1111) conducted ceremonies in which participants chanting the *nembutsu* circled round a statue of Amida. According to legend, one day the statue got off its pedestal and joined in. Eikan was rooted to the spot in astonishment, at which the statue turned round and called out, "Come on, Eikan, you're dawdling." The place where this happened, now the temple of Eikando, houses a commemorative statue known as the Turning Amida. It is a small figure, only thirty inches tall, but with a greater force than many larger figures. Unusually for an altar statue, the head is turned round and looking back. It suggests that the faithful are never alone, for Amida is leading the way and calling them ever onwards to the Pure Land. More than most, the image lingers in the mind.

In the 1160s came the culmination of Amidism with the building of Sanjusangendo. It is the longest wooden building in the world—387 feet in total—and houses 1,000 standing Kannon on either side of a huge sitting statue. As with the Phoenix Hall, the present building was just the private chapel of a large estate: it belonged to Go-Shirakawa (1127-1192), a retired emperor who continued to control affairs even after his abdication (typical of the "cloistered emperor" system). He was a devout Buddhist, who while on retreat became overwhelmed by the presence of Kannon (the personification of Amida's mercy).

A visit to the hall is a breath-taking affair, for the scale is stunning. Commentators have written of the curious effect in passing before the assembled statues, lined up as they are like a heavenly choir. On either side of the central seated figure are ten rows of fifty statues. They have eleven heads, to show Kannon's all-seeing nature. They also have forty-two arms, consisting of two ordinary and forty symbolic arms. These signify the deity's all-giving mercy, for each arm bears an item of comfort. Only on closer inspection do the differences between the statues become apparent. Some are thinner than others, some have wider eyes, and some have drapes with larger folds. The expressions, too, have an individual character. Sooner or later, Japanese say, one will find the likeness of a relative.

The whole collection is aligned so that the viewer looks westward, towards the Pure Land. The sense of the afterworld was more intense in the past, as the original building was painted in vivid colours—blue, red, white, yellow, and green. Look at the beams and you can see the faded remains of flowers, clouds and Buddhas representing the joyful paradise. In the early morning when the doors were thrown open, the sun would creep over the eastern hills to kiss the golden heads of the statues.

In 1249 the hall burned down, and though priests risked their lives to save what they could, 875 of the Kannon were destroyed. The job of

replacing them was given to a team under master-sculptor, Tankei (1173-1256). Unbelievably, he was eighty-two when he completed the magnificent sitting statue at the centre of the new collection. Tankei was the son of Unkei (d.1223), and the Kei family dominated the sculpture of the age. They claimed descent from Jocho of Byodo-in fame, and in their work can be felt all the vigour of the "golden age of sculpture", when wood was used to create figures of strength and muscularity. The rugged individualism, given a final sparkle by crystal eyes, is evident in the figures placed before the Sanjusangendo Kannon to protect them. The awesome creatures consist of twenty-eight guardian spirits, plus Raijin (the god of thunder) and Fujin (the god of wind). The two native deities are only three-and-a-half feet tall, but the dynamic power with which they surge from behind banks of clouds makes them seem much taller.

Some of the very best Kamakura sculpture is on display in a small and nondescript hall, unknown to the millions who do the rounds of the city's tourist sights. It stands at the back of Rokuharamitsu-ji and includes self-portraits of Unkei and Tankei that are particularly moving. Carved in black wood, the genial sculptors seem so lifelike that one wants to reach out and thank them for their creations. Nearby stands a statue of the *nembutsu* preacher Kuya, founder of the temple, considered one of Japan's finest sculptures. It was carved by Unkei's fourth son, Kosho (d. 1237), and shows a small emaciated man in tattered clothes holding a staff surmounted by a deer's horn. In his right hand is a wooden hammer with which to strike a bell hung around his neck. Six small Buddhas extend on a wire from out of his mouth—one for each Chinese character in "Namu Amida Butsu".

With his twisted hips, sunken cheeks, and distant gaze, Kuya looks every inch the barefoot mystic. Amidism has left us many grand memorials, but the solitary mendicant is a striking reminder of the strength of belief in an age of despair. Here in this stunning piece of sculpture the whole force of the faith is brought to life.

Pure Land Devotion

Just as the foundation of Heian-kyo led to the emergence of Esoteric Buddhism, so the unrest at the end of the era created the conditions for new sects. Yet again Mount Hiei proved fertile ground, as Tendai's practices were broken down into constituent parts. It was at this time that belief in Amida was made into a fully-fledged sect, thanks to a monk named Honen (1133-1212). According to tradition, he had gone to study on Mount Hiei after being orphaned at the age of eight when his father was attacked by robbers. The dying father begged his son not to take revenge, but to pray for the salvation of mankind. It shaped his life.

Honen proved an eager student and a quick learner: "If you told him one thing, he understood ten," said his teacher. Although his ability promised a bright future, he grew disillusioned with the worldliness of the clergy and at eighteen joined a hermitage instead. He remained devoted to study and went through the whole Buddhist canon five times, though his mastery left him unfulfilled. "By renunciation I have become a hermit," he wrote, "but my body and soul are not at peace."

One aspect that troubled Honen was the remoteness of Buddhism from the poor. When he happened across an old Chinese text about the merits of the *nembutsu*, he came to see it as more than just a way of reaching out to the masses, but as the one and only means of salvation:

> *Learning a lot of dogma and practising asceticism is to little avail. The only real requirement is to chant* nembutsu. *In this way anybody can be born into the Pure Land through the agency of Amida's saving power.*

Fired by his belief, Honen left Hiei and moved to Otani, a burial ground to the east of the city. His reputation soon spread, though his teaching was considered heretical by Tendai. This led to tragic consequences for two of Honen's followers, Anraku (d. 1207) and Juren (1169-1207).

The two monks had persuaded a couple of ladies-in-waiting to convert to Pure Land thinking and leave the court. Whether the attraction was the men or their message is unclear, but it infuriated the emperor who numbered them among his favourites. Taking advantage of the Tendai stance, he had the monks charged with heresy, and when they refused to recant they were executed. The resolution the men showed in the face of death proved a great boost to the new teaching. Legends grew up around the event, and rumours spread that purple clouds had gathered at the moment of Anraku's execution as Amida descended to welcome his soul.

In the crackdown on the sect, Honen was exiled to Tosa in Shikoku. He was seventy-four, but he took it as a welcome opportunity to spread his message to the provinces. Four years later, he was allowed back to the capital after the emperor had a nightmare warning him about his mistreatment of the monk. The next year Honen died, at the age of seventy-nine. He refused to take hold of a cord attached to an Amida statue, saying that he could already see the deity descending. His belief was absolute, for he felt that he had been personally saved by Amida when his Tendai faith failed him. Such was his devotion that he recited the *nembutsu* up to 60,000 times a day.

Whereas Esoteric Buddhism emphasized the struggle for enlightenment, Honen laid stress on faith. Instead of reliance on one's own power (*jiriki*), he preached reliance on another (*tariki*). In place of wisdom and asceticism, he preached devotion and charitable works. It was a reformation which opened up Buddhism to ordinary people.

Amida-Buddha's compassion is not limited to particular people, such as monks or the rich, but is for all beings: therefore, anyone can be liberated, regardless of their gender, status or financial position. All we have to do is chant "Namu Amida Butsu."

With its populist streak, Honen's sect became a mass movement, and at one point it is estimated that a third of all Japanese were converts. "Tendai for the royal family, Shingon for the aristocracy, Zen for warriors, and Pure Land for the masses", ran a popular saying. Today the sect remains among the biggest in Japan.

The head temple is the magnificent Chion-in, standing on the site where Honen lived and died. The complex burnt down in the seventeenth century, after which it was re-established in its present form. Set on the eastern hills, it is entered up a steep slope on which is an imposing set of steps (featured in *The Last Samurai*) that lead to the largest gate in Japan. As well as honouring Amida, Chion-in is also something of a shrine to the founder. The place where Honen died is now a hall of worship, and on the nearby hill is his tomb before which prayer mats are laid out. The sound of the *nembutsu* seems to hover over the area.

One of the treasures of the temple is a huge series of hand scrolls entitled *The Illustrated Biography of Priest Honen*. The Kamakura era was rich in such "lives of the saints", and with forty-eight scrolls this is the longest of them all. The first covers Honen's childhood up to the age of eight when his father died, and interestingly there is a scene where he appears twice. On one side of the picture he is riding a bamboo stick like a horse, while on the other he is standing before a wall in prayer. The latter was inserted later, to show that even as a boy he was drawn to the Western Paradise. It is not often one gets such a graphic example of hagiolatry in action.

The heart of the temple is the huge Founder's Hall, built on the site where Honen once preached. It houses a sacred image of him, which is cleaned on 25 December each year in a special ceremony. It is quite an occasion, with over a thousand people banging on wooden drums (*mokugyo*) as young priests prostrate themselves full-length. It is the kind of treatment normally reserved for august deities, and, seated among the believers, I was overwhelmed by the reverence shown to the Pure Land prophet. Here, as in many religions, the messenger is feted for the message.

True Pure Land Devotion

One of Honen's followers was a priest called Shinran (1173-1262), who was also raised on Mount Hiei from a young age. The orphaned son of a minor aristocrat, he had started out by becoming a dedicated ascetic who performed the most rigorous of practices. Yet he was alienated by the "politics" at the temple, and he found that asceticism did not tame his desires. At the age of twenty-nine, while on retreat in the city at Rokkaku-do, he had a vision which altered the course of his life. The temple was dedicated to Kannon, and the deity appeared in a vision offering to manifest as a woman for his pleasure while at the same assuring him of entry to the Pure Land. It spurred Shinran to abandon asceticism for study with Honen, forty years his senior. He became a devoted disciple.

In 1207, at the time of Honen's exile, Shinran was also banished. He went first to Echigo (now Niigata), then to Hitachi province (now Ibaraki) where he spent twenty years. Unlike Honen, he did not keep monastic rules, but married, had children, and ate meat and fish. He was an individualist, dedicated to pursuing truth in his own way— "neither monk nor laity", as he put it. In terms of traditional Buddhism, he was a heretic. Compared with Honen, he laid greater emphasis on conscience, which is why he has been compared to Martin Luther. Calling on Amida seemed to him meaningless if not said in sincerity. Instead of countless repetitions of the *nembutsu*, he claimed that salvation was possible from a single utterance if it was said "from the gut".

Following his return to Kyoto, Shinran devoted himself to theoretical work in support of *tariki*, or salvation through "other power". This required a subjugation of the ego, as can be seen through the startling declaration that "Even the good person is born in the Pure Land, so without question is the person who is evil." The thinking behind this was that whereas good people assume they have earned the right to paradise, evil people are driven by the burden of imperfection to submit their very souls:

And from that time on, there is no necessity for any other good deed...
there is no need to fear committing an evil action, for no evil can
stand in the way of the original vow of Amida.

Shinran died at the age of eighty-nine. "When I die, throw me into
the Kamo River and let the fish eat my body," he had told his followers.
It showed a lack of worldly attachment, as well as a desire to avoid
posthumous veneration. Nonetheless, a mausoleum set up for him in
Yamashina became a focus for followers, from out of which grew the
True Pure Land Sect (Jodo Shinshu). For many years the sect was
subject to persecution and suffered hard times, but thanks to the efforts
of Rennyo (1415-99) there was a dramatic upturn in its fortunes as it
reached out to farmers and the rural poor. In 1591 came an important
breakthrough when the sect was granted land in central Kyoto, to
which it moved the head temple of Hongan-ji (meaning Temple of the
Primal Vow, a reference to Amida's promise to save mankind).

At the start of the seventeenth century, a dispute over succession
arose between two brothers, resulting in the division of the sect. The
result can be seen in the two mighty temples that today dominate the
area north of the railway station. Nishi (West) Hongan-ji stands on the
original site, while Higashi (East) Hongan-ji is a block away. Property
was divided between them, including Shinran's remains. As a result, the
founder now has two tombs: one in West Otani and one in East Otani.

The Hongan-ji temples are palatial affairs, set in their own moated
compounds. They bear joint witness to the popularity of Shinran's
teaching, for ironically the man with no intention of starting a sect
became the founder of the largest of all. By the late nineteenth century,
it is said that Nishi Hongan-ji alone had a bigger budget than the whole
of Kyoto Prefecture.

Of the two temples, Nishi Hongan-ji is of greater interest culturally.
It was given parts of Hideyoshi's palace in the seventeenth century
(which we will come to in the chapter on Momoyama arts), and it
houses an Amida Hall in which are portraits of Pure Land prophets,
starting with Honen and stretching back through China all the way to
India. In the Founder's Hall is a seated statue of Shinran, which is two
and a half feet tall, made of Japanese cypress and dating from Kamakura
times. Legend has given it an aura of mystique, for it is said to be carved
by the founder himself and varnished with ash from his cremation.

Higashi Hongan-ji sadly suffered a devastating fire in the late nineteenth century, which meant that it had to be rebuilt. Its chief glory is the massive Founder's Hall, not only the largest wooden building in Kyoto but one of the biggest in the world. This being Japan, the dimensions are precisely spelt out: 253 feet long, 193 feet wide, 127 feet tall, 175,967 roof tiles, and a floor space comprising 927 *tatami* mats. As with the Pure Land Sect, it seems that the messenger outranks the message, for this gigantic Founder's Hall overshadows the Amida Hall that stands beside it.

Among the exhibits are some thick ropes made from women's hair. These were donated to help with reconstruction of the temple and were used to hoist the massive beams into place. The longest is thirty-six feet long and fifteen inches in diameter. It is all the more impressive when one remembers that a woman's hair was traditionally regarded as her crowning jewel. "As the hair of the Japanese woman is her richest ornament, it is of all her possessions that which she would most suffer to lose," noted the writer Lafcadio Hearn (1850-1904). The sacrifice shows the strength of belief, and in their way the ropes are as impressive as the buildings they helped erect. It is as if each single strand bears testimony to the legacy of Shinran and the Pure Land prophets before him. Most people associate Kyoto with Zen; it is just as much the city of Amida.

Chapter Four
CITY OF HEIKE

Epic Origins

Two great names from the past haunt the imagination of modern Japanese: the Heike and the Genji. These two powerful clans clashed in the Gempei Wars of 1180-1185. The struggle between them not only shaped the course of Japanese history, but it also furnished the material for an epic work of literature that relates many of the best-known incidents in Japanese history. More Noh plays are based on *The Tale of the Heike* than on any other source.

Though the epic centres on the military conflict, it contains far more than battle scenes, for the warfare is interspersed with lyrical passages and tragic love affairs. The authorship is uncertain, though the original is thought to have been by a thirteenth-century nobleman, after which the story was taken up by blind, lute-playing priests who travelled the country performing memorized chants. This has led to comparisons with Homer's *Odyssey*. The priest-performers gave the account a strong Buddhist slant—human life is illusory: all things must pass; even the mighty are destined to fall. The themes are repeatedly spelled out, as here in the opening passage, which is learnt by heart by schoolchildren:

> *The sound of the bell of Jetavana echoes the impermanence of all things. The hue of the flowers of the teak-tree declares that they who flourish must be brought low. Yea, the proud ones are but for a moment, like an evening dream in springtime. The mighty are destroyed at the last, they are but as the dust before the wind.*

The priest-performers developed individual variations of the tale, and the text used today was taken down from a performer shortly before his death in 1371. It is a sprawling affair, not much read these days because of its medieval language. In 1951, Yoshikawa Eiji brought out a popular modern version entitled *Shin Heike Monogatari* (New

Tales of the Heike). It not only updated the language, but tightened the narrative and toned down the Buddhism. The book was serialized by the Japanese Broadcasting Corporation (NHK), and formed the basis for a lavish film by Kenji Mizoguchi. For a whole new generation, the Heike lived again.

At the heart of the epic is the rise and fall of the Heike, who were the first non-aristocrats to take power. Like the Genji, they were formed from the illegitimate offspring of emperors and became samurai, which literally means "to attend upon". As such, they were looked down on by the aristocracy, whose dirty work they carried out. Confusingly, the two clans have alternate names, since the Chinese characters involved can be read in two different ways. Members of the Heike (literally, "house of Hei") bear the family name of Taira. The Genji ("the clan of Gen") have that of Minamoto. Thus the Heike leader, Taira no Kiyomori (1118-81), was opposed by the Genji leader, Minamoto no Yoshitomo (1123-60).

During the twelfth century, the samurai became steadily more powerful. Instead of simply serving, they began to assert themselves. Things came to a head in the Hogen (1156) and Heiji Insurrections (1159), which put an end to Fujiwara rule and divided the aristocracy and their allies. From out of the turmoil, Taira no Kiyomori emerged on top. It was to change forever the social order.

The Tyrant

Following their military success, the Heike replaced the Fujiwara as the dominant family at court. Kiyomori emulated their marriage politics by having his daughter marry the heir to the throne and lived to see his grandson enthroned as emperor, a historic first for a non-aristocrat. The Heike chief had brutally killed off his opponents and was known for his cruelty, but there were two notable exceptions. These were the half-brothers, Yoritomo and Yoshitsune, who were the sons of his great rival, Minamoto no Yoshitomo. The eldest son, just thirteen, was sent to a temple in Kamakura to pray for his deceased kin. Yoshitsune, only two, was spared as a sop to his mother, the beautiful Tokiwa Gozen, who was made Kiyomori's mistress.

It would be pleasing to write that Kiyomori was rewarded for his unusual act of mercy, but it proved in fact to be his undoing and even served as a warning to posterity never to be lenient. When Yoritomo grew up, he assumed leadership of the Genji and took control of the Kanto plain (around modern-day Tokyo). Here the clan bided their time, waiting until they were strong enough to move against the Heike. It was a classic case of clan warfare, with revenge the driving force.

By the time fighting broke out in 1180, the Heike had taken on some of the courtly elegance of the aristocracy. One of the sub-themes of *The Tale of the Heike* is the contrast between the provincial Genji and their more sophisticated rivals. The episode of young Atsumori is a case in point. While fleeing Kyoto with the rest of his clan, he was caught on the beach by a Genji opponent named Kumagai Naozane:

> *The horse he rode was dappled-gray, and its saddle glittered with gold mounting... the warrior turned his horse and rode back to the beach, where Kumagai at once engaged him in mortal combat. Quickly hurling him to the ground, he sprang upon him and tore off his helmet to cut off his head, when he beheld the face of a youth of sixteen or seventeen, delicately powdered and with blackened teeth...*

Kumagai had a son about the same age as Atsumori, and though he was reluctant to kill his opponent, there were others approaching and he made a quick end of the youth. Afterwards, in searching his belongings, he was astonished to find a flute. "Among all our men of the Eastern Provinces I doubt if there is any one of them who has brought a flute with him. How gentle the ways of these courtiers!" he exclaims.

Another incident involving Taira no Tadanori, younger brother of Kiyomori, also illustrates the Heike refinement. Before fleeing Kyoto, he handed a poem to Fujiwara Shunzei in the hope that it would be included in an imperial collection. Though he was killed in battle, his wish came true for Shunzei did include the poem, but listed it as anonymous. The incident forms the basis of the Noh play *Shunzei Tadanori*, in which the warrior's restless spirit expresses anguish at the omission of his name. Rather than defeat, it is his reputation as a poet that worries him most.

Such were the cultured warriors of the Heike. Yet they are remembered in negative terms thanks to their portrayal in *The Tale of the Heike*, where their defeat is put down to their selfish ways. Nowhere is this clearer than in the account of Kiymori's death, which came while the war was still under way. He developed an acute fever that even immersion in cold water failed to soothe, and the narrative ascribes his suffering to the sin of pride. The passage concludes with a homily about the nature of death, which makes sombre reading:

> *He was sixty-four years old this year. He cannot be said to have died of old age, for when the result of man's karma comes upon him the most potent Sutras have no efficacy, nor can the power of the gods and Buddhas avail anything; yea, all the deities of heaven cannot protect him, so what can ordinary men do? And so alone and without a companion he must go down to Hades... And the evil karma that he has made will take shape as the jailers that come to meet him.*

It is worth remembering here that the account was written in an age dominated by the ruling Genji. History is written by victors, it is said, and doing down Kiyomori made sense not just in Buddhist terms but in worldly terms too. "He who controls the present controls the past," said George Orwell. *The Tale of the Heike* may be a case in point.

The Hero

Yoshitsune has been called "Japan's most glamorous hero". Brought up in Kyoto, he was a man of good looks and brilliant victories. Yet his fall from grace was as sudden as it was unjust, and his early death brought him posthumous glory. To later generations, he represented the ideal kind of warrior.

After his father was killed fighting Kiyomori, Yoshitsune was brought up in the house of a Fujiwara noble whom his mother had married. At the age of seven, in accordance with Kiyomori's instructions, he was sent to train as a monk at Kurama Temple. Here he was called Ushiwakamaru (Young Cow Lad), a name still fondly used of him. The temple stood high on a mountain side. Though only eight miles to the north of Kyoto, Kurama was a remote and wild place in Heian times; its great woods enfolded a shadowy world in which moved strange creatures. "Kurama is so steep that even when you decide to go there on pilgrimage, you end up not going out of fear," wrote the author of the *Sarashina Diary*.

When Yoshitsune was ten, he learned of his father's death and became set on revenge. No doubt his resolve was strengthened by rumours of his mother's relationship with Kiyomori. Tradition tells of how he developed his fighting skills by practising in the woods with *tengu*, mythical creatures with red faces and long noses. Were these perhaps ninja-like figures training in secret, or could they have been martial arts experts sent by his brother Yoritomo?

By all accounts, Yoshitsune was a small man, somewhat effeminate in manner. There is a stone on the Kurama hillside against which he supposedly measured himself at sixteen, and it barely even reaches my chest. This suggests that he was remarkably short—well under five feet. It is worth noting, for it bears on his legendary encounter with the giant Benkei. Like Robin Hood against Little John, it was a test of the little man's resourcefulness.

Benkei was a warrior-monk attached to Enryaku-ji who was on a mission to win 1,000 swords to fund the building of a temple. He had already collected 999 when he came upon the slightly-built Yoshitsune playing a flute on Gojo Bridge. Seeing a chance to complete his collection, he challenged him to fight but found himself outwitted, as his agile opponent skipped along the parapet of the bridge. Benkei admitted defeat and pledged to be his victor's loyal follower.

With Benkei to protect him, Yoshitsune ran off to join the Genji forces in the west. He was given charge of an army by Yoritomo, and proved a brilliant general in a series of remarkable victories. One of these was against his cousin, Kiso no Yoshinaka (1154-84), who had overrun Kyoto and threatened to seize control for himself. Following this success, Yoshitsune turned on the Heike, driving them to Shikoku and along the coast of the Inland Sea. The campaign culminated in 1185 in the decisive sea-battle of Dan-no-Ura, in the straits between Honshu and Kyushu, where the clan was wiped out. Back in Kyoto, the young general, still in his mid-twenties, was acclaimed as a liberating hero. Storm clouds were gathering, however, since his popularity drew the suspicion of Yoritomo in his power base at Kamakura. *The Tale of the Heike* makes a clear distinction between the brothers, contrasting the warm and spontaneous Yoshitsune with the more calculating Yoritomo.

At this point the cunning Go-Shirakawa, the man behind the Sanjusangendo, enters the story. The ex-emperor was a wily politician who had used the Taira to see off the Fujiwara. Now he saw an opportunity to split the Minamoto. He fostered close ties with Yoshitsune to heighten Yoritomo's anxiety, while at the same time feeding the younger man rumours that his half-brother was scheming against him. The situation became so tense that Yoshitsune was accused of treason and forced to flee for his life. With just a handful of followers to accompany him, Yoshitsune made his way north to Ataka where at the border-post was played out an incident that is well known through depictions in Noh (*Ataka*) and Kabuki (*Kanjincho*). To escape detection, the group's members disguise themselves as *yamabushi*, with Yoshitsune dressed as a porter. Benkei assumes charge, and when challenged by Lord Togashi he pretends to read out a travel-permit from Nara's Todai-ji. The group is allowed to proceed, but as they do so there comes a heart-stopping moment, for just as Yoshitsune is passing the border his identity is suspected. Realizing the need for action, the quick-thinking Benkei scolds "the porter" and slaps him for causing a delay. Since no follower would ever dare act in such a manner towards his lord, it seems to prove his innocence. Although Togashi suspects the truth, he is so impressed that he lets the group through, and afterwards a distraught Benkei is overcome with remorse at his action.

Yoshitsune later found refuge in Tohoku with an ally, whose death exposed him to Yoritomo's forces. How exactly he died is unknown, though one account touchingly tells of the loyal Benkei defending Yoshitsune to the end, his huge body pierced with arrows so that his master has time to die in dignity. As with heroes in other countries, rumours spread that he had not died at all but survived to fight another day. Some said he was among the Ainu in the north, while others, more imaginatively, claimed he had escaped overseas to become Genghis Khan.

Yoshitsune's life brought together many of the elements that comprise a hero. Dedicated to revenge, he was a brave and selfless figure who risked death on more than one occasion. He even once led a cavalry charge down an almost vertical cliff. His early demise evokes the famous comparison with the cherry blossom falling at its peak, and his youthful features remain frozen in the collective memory. As Ushiwakamaru, he remains close to Kyoto's heart and is forever associated with Kurama and the *tengu* there that trained him. A small brave figure who was victimized and misunderstood: could anything be more Japanese?

The Tragic Female

The final episode of *The Tale of Heike* concerns Kiyomori's daughter, Kenreimon'in (c.1155-91). Hers was a tragic life. She was married to the younger brother of Go-Shirakawa at fifteen, and her son became the boy-emperor Antoku. When the Genji forces came marching in, she fled the capital with the rest of the Heike, and she was at Dan-no-Ura when the final defeat of the clan took place and all her nearest and dearest died. To escape capture by the Genji, her mother and son drowned themselves. She tried to follow them, but was hauled out of the sea by her hair and returned to the capital. She became a nun and entered Jakko-in at Ohara, a village to the north-east of Kyoto.

> *The place she had chosen to dwell was ancient and surrounded by mossy rocks. The reeds in the garden were now covered with hoar-frost instead of dew, and when she gazed on the faded hue of the withered chrysanthemums by the wall she could hardly fail to be reminded of her own condition... They built for her a small cell ten feet square beside the Jakko-in, and in it were two rooms; in one she put her shrine of Buddha and in the other she slept. There she spent her time continually repeating the* nembutsu *and performing Buddhist services by night and by day.*

On one occasion, Go-Shirakawa decided to pay his sister-in-law a visit. The occasion forms the basis for Zeami's Noh play, *Ohara Goko*, over half of which is made up of direct quotations from *The Tale of Heike*. It begins with Go-Shirakawa arriving while Kenreimon'in is out with a companion gathering flowers, and he composes a poem suggestive of Heike bodies floating on the sea:

> *The cherry tree leans*
> *Over the quiet depths*
> *Of the pool*
> *While fallen petals float*
> *On the silent ripples.*

When Kenreimon'in returns, she tells him of her terrible experiences and he is moved to tears. The play reaches its tragic climax with her account of the battle of Dan-no-ura, when, with the enemy closing in, the seven-year old Antoku is guided by his grandmother to face his final moments.

With its Heike associations, Jakko-in is a popular destination for the literary pilgrim. One can hardly fail to be moved. The temple garden remains almost exactly as it was a thousand years ago: the pond is still there, as well as a descendant of the cherry tree about which Go-Shirakawa composed his poem. It was here at this humble temple that the former empress spent her final days, and her tomb lies to the right of the temple, up a steep set of steps. More than most, she could bear witness to *The Tale of Heike's* opening words: "The sound of the temple bell echoes the impermanence of all things." The epic closes with the sound of another bell—that of Jakko-in. Like *The Tale of Genji*, it is a sprawling story that begins with the deeds of worldly men and ends with a solitary female in a temple sanctuary. It is a finely crafted trajectory, leading with a sense of inevitability from the vanity of this world to contemplation of the next.

The Poet Wanderer

It is curious that during the late twelfth century, when Kyoto saw some of its most turbulent years, there were several remarkable figures at work in the city. It is as if they sought refuge from the turmoil in a world of their own creation. One of these was the poet Saigyo (1118-90). Born into the warrior class, he had a prestigious job in his youth as an imperial bodyguard, but at twenty-two dropped out to become a Shingon priest. "Saigyo" was his religious name, meaning "western journey", a reference to Amida's Pure Land. According to tradition, he took orders at Shoji-ji in Katsura, in south-west Kyoto, where he lived in a hut near a cherry tree:

Gazing at them
The blossoms have grown
So much a part of me,
To part with them when they fall
Seems bitter indeed.

Identification with cherry blossoms is a thread that weaves through Saigyo's poems, and in his honour Shoji-ji has transformed itself into the Hana-dera (Cherry Blossom Temple). The hundreds of cherry trees make the hilly retreat a popular place in spring, and, ironically, one of the poet's most famous verses complains of the disturbance caused by such visitors:

> They disturb the peace
> The crowds of people who come
> To view the blossom:
> Who is there to blame except
> The blossoming tree itself?

The poem was taken up in Zeami's fifteenth-century play, *Saigyo's Cherry Tree*, in which the spirit of the tree talks of its Buddha-nature and extols the beauty of the groves in the Flowering Capital.

For a few years after leaving Shoji-ji, Saigyo lived in retreats on the fringes of the city. His poetry speaks of concern about remaining too long among familiar surroundings:

> I have cast off the world
> But there are thoughts
> I cannot cast away—
> I who have yet
> To part from the capital.

Once Saigyo made the break with Kyoto, he took to the life of a wandering poet. He cultivated solitude, and spent time in religious exercises. He was drawn to the atmosphere of remote places, almost in a Wordsworthian way, and his verse is marked by an aesthetic known as *sabi* in which existential loneliness is offset by the consolations of nature. His poetry furthered his spirituality, and his spirituality deepened his art. "Every time I finish a poem, I feel like I have created a statue of the Buddha," he wrote.

In the intervals between his travels, Saigyo returned to the Kansai area where he based himself at Mount Koya, headquarters of the Shingon sect. His poetry makes plain the tension felt by the hermit between the need for companionship and the desire for solitude, as here in this charming verse:

Someone who has learned
How to manage life in loneliness:
Would there were one more!
He could winter here on the mountain
With his hut right next to mine.

As well as cherry blossoms, Saigyo sang of the moon. It was a powerful subject, which combined the aesthetic of moon-viewing with Buddhist significance. The ever-changing phases were a cosmic reminder of impermanence, while the full moon was a traditional symbol of enlightenment, shown in pictures of the dying Buddha. For the poet, the pale orb was a spell-binder, a mood shifter, whose ethereal beauty spoke of eternal truths and the illusory nature of existence. But there was also a personal connection, for the nightly passage across the sky mirrored his solitary wandering. The more Saigyo contemplated it, the more entranced he became:

Back in the capital
We gazed at the moon, calling
Our feelings "deep"—
Mere shallow diversions
That here don't count at all.

In a poem combining his two passions, Saigyo wrote of wishing to die under a full moon in cherry blossom time, and it seems that he did. To later centuries he became a folk hero, who stood for mankind's search for truth. The haiku poet, Basho, was a strong admirer, and when he visited Kyoto he paid homage by visiting the site where his predecessor had once lived (Saigyo-an, next to present-day Maruyama Park).

Saigyo's death came at the dawn of a new age, when the Heike who had dominated his time were replaced by the Genji. His concerns lay elsewhere, with more transcendental matters. From the capital he blazed a lonely trail, creating small gems like some early version of a beat poet. At Shojo-ji there is a small statue which shows him with a puzzled expression, as if trying to make sense of the world. More than most, one feels he did.

Court Verse Revisited

With the defeat of the Heike, Yoritomo (1147-99) was made shogun, or supreme general. He set up a military government at Kamakura near modern-day Tokyo, far removed from the corrupting influence of Kyoto's court. For the next 140 years his family remained nominally in charge, though behind the scenes the Hojo family held power. Provincial lords took oaths of loyalty, and the ties of feudal obligation established a measure of stability. Though there were occasional attempts to restore imperial power, the emperor was relegated for the most part to a symbolic role. The long centuries of samurai rule had begun, only to end in 1868.

Though the court had lost political power, the aristocracy continued to be the dominant force culturally. A notable example is Fujiwara no Sadaie (1162-1241), who wrote under the name of Teika and is famous as one of the "four greatest Japanese poets". His collection of *One Hundred Poems by One Hundred Poets* (c.1229-41) remains an ever-green favourite. From his father Fujiwara Shunzei, he inherited a taste for the aesthetic of *yugen*, which combines elegance with profundity. It is the art of the implicit, creating the suggestion of hidden depth. For Teika's contemporary, Kamo no Chomei, its essence lay in the creation of "an unseen world that hovers in the atmosphere of the poem."

Teika was one of the compilers of an imperial anthology in 1205, entitled *Shinkokinshu* (New Collection of Ancient and Modern). As its title suggests, it was modelled on its famed predecessor, and its completion was timed to coincide with the three hundredth anniversary. Saigyo was the star of the collection, with ninety-four poems to Teika's forty-six. Taken overall, the verse has an autumnal feel, with separation and melancholy predominating. The bleakness was intentional, for the editors were aware of living in unfortunate times. The tone is typified by a sombre poem by Teika. It amounts to an elegy for the passing of an aristocratic age when "blossoms" and "crimson leaves" were treasured for their beauty.

Looking at the bay
I see no cherry blossoms
Or any crimson leaves

But a simple fisher hut
On this autumn evening.

The new mood is reflected in the art of the age, as exemplified by a colour portrait of Yoritomo on a hanging scroll at Jingo-ji, in the north-west of the city. It shows a stern-looking shogun sitting cross-legged in a stiff robe, his square shoulders jutting out in exaggerated manner. The effect is of an unbending and forceful personality, typical of the samurai ethos. Contrast it with earlier portraits of Fujiwara statesmen at ease in their flowing robes, and you can well understand why Teika thought the blossom had disappeared from life. In the new order there were only stark realities.

Chomei's Hut

Hojoki, or *The Record of a Ten-Foot Square Hut* (1212), is a remarkable book. It was written by an aristocratic drop-out named Kamo no Chomei (c.1153-1216) and articulates a back-to-nature credo centuries before the likes of Walden. It speaks to the deepest recesses of the human heart, for it tells of a lifestyle set in the forgotten Eden of our ancestral memory. The author came from a long line of Shinto priests attached to Shimogamo Shrine, and as a young man his poems were included in the *Shinkokinshu*. But he was disappointed in his career, and after becoming a monk he went to live on a hill near Uji. Here he built a ten-foot square hut:

> *It is a hut where, perhaps, a traveler might spend a single night; it is like the cocoon spun by an aged silkworm. This hut is not even a hundredth the size of the cottage where I spent my middle years... A bare two carts would suffice to carry off the whole house.*

A model of the hut is on display at Shimogamo Shrine. It looks not unlike a modern summer house, with a small porch for sitting out and two Heian-style shutters which open upwards and outwards. In summer it was open to the elements, and in winter a fire converted it into a smoky haven. It is the kind of place one could happily spend a weekend.

Chomei's account of his life is a meandering affair, wandering from subject to subject in the *zuihitsu* or follow-your-pen style. It begins with

71

descriptions of natural disasters that leave one gasping at the fragility of life in those days. Fire, whirlwind, famine and earthquake follow in quick succession. Corpses lie in the streets, and infants suck at the breasts of dead mothers. The lesson the author draws from all this is the folly of building houses in the capital. Thoughts of death are never far from his mind, and, like Shakespeare, he believes that "readiness is all." Indeed, the whole seasonal round seems to him like one year-long reminder:

> In the spring I see waves of wisteria like purple clouds, bright in the west. In the summer I hear the cuckoo call, promising to guide me on the road to death. In the autumn the voice of the evening insects fill my ears with a sound of lamentation for this cracked husk of a world. In winter I look with deep emotion on the snow, piling up and melting away like sins and hindrances to salvation.

Yet the author describes his life in appealing terms. It must have been lonely and at times miserable, but he makes it sound idyllic. "The best friends one can have are flowers and moon, strings and pipe," he says of his solitude. He uses fresh rainwater for tea and soup; eats home-grown mushrooms, herbs and fruit; and for exercise, he wanders to a nearby temple, or makes sorties to places of poetical interest. He enjoys the company of a youth who lives nearby, and he plays music which harmonizes with the rhythms of nature: "My body is like a drifting cloud—I ask for nothing, I want nothing. My greatest joy is a quiet nap; my only desire for this life is to see the beauties of the seasons."

There is a heart-warming quality to the reclusive Chomei because of the pleasure he takes in small things. "I seek only tranquillity; I rejoice in the absence of grief," he writes. This modest man even ends his account by wondering if he has not become too attached to his simple lifestyle: "It is a sin for me now to love my little hut, and my attachment to solitude may also be a hindrance to enlightenment." He had grown up under the Heike and lived through the Gempei Wars, when there had been fierce fighting in the streets. Yet of all this he mentions not a word. It is as if such transient affairs are of little concern to him. Freed from "the dust of this world", he was able to muse on other matters in his mountain retreat, and the reader is the beneficiary.

Kenko's Idleness

A century after Chomei, another collection in the *zuihitsu* style appeared. It is one familiar to Japanese, for passages from it are included in school textbooks. Observations, anecdotes, and musings follow one after another, sometimes a mere sentence in length. The opening suggests its spontaneous style:

> *To while away the idle hours, seated the livelong day before the inkslab, by jotting down without order or purpose whatever trifling thoughts pass through my mind, verily this is a queer and crazy thing to do!*

Tsurezuregusa (c.1331), literally "Grasses of Boredom", has been given the English title of *Essays in Idleness*. It was written by a Buddhist recluse called Yoshida Kenko (1283-1350), who lived on a hill in the west of the city called Narabigaoka. His background was not unlike that of Chomei. Both were literary men with court connections and Shinto lineage. Both dropped out to become Buddhist recluses. But there was a major difference between them, for Kenko remained on the edge of the city and his concerns were mainly social. It shows in his book: only five of the 234 items deal with nature.

Kenko had once been a specialist in court ritual, and he is given to grand pronouncements about matters of etiquette. "It is a fine thing," he writes, "when a man who thoroughly understands a subject is unwilling to open his mouth, and only speaks when he is questioned." Like Shonagon, he appreciates fine manners and dislikes vulgarity. Though a priest himself, he also likes to make fun of religious figures, which reminds us that he was living in the age of Chaucer and worldly monks. One of his anecdotes concerns a novice at Ninna-ji who got drunk at a party, put an iron pot over his head, and performed a comic dance. Afterwards he was unable to get it off, and in the end it had to be pulled off by force, ripping away his ears and nose. The tale leaves a sense of Kenko, aloof on the neighbouring hill, smiling at the foibles of mankind like Democritus, the laughing philosopher.

It is in the field of aesthetics, however, that Kenko has won most praise: Donald Keene calls his book "a central work in the development of Japanese taste". He not only argued against the ornate and in favour of the plain, but he advocated the irregular and the imperfect. "In everything, no matter what it may be, uniformity is undesirable," he remarks: "Leaving something incomplete makes it interesting, and gives one the feeling that there is room for growth."

> *The moon that appears close to dawn after we have long waited for it moves us more profoundly than the full moon shining cloudless over a thousand leagues. And how incomparably lovely is the moon, almost greenish in its light, when seen through the tips of the cedars or when it hides for a moment behind clustering clouds during a sudden shower.*

Irregularity and asymmetry have been central to the Japanese tradition. It is evident in the layout of gardens, in the preference for odd numbers, in the distinctive arrangements of *ikebana*, and in the tea ceremony where the most prized bowls are irregular in shape and pattern. Kenko was the first to articulate the aesthetic.

Another of the author's preoccupations was transience, and here again he proved an original thinker. For Heian poets, impermanence led to a melancholy view of life, but for Kenko it was a precious gift:

If man were never to fade away like the dews, never to vanish like the smoke, but lingered forever in this world, how things would lose their power to move us! The most precious thing in life is its uncertainty. Consider living creatures—none lives so long as man. The Mayfly waits not for the evening, the summer cicada knows neither spring nor autumn. What a wonderful unhurried feeling it is to live even a single year in a perfect serenity! If that is not enough for you, you might live a thousand years and feel it was but a single night's dream.

Kenko's life was spent on the hilly retreats of Kyoto, half in and half out of the city. By birth he was connected with the priests on Yoshida Hill; he took orders on Mount Hiei; and on Narabigaoka, where stood his hut, was his final resting place. "The pleasantest of all diversions," he wrote, "is to sit alone under the lamp, a book spread out before you, and to make friends with people of a distant past you have never known." He lived at the end of the Kamakura era, when the seat of government was about to return to Kyoto in the form of the Ashikaga. The new rulers saw themselves as following in the tradition of the Heike, though the artists they patronized drew inspiration from the teachings of Zen. It was to open up an exciting new chapter for the capital.

Chapter Five
CITY OF ZEN

The Wordless Way
In the 1960s and 1970s, when the alienated youth of the West looked east, many turned to Zen for inspiration. The Beats had earlier taken up Buddhism; now the writings of D. T. Suzuki and Alan Watts proved hot sellers. Hippy communes practised meditation, while enterprising souls set out on spiritual odysseys. Kyoto, home to large monasteries, was a popular destination. Some, like the poet Gary Snyder, remained in the city for a while and returned home invigorated. Others stayed on to become priests, and a few still haunt the streets of north Kyoto.

Much of the fascination derived from D. T. Suzuki's influential *Zen and Japanese Culture* (1938, revised 1959), which made some expansive claims, such as, "Zen is the Japanese character." The book has been criticised for overstating its case, but it would be impossible to deny the vital role of Zen in Japanese arts, and in the culture of Kyoto in particular. So what is it exactly? Books on the subject like to state, ironically, that it cannot be understood through words, that it has to be experienced. Intuition, not understanding, is the means to wisdom. It takes its lead from the "flower sermon" of Buddha, when in front of an assembled crowd he silently held up a single bloom. Of all those present, only one smiled in comprehension. He became Buddha's successor.

The distrust of language stems from the way words define and divide. The striving of Zen, by contrast, is for oneness. It seeks to cut through verbiage by going beyond words. This requires a stilling of the ego, which thrives on rationalization. For Zen, the self is an illusion which masks a deeper truth, that inside every being is "Buddha-nature". The means of realizing this is by *zazen*, or sitting meditation. It is implicit in the sect's name, for "zen" derives from the Sanskrit for meditation. The idea is that through watching one's thoughts, they will slowly settle and disperse. A common analogy is to a glass of muddy water that is left to stand; the sediment sinks to the bottom, allowing the water to become clear. In this way one comes to see one's true self.

It is this wordless nature of Zen that lies behind many of the sect's eccentricities. "Those who know, do not speak; those who speak do not know," said the Taoist sage, Lao Tzu. Truth—like love and faith—is not a matter of words. The point is made in a story of an abbot who had to choose the head of a new monastery. He assembled his monks and placed a pitcher on the floor before them, saying "If you can't call this a pitcher, what would you call it?" The senior candidate mused thoughtfully, "You certainly can't call it a stump." The cook, however, simply got up and kicked it over. It was he who got the job.

The man given the credit for introducing Zen to Japan is a Tendai priest named Eisai (1141-1215). There had been earlier attempts to spread the teaching, but these had come to nothing. With the Kamakura era, however, came a fresh opportunity, as the new rulers sought a break with the old order. Whereas the aestheticism of the Esoteric sects suited the aristocrats, the rigour of Zen suited the warriors.

Eisai had studied on Mount Hiei from the age of fourteen, and to deepen his knowledge he made two visits to China (in 1168 and 1187). On the second occasion he took up the study of Zen, and on his return established a temple in Kyushu. Following this, he made his way to Kyoto, where in 1195 he met with Yoritomo. The shogun took a liking to him, and invited him to Kamakura. Eisai's preaching soon found favour among the samurai, and he published a treatise *On the Propagation of Zen for the Protection of the Nation* (1198). That an introspective religion should so appeal to warriors might well seem strange: what do fighting and killing have to do with meditation and enlightenment? The answer is that both monks and warriors shared an emphasis on discipline, and both had hierarchical structures in which the self was suppressed. Moreover, the focused concentration of Zen helped promote the alertness needed in swordfights, while the striving to transcend the fear of death provided the samurai with a means to prepare for battle. Over time the way of the warrior became closely identified with that of Zen.

In 1202 Eisai was given charge of Kennin-ji in Kyoto, and he made it into a centre of Zen practice. The teaching derived from a Chinese monk named Linji (d. ca. 867), who is called Rinzai in Japanese. It has the reputation of being a "rough school" which is hard to enter and which seeks to jolt members into enlightenment. One of the techniques makes use of *koan* (riddles) such as "What is your original face, before you were born?" There are some 1,700 of these riddles in the Rinzai canon. As Suzuki says, the questioning "has a most definite objective, the arousing of doubt and pushing it to its furthest limits." This can help trigger awakening.

There are two other Zen sects in Japan. Largest in terms of numbers is Soto, introduced from China by a one-time pupil at Kennin-ji named Dogen (1200-1253). It takes a more gradual approach than Rinzai and is known as the "gentle school". Whereas for Rinzai meditation is a means to an end, for Soto it is more of an end in itself since it leads step by step along the path to true understanding. You can tell the sects apart by the style of meditating: the Soto style faces the wall, whereas Rinzai faces away from it.

The third Zen sect is Obaku, founded in 1661 by a Chinese immigrant called Ingen Ryuki (1592-1673). It accounts for some eight per cent of practitioners, and though it is close to Rinzai it retains distinctive elements such as the recital of the *nembutsu*. The head temple is Manpuku-ji at Uji, which has 460 branch temples around the country. With its coloured pillars and fat-cheeked Buddhas, the temple has a strongly Chinese atmosphere.

Of the three sects, it is Rinzai that dominates Kyoto, and within two centuries of Kennin-ji the teaching had six other large monasteries in the city. (By contrast, Soto preferred the quiet of the provinces.) The new monasteries stood on the fringes of the city. To the south-east lay Tofuku-ji (1236), while on the eastern edge was Nanzen-ji (1291). Myoshin-ji (1318) and Daitoku-ji (1324) were located in the north-west. Tenryu-ji (1339) lay further west, at Arashiyama. Shokoku-ji (1392), the last to be established, occupied the most central position thanks to the patronage of the shogun, who lived nearby.

By and large, the monasteries conform to a common pattern. The central compound is Chinese in style, with buildings that have solid walls, slate floors, and swinging doors. Around this are grouped sub-temples, which are more Japanese in style. Here one finds sliding screens, *tatami* mats, and an "organic" development of asymmetrical shapes. The main temples contain splendid ceiling paintings of dragons, often by top artists. The custom was imported from China to bestow protection, for the composite creature was an emissary from heaven bearing a jewel of wisdom (you can distinguish Japanese dragons from Chinese because they have three claws instead of five). Since the serpent-like being inhabits watery depths, it also offers protection against fire. In the creature's symbolic union of yin and yang lies the embodiment of the universal life force, a reminder of the Taoist roots of Zen.

In the past the monasteries were small townships, hosting scores of sub-temples. Myoshin-ji still retains something of the atmosphere of the past, with forty-six sub-temples in a walled enclave like a medieval village. Among the others, Daitoku-ji retains twenty-six sub-temples, Tofuku-ji twenty-three, and Shokoku-ji just nine. These are held privately, and many have been passed down through successive generations. One of the curious things about Japanese Zen is that it is largely hereditary.

To an outsider, the martial discipline of the monastic lifestyle can seem almost frightening in its precision. I remember the shock I experienced at the first meal I attended, when the monks paraded into the dining hall and sat in perfect rows with bowls and chopsticks laid out identically. There was a chilling, impersonal element which I had not expected. Following the recitations, soup and rice was eaten with concentrated silence. While I was secretly surveying the scene, wooden blocks were clapped to announce the end before I had hardly started, and since custom dictates that no morsel should be wasted, I had to gulp down the last mouthfuls. Bowls were then washed in order of size, wiped clean, wrapped back up, and to the next clap of the wooden blocks the monks left in the same ordered procession as they had entered. It was a performance of which the most disciplined samurai could be proud.

For the monks, the daily round begins with a 4.30am meditation, followed by breakfast and sweeping the garden. The physical work not only maintains a healthy mind-body balance, but is a tool to cultivate mindfulness. According to a Zen saying, first comes cleaning, then religious practice, and thirdly study. The thinking is that a menial task like sweeping can help bring one closer to one's true self. Cleanliness is indeed next to godliness.

In the past the opportunity to practice meditation at the monasteries was hard, for aspirants had first to prove their sincerity. These days, however, there are several places open to visitors. It is customary for the abbot to say a few words to those staying overnight, and on one such occasion the group I was with were told about the impending visit of foreign priests. "We Japanese have a long history of Zen. Eight hundred years. Perhaps we have grown lazy," the abbot smiled. "Foreign priests are very strict. They follow rules very hard. We are nervous to do our best," he giggled, "I hope we do not disappoint them." Then, as if to reassure us after confessing such mundane worries, he taught us a Zen wisdom: "Before a person studies Zen, mountains are mountains and waters are waters. After a first insight, mountains are no longer mountains and waters are no longer waters. But after enlightenment, mountains are again mountains and waters are again waters." He giggled once more, and left us to ponder the deeper meaning.

Constructs

Although Zen was introduced in Kamakura times, its development took place in the Muromachi era (1333-1573). This was when political power moved back to Kyoto in the form of the Ashikaga shoguns. There were fifteen in all, and for the last hundred years of the era they had control over little more than the capital—and not even that at times. It is known as the Warring Countries period, when provincial warlords vied with each other for power.

The breakdown of central control brought with it an impoverishment of the aristocracy as their provincial estates were taken over. Even the imperial family was bankrupt. One emperor was reduced to selling his own calligraphy, while another remained unburied for six weeks because funeral expenses could not be met. Yet the uncertain times encouraged flight to the monasteries, and the warrior class proved powerful patrons. Privileges were channelled to five main temples in an arrangement known as the *Gozan* system. This was a hierarchical arrangement following Chinese practice by which resources flowed downwards from the top (*Gozan*, meaning Five Mountains, was a reference to the founding of temples on mountains).

There were *Gozan* temples in both Kamakura and Kyoto, and though the listing changed somewhat over time the latter comprised Nanzen-ji, Tenryu-ji, Kennin-ji, Tofuku-ji, and Shokoku-ji. These were given special licences to trade with China, and they became agencies for imported goods. They were also important centres of learning, from out of which arose "*Gozan* literature" based on Chinese models.

A key figure in the establishment of the system was Muso Soseki (1275-1351), famous for creating the meditation garden. He had studied Tendai as a teenager, but gave it up for Zen and a life of seclusion. In 1325 he was made abbot of Nanzen-ji, a powerful position, and not long afterwards the new shogun, Ashikaga Takauji (1305-58), entrusted him with the construction of a family temple at Toji-in. It is a delightful but little-known complex in the north-west, one of my personal favourites. As well as a charming pond-garden, it houses a small room with statues of the Ashikaga shoguns doing *zazen*—frozen for all eternity in suspended meditation.

Muso's connection with the shogun also bore fruit in the construction of another temple, that of Tenryu-ji at Arashiyama. It was dedicated to the spirit of Emperor Go-Daigo (1287-1339), who had been betrayed by Takauji and forced into exile. He set up court at Yoshino, inaugurating a fifty-year period known as the Nambokucho when there were two rival emperors. Following Go-Daigo's death, Muso had a vision in which the former emperor's angry spirit rose up like a Golden Dragon. To pacify it, he persuaded Takauji to build a temple by the River Oi where Go-Daigo had grown up. The project took five years, and it is said that as penance Takauji himself helped in the construction by carrying rocks and digging out the pond.

Takauji was by no means the only Ashikaga to leave his mark on the capital. The dynasty saw themselves as cultural heirs to the Fujiwara, and they became generous patrons. Two in particular are remembered for their legacy: Ashikaga Yoshimitsu (1358-1408) and his grandson Yoshimasa. Yoshimitsu was a strong military leader who took Zen orders and established the monastery of Shokoku-ji, which became an important centre of fine arts. For his retirement, he built a Golden Pavilion in the midst of a large estate. It was a huge project, intended to reflect the greatness of its maker, and here, in 1408, is where the first recorded stay of an emperor in the house of a non-aristocrat took place.

The flourishing arts of the period are known as the "Kitayama Culture" after the area in which the estate was situated. The shogun had a liking for novelty, and he encouraged the development of Noh and the tea ceremony. Under his auspices, craftsmen produced works of the highest quality, including swords, lacquerware, brocade and pottery.

Of Yoshimitsu's original estate, the Golden Pavilion alone survives. It has three storeys, which integrate different styles of architecture. The lower floors with their shingled roofs and grilled wooden shutters are in the residential *shinden* style of the nobility. The upper floor, a private retreat for meditation and tea gatherings, is more Chinese in appearance, with bell-shaped widows and panelled doors. It is a reminder that Zen was an imported religion that came with foreign fashions, yet it is so perfectly blended with the native tradition that the gold-leaf building presents a dazzling display of harmony. "The beauty of the pavilion is superior even to Amida's Pure Land," one of Yoshimitsu's ministers declared. In later years, the pavilion was turned into a Zen temple and put under the charge of Shokoku-ji. Those familiar with Mishima's novel, *The Temple of the Golden Pavilion* (1956) will know of its role as a seminary, for the book was based on the story of a novice who set fire to the temple in 1950. Five years later it was

rebuilt, and today it is a flourishing tourist sight which glistens (a little too brightly for some) in the pond before it.

The Golden Pavilion is matched in the north-east of the city by a Silver Pavilion built by Ashikaga Yoshimasa (1435-90). He sought to emulate his grandfather by building an equally grand estate for his retirement, though surprisingly it was planned in the midst of the worst fighting ever seen in Kyoto—the Onin War (1467-77). It had broken out in a dispute over the succession to Yoshimasa. The shogun was an aesthete, with little taste for politics, and he had nominated his brother as his successor. Yet when his wife Hino Tomiko (1440-96) unexpectedly bore him a son, she pressured him to revoke the agreement. This led to fighting as warlords sought to take advantage of the situation, and for ten years the front lines raged back and forth across the city, long after the original cause had been forgotten. Historians consider it to be among "the most futile wars ever fought", and it was certainly among the most destructive. No clear winner emerged, yet by its end it had reduced a population of hundreds of thousands to a mere forty thousand. It is said that the River Kamo was blocked by the dead and that the city stank from unburied corpses.

Yoshimasa spent the war years preoccupied with the pursuit of arts, blithely ignoring the suffering of the people. Afterwards he built a retreat, which lay by the eastern hills. In the grounds stood a dozen pavilions dedicated to such pursuits as moon-gazing, poetry composition, incense appreciation and flower-viewing. From the scorched earth of post-war Kyoto sprang up a vigorous growth known as "Higashiyama culture" after the location of the estate. Prominent among the flourishing arts were Noh, garden design, tea ceremony, *kodo* (the way of incense), and *renga* (linked verse).

Following Yoshimasa's death the estate was turned into a Zen temple. Then, in the sixteenth century, it was devastated by fire, and only two buildings survived. One was the Silver Pavilion. Tourists often have a shock when they see the building because it is not silver at all, but unpainted wood: Yoshimasa died before his plan could be completed, but ironically this makes it all the more attractive and in keeping with the culture of *wabi* (refined simplicity) that guided Zen arts.

Yoshimasa's original vision had been of a silver-coated pavilion gleaming in the moonlight. Here was to be the moon-viewing heart of the Moon-Viewing Capital. The retired shogun loved to spend his evenings keeping watch as the shimmering mystery appeared from behind the woods of the eastern hills, and his poem on the subject captures the intensity of his anticipation:

For my villa stands beneath
The Moon-Awaiting Mountain.
Under this dark hill
How my longing grows tonight
With the sky's impending light!

The pond garden of Yoshimasa's time was later supplemented by a Sea of Silvery Sand, designed to reflect the rays of the moon, and, according to a recent NHK programme, at one time silver paint was added to the under-eaves of the pavilion to direct the reflected moonlight into the bottom room. Reflections of reflections of moonlight: could anything better capture life's dreamlike nature?

Apart from the pavilion, the only other building to survive from the original estate is the Togudo Hall, which was Yoshimasa's private residence. It contains a study built with *tatami* floor, paper window, and *tokonoma* (alcove area); this new style was in time to become the standard for Japanese housing. The hall also comprises a tearoom, which represents the first specially designed space for this emerging practice. It is four and a half mats in size, with a sunken hearth, and the prototype for later models. It exemplifies why the estate is of such significance, for the developments that took place here shaped the Japan that we know today. There are annual "open days" when one can visit the hall and stand in the midst of this historic space. For anyone mindful of Japanese culture it is an undoubted thrill, for it was here, in the words of Donald Keene, that "the soul of Japan was forged."

The Wild Man
The emphasis in Zen on inner truth breeds an individualism that runs to the eccentric. Beneath the emphasis on self-discipline lies a playful anarchy, for authority is ultimately disposable. Buddha himself said that his teaching was only a raft to be discarded on the far side of the river. Hence some apparently outrageous attitudes: "If you encounter the Buddha, slay him," said Rinzai.

The history of Zen is full of odd characters, whose quirky behaviour makes for enjoyable reading. Kyoto's representative is Ikkyu Sojun (1394-1481), the illegitimate son of an emperor, who became the wild man of Zen, living as an outsider and frequenting prostitutes. To shake people out of their comfortable certainties he acted the holy fool, and when he came across hypocrisy he reacted with furious outbursts. He was probably fathered illegitimately by Emperor Go-Komatsu (1377-1433), and at five he was sent to a temple for training. He was unusually bright, and his reputation reached the ear of Yoshimitsu, who arranged to meet him. Pointing to a picture of a tiger, the shogun tested the boy by asking him to tie it up. "I'll tie it up if you first drive it out," came the quick-witted reply.

At thirteen Ikkyu entered Kennin-ji, but by sixteen he was complaining of the corruption there. He moved out to study under a spiritual master, whose death so moved the twenty-year old that he contemplated suicide. Tradition says that he was talked out of it by a messenger sent by his mother. Following this, Ikkyu sought one of the strictest masters of the day, a monk called Kaso, who lived in a run-down temple by Lake Biwa. As was customary, his request was refused as a test of his resolve, but the applicant continued to wait patiently outside the temple. One day as he was going out, Kaso ordered a servant to throw dirty water over him, and when he returned later he was surprised to find a drenched Ikkyu still in the same position. It was enough to convince the master.

Training under Kaso was hard. The temple had no money, and to help it survive Ikkyu made dolls' clothes and perfume sachets. It was at this time that he was given the name of "Ikkyu", meaning a pause. A poem he wrote suggests the significance:

From the world of passions
Returning to the world beyond passions
There is but a moment's pause:
If it is to rain, let it rain,
If it is to blow, let it blow.

Ikkyu's "awakening" came in his mid-twenties when he was startled by the cawing of a crow while he was meditating in a boat. The sound seemed to him to fill the universe. But when Kaso issued a certificate of enlightenment, Ikkyu threw it down in disgust and walked out. Such was his distaste for ceremonial trappings: it was the spirit of Zen that mattered most to him.

After leaving Kaso, Ikkyu embarked on a wandering lifestyle. Though he rarely stayed long in one place, he based himself in Sakai at Osaka. He led a double life, performing austerities by day while carousing by night. Contrary to the teaching of Zen, he took lovers, drank saké, and ate fish. He was a born rebel: "Those who keep the precepts become donkeys, those who break them, men," he once said. His behaviour could be outrageous. On one occasion he went around waving a wooden sword, explaining that it was a sham and could not kill anyone—just as the large temples were a sham and could not save anyone. On another occasion he appeared in a dirty black robe for a memorial service at Daitoku-ji when everyone else was in their best outfits. "I alone ornament this assembly," he declared defiantly, "I do not intend to ape the way of false priests."

As well as practising art and calligraphy, Ikkyu was also a writer whose poems come from the heart. "I'm pure shame: what I do and what I say never the same," he admitted. He chose the penname of "Crazy Cloud", cleverly combining a sense of worldly detachment with a rejection of rationality. He was open about his love life, and it seems at some stage he had a son. He even claimed that the brothel offered a better means of salvation than the temple. His contempt for hypocrisy became focussed on one man in particular, a priest named Yoso, who became the head of Daitoku-ji. There are over a hundred poems about this "poisonous snake" and "unparalleled villain". The hostility seems to have arisen from Yoso's practice of raising money for the temple by selling certificates of enlightenment to rich merchants.

Despite—or perhaps because of—his lifestyle, Ikkyu remained vigorous all his life. His seventies proved eventful, for he fell in love with a blind singer called Mori. She was one of his acolytes, and some forty years younger. The affair inspired several love poems, among which is this heartfelt ode of gratitude:

After the tree withered and the leaves fell, spring returned:
The old trunk has flowered, old promises renewed.
Mori—if ever I should forget how much I owe you
May I be a brute beast in hell through all eternity.

It was around this time that Ikkyu was asked by the emperor to be head of Daitoku-ji. It seems an odd choice, but the request came after the destruction of the Onin War when the temple was on the point of collapse. Ikkyu was an admirer of the founder, Daito Kokushi, a.k.a. Shuho Myocho (1262-1337), and did not wish to see his institution collapse. He threw himself into the job, bullying the merchants of Sakai into contributing money, and under his short management the fortunes of the temple revived.

Before his death, Ikkyu made a speech to his disciples, which showed that even at eighty-seven the old rebel had not mellowed:

> *After my death, among my disciples will be those who will go to the forests or mountains (to meditate), and some who will drink saké and enjoy women, but those disciples who lecture to an audience to make money, talking about Zen as "the moral way", these men misappropriate Buddhism and are, in reality, Ikkyu's enemies.*

In Edo times (1603-1868) a collection of anecdotes projected Ikkyu as a lovable buffoon, and in modern times he has been portrayed as a boy genius. Yet there was much more to him than that. As well as being a humanitarian and an inspirational teacher, he was an artist of note and a talented calligrapher. Among his entourage were some of the most talented figures of the age. But it is for his human qualities that one warms to him most. He was an irascible sort, but underlying his anger one senses a purity of spirit, for he believed he was single-handedly maintaining the tradition of Rinzai. "For thirty years," he wrote in a poem, "the weight on my shoulder has been heavy: alone I have borne the burden." An ink portrait of him done by his disciple Bokusai shows an aging but vigorous man with a craggy face and thick head of hair. The piercing gaze, in the words of one commentator, is "attractive but unsettling". The same could be said for the man as a whole.

The Art of Zen

Walking around Zen temples, one often comes across portraits of humans, though statuary of deities tends to be scarce. It reflects the thinking of a sect that believes the truth lies within rather than in external images. It shows, too, the importance of the teacher-pupil relationship in which teaching is transmitted "outside the scriptures". Role models are thus the most revered. These include, above all, the historical Buddha, known as Shakyamuni, and the sect's founder, Bodhidharma (b. 470), known in Japan as Daruma.

There is a tradition of exhibiting large paintings of Shakyamuni on the anniversary of his death. These are called "charts", since the paintings are based on the same model: they show the dying Buddha in a grove of trees surrounded by mourners, with grieving animals in the foreground. The largest is at Tofuku-ji, and was painted in 1408 by Cho Dentsu, a.k.a. Mincho (1352-1431). It is a full fifteen yards in length and famous for including a cat, for the animal was usually left out of such work as being unfaithful.

As the founder of Zen, Daruma is also a popular subject for artists. With his bushy eyebrows, glaring eyes, and round, almost comical, face, he is instantly recognizable. One fine example is at Nanzen-ji, painted by Shokei (late fifteenth-century). It shows the patriarch with wispy beard, overhanging eyebrows, and spiky hairs sticking out from nose and ears. In other pictures he is depicted as round in shape, for according to legend he lost his arms and legs through facing a cave wall for nine years meditating. The story serves to motivate practitioners, and his glare of resolve is like a whip to the conscience.

Another type of portrait is the *chinzo*, a genre that portrays distinguished monks. They were done in a "warts and all" style with little attempt at flattery. The spirit of the man was the point: the appearance was merely ephemeral. Tofuku-ji has a nine-foot portrait of its founder, Enni Benen (1202-80), which is a case in point. It shows an old man, blind in one eye, with grumpy mouth and slippers on a stool before him. The effect is to emphasize the human frailty of one who strove for perfection.

The Tofuku-ji portrait came at the start of a seismic shift in the arts as Zen gained ground. If the purpose of meditation was a "direct pointing at the heart of man", then art for Zen was a "direct pointing at the heart of things". Capturing the essence was the objective, and this required stripping away all that was unnecessary to a clear vision. Simplicity and minimalism were the chief characteristics. The impulse found outlet in the imported ink-painting of China, for the monochrome art-form seemed to express the underlying unity of the universe. Idealized landscapes told of an identification with nature, and the tiny human figures dwarfed by their surroundings indicated the larger scheme of things. Early pictures were accompanied by calligraphy describing such feelings in poetry.

The passage from figure painting to landscape is exemplified in the work of a Chinese immigrant named Josetsu, naturalized in 1370. Known as "the father of Japanese ink paintings", he not only popularized the new style but also initiated the line of teacher-pupil relations at Shokoku-ji which produced some of Japan's most prestigious painters. The best known of his paintings belongs to Taizo-in, the oldest of Myoshin-ji's sub-temples. Entitled "Catching a Catfish with a Gourd" (c. 1413), it shows a comical-looking man fishing against a background of winding river and bamboo grove. It is a patent piece of absurdity, since the large fish cannot fit into the narrow neck of the gourd. The painting is thought to have been inspired by a riddle set by the shogun: "How do you catch a catfish with a gourd?" Written across the top are thirty-one poems on the subject by Gozan priests. The gourd was a Taoist symbol, signifying the potential of new beginnings, yet the symbolism is undercut by the bizarre features of the fisherman with his huge whiskers. Is this a piece of Zen humour—or a piece of nonsense? Perhaps like a *koan* in visual form, the intention is to provoke the viewer into new ways of "seeing".

Shokoku-ji was the motor-engine of Muromachi art, and among Josetsu's pupils was Shubun (fl. 1430) whose "Ten Ox-Herding Pictures" illustrating the stages of enlightenment can be seen in the temple museum. The ox herd represents the real self. The pictures are all circular in shape, and the eighth shows "nothing": in other words, it is an empty white circle. Like a full moon, it signifies enlightenment. Thereafter the truth of the world becomes clear.

It was Shubun's pupil, Sesshu Toyo (1420-1506), who was to become the greatest of the Shokoku-ji artists. Famous for his angular strokes and pointillism, the "genius of ink painting" was constantly chasing new horizons. Among his achievements was mastery of both styles of Chinese painting: the hard "northern" style, with its rugged strokes, and the softer "southern" style with its misty features. There was a special exhibition of Sesshu's work at the Kyoto National Museum in 2002, which was packed and rightly so—according to curators, it was a once-in-a-lifetime event. Yet despite the crush, I doubt that a single person came away who was not overwhelmed by the brilliance of what they had seen. Piercing mountain peaks cut savagely into the sky as tumbling waterfalls cascaded down vertical cliffs to peaceful valleys far below. The bold lines sliced through space with such ferocity that the landscapes leapt out of the canvas in three-dimensional form.

Sesshu was only twelve when he went to study at Shokoku-ji. He was a restless youth, always rushing off to do a painting or drawing. To discipline him, one of the monks tied him to a pillar, and on his return he was startled to see a mouse. This turned out, however, to be a drawing by Sesshu which he had done with his foot from a pool of tears. Like others of his time, the young artist looked to China as the home of culture, and in 1467 he travelled there with a trade mission. On his return he went to live in Kyushu, for Kyoto was in the midst of the Onin War. Natural landscape, with steep mountains and gnarled trees, was his forte. He was an experimentalist, too, breaking convention by omitting text and introducing colour.

One of Sesshu's later pictures, "Amanohashidate", stands tribute to his vigour. Painted when he was over eighty, it is a rare example in his paintings of an actual location. The inlet on the Japan Sea is celebrated as one of the three most beautiful views in Japan, and features a pine-covered sandbar that runs across an inlet. Sesshu depicts it from high on a hill, though how the aging painter managed this remains unclear. Even among the treasures of the Kyoto National Museum, the painting is one of the most cherished.

Like others of his time, Sesshu moved towards a more secular approach as he grew older. There was greater detail and colour in his paintings, greater realism one might say. It was part of a wider tendency, which can be seen in the early work of the influential Kano School (see Chapter Seven). The founders, Masanobu (1434-1530) and Motonobu (1476-1559), were from the samurai class and more concerned with real life than were the priests of Shokoku-ji. Under their influence, Japanese art moved away from monochrome idealism towards a more sensuous approach. The great age of Muromachi ink painting was drawing to a close.

Dry Landscapes

The impact of Zen was not limited to painting, but extended across the full range of arts. Calligraphy, for instance, was transformed from an aesthetic activity into a spiritual pursuit in which participants sought to produce writing that breathed with cosmic vitality. Stylized and yet individual, it can be hard if not impossible to read. Another exciting development was in garden design, and nowhere can this be better seen than in Kyoto. Under the influence of Zen, the notion of viewing gardens for quiet contemplation began to take hold. This was in contrast to the traditional pond garden or paradise garden that one could walk around. It required a radical rethinking in terms of design: rather then entering physically, one entered mentally.

The transition can be seen in the work of Muso Soseki, the founder of Tenryu-ji. The garden he designed there has a pond in the traditional style, but it is principally for viewing. The focal point is a group of vertical rocks, which are reflected in the water. Beyond them lies Japan's oldest example of *shakkei*, or borrowed scenery, whereby the hills in the background are skilfully drawn into the composition. It is a fine example of the garden as three-dimensional art.

A second garden by Muso is the Moss Garden at Saiho-ji, which consists of two levels. One centres round a landscaped pond in four and a half acres, where over a hundred kinds of moss present a seamless mosaic in shades of green. The upper section contains a rock garden and place for meditation: a large flat stone is said to be where Muso himself sat in contemplation. "People who understand that mountains, steams, earth, plants, trees and rocks are all one with the fundamental self can make these natural features part of their meditation," he wrote. In this way the garden bridges the Heian pond garden and the Muromachi Zen garden.

In the century that followed, there was a movement towards simplification as garden features were steadily reduced. This was driven by the essentialism of Zen, but other factors played a part. Money was scarce following the Onin War, and the impoverished aristocrats could no longer afford large estates. The reductionism is best seen in the auspicious "crane and turtle" combination. Taken separately, the two animals symbolize wisdom and longevity, based on their supposed characteristics, but taken as a pair there is a Taoist significance, for the turtle in plunging the depths and the crane in soaring heavenwards represent the balancing of yin and yang. In the pond garden, the combination took the form of islands: a low-lying turtle is juxtaposed with a craggy crane island showing the bird about to take off. Later, the pair were represented by groupings of rocks arranged to show a standing "crane" offset by a lower "tortoise". In time this was further reduced to a single pair of rocks, one vertical and one horizontal.

It was in such circumstances that the "dry landscape garden" (*karesansui*) gained popularity, as one of its virtues was that it could fit into small temple courtyards. The rock garden is thought to have originated on the desert fringes of western China, where sand or pebbles were used as a replacement for water. It appealed to Zen, for it captured the representational essence of nature. Complex notions governing proportion, placement, and the use of space added an aesthetic dimension. Like a *koan*, it sought to bypass the rational in order to trigger intuitive insight. It was, in short, a "dry" way to enlightenment.

Kyoto boasts many fine examples, but two are particularly well-known. One is at Daisen-in, a sub-temple of Daitoku-ji. It was made in 1509 in the narrow space around a rectangular building. "If you look at this garden after seeing the landscape painted by Soami on the sliding doors," says the temple pamphlet, "you may find out that such a garden is nothing but a three-dimensional reproduction of monochrome landscape paintings." The extrovert priest who guides visitors around offers an interpretation of the garden elements. A "river of life", barely nine feet wide, flows along the side of the building past crane and turtle formations towards a representation of Mount Horai, with which the combination is associated. The mountain is the legendary centre of the universe, and here in the garden it acts too as pivotal point. At its top is the "source" of the river, which issues forth in the form of a dry waterfall from a (vaginal) cleft between two rocks. The stream below seems to swirl around before being checked by a rocky wall. According to the shrine literature, this is where "the soul is confronted by the problem of the 'why' of existence."

Reducing the garden to symbolism in this way ignores the garden's other properties, for proportion and placement are crucial to the effect. This is more clearly evident at Ryoan-ji, considered by many to be the dry garden *par excellence*. Built around 1500, it is contained in a small courtyard bounded by aging walls. The elements are simplicity itself: raked gravel and fifteen rocks bordered by a little moss—nothing more.

Like the Mona Lisa, much of the appeal lies in the enigmatic quality. It has been pointed out that all fifteen stones cannot be seen at once, as if "the larger picture" can never be known. The most common meaning given to the garden is that the rocks represent islands of consciousness in a sea of emptiness. There are other fanciful ideas: boats sailing towards Mount Horai, mountain-tops sticking up through clouds, even the abstract design of a dragon. The groupings of stones are also said to match the numbers involved in a Confucian puzzle about a tigress with five cubs which has to cross a river. Though she can only carry three cubs at a time, a leopard lurks nearby threatening to attack any that are unprotected.

Those for whom such explanations belittle the garden talk of the profound emotional response that prolonged contemplation brings. In his book *By the Walls of Old Kyoto* (1981), the poet Harold Stewart unpacks the different levels in a dazzling *tour de force* involving numerological, calligraphic, and cosmological treatments. There is also a Taoist reading in which river and mountain, light and shadow, rough and smooth, horizontal and vertical are offset in a dynamic tension of opposing forces.

With Ryoan-ji, then, the dry garden took its place among the proudest accomplishments of Zen art. The abstraction from nature encapsulates the marriage of simplicity and profundity that characterizes the sect. For the priest Tessen Soki, the value of a garden lies in its ability to create "a distance of thirty-thousand leagues condensed into a few feet". In the rock garden, it sometimes seems limitations of space are transcended altogether.

Chapter Six
CITY OF NOH

Torchlight Drama

In the vast expanse of the Heian Shrine an expectant crowd of some 3,000 people waits on a pleasant afternoon at the beginning of June. Before them is a stage framed by bamboo poles and festooned with Shinto rope. The green roof and orange pillars of the buildings sparkle in the late afternoon sunshine, and in the midst of the eastern hills the large Chinese character for "Dai" is clearly visible. Musicians and chorus take their place on stage. Suddenly the piercing sound of a flute brings the audience to attention. The chorus are already kneeling in a straight line with fans placed before them. The play has begun, and though nothing much seems to be happening, the peculiar "ya-oh" of the drummer is arresting. Slowly one becomes aware of a figure moving—or gliding—towards the stage, the back tilted forward, the knees slightly bent, the movement controlled and gradual. The effect is eerie. A long recitation follows, after which there is a rustling of the curtain over the entrance area and a masked figure enters, dressed in the most gorgeous of yellow robes. The visual splendour, the intriguing music, the orange glow of the setting sun conspire to produce a sense of theatrical wonder that, for the moment at least, replaces the need for meaning.

At 6.30 Shinto priests emerge in the gathering gloom to light the braziers. The spirit of Rokujo, on stage now, looks haunting in the flickering firelight. The main building of the shrine, tastefully lit from inside, provides a decorative backdrop as syncopated sounds rise heavenwards and a ghostly silhouette moves imperceptibly in a dream-like dance. Darkness descends, and the audience grows noticeably more absorbed in the other-worldly scene. As the flames die down, the darkness grows more intense. An outburst from the flute seems to startle the dying embers back to life, then suddenly and without ceremony all is over and the performers leave the stage. The spell is broken, the crowd begins to disperse, and reality returns. Kyoto's Takigi

Noh is over for another year.

The event has been held every year since 1949. It was started in imitation of a medieval rite, and the revival proved such a success that it spawned some two hundred other events around the country. Those who come to Noh in this way delight in the easy-going atmosphere. With its masks, chorus, music and all-male cast, the drama has been compared to that of ancient Greece, but viewed in this way it has something of the great religious dramas of south-east Asia: a statelier version of the Balinese re-enactments of the Ramayama, perhaps.

Yet for all this, Noh has the reputation of being unbearably boring. It is the great polarizer of Japanese art-forms: you either love it, or loathe it. A theatre with no conflict, no humour, and no facial expression adds up in the minds of many to "Noh interest". For its detractors it is an outmoded relic of medieval times: a plot of two minutes that takes an hour to unfold; a snail's pace to cross the stage; dances that are stiff and solemn; arcane language and archaic music.

What is remarkable, then, is that the drama remains alive and flourishing. Some ascribe the survival to its multi-level appeal. Music, dance, costume, acting, and script combine in a highly refined art. Others see it as a tribute to the great performing families, for like much else in Japan's traditional world, the system is largely hereditary. For generations now it has been handed down with reverential care, refusing to adapt to the modern age. There is no scenery or lighting, nor is there any modernizing of the language. It is as if Elizabethan theatre had survived intact, and along with its original form kept something of its original force.

Noh Genius

Unusually for theatre, Noh has a precise starting point. In 1374, the seventeen-year-old Yoshimitsu, of Golden Pavilion fame, attended a performance at Imagumano Shrine in north-west Kyoto put on by a Shinto priest named Kan'ami (1333-84). The play drew on the traditions of *dengaku*, which involved music and ritual, and *sarugaku noh*, in which actors entertained festival crowds. To suit upper-class tastes, Kan'ami incorporated an elegant style of dance movement. It appealed to the young shogun, as did the priest's eleven-year old son. As a result Yoshimitsu bestowed his patronage on the troupe, meaning that they could remain in Kyoto to perfect their art.

Kan'ami's son, named Zeami (c.1363-1443), became a firm favourite of the shogun. Despite the difference in age, the pair were on intimate terms, and at the Gion Festival parade of 1378 they appeared together in public. It caused raised eyebrows, and a nobleman was prompted to record the following:

> *For some while the shogun has been making a favourite of a* sarugaku *boy from Yamato, sharing the same mat and eating from the same plates. These* sarugaku *people are mere mendicants, but he treats them with as much esteem as if they were Counsellors. Those who give the boy presents ingratiate themselves with the shogun... It is a most vile state of affairs.*

Zeami was educated by the top artists of the day, and he became an outstanding performer. Following his father's death, he took charge of the acting troupe and dedicated himself to furthering the art. Freed from the need to attract a commercial audience, he produced performances designed to appeal to the most sophisticated of tastes. The peak of his career came in 1408 when he appeared at the Golden Pavilion before both shogun and emperor.

Though Zeami knew success, he suffered bitter misfortune in later life. In 1429 he fell out of favour with a successor of Yoshimitsu and was banned from major events. The next year his younger son gave up Noh to become a monk. Then, in 1432, his oldest son and heir died. It was a crushing blow, followed two years later by exile to the island of Sado in the Japan Sea.

Zeami's legacy is impressive. Almost single-handedly he established a complex art-form, and his skills were passed on in direct transmission to his son-in-law Komparu Zenchiku (1405-68). He was the author of a good many of the 250 plays still being performed, and in addition he wrote influential treatises that continue to set the guidelines for the drama form. It is as if even now, six hundred years after his death, he continues to direct Noh from beyond the grave.

Zeami's most famous work, *Fushikaden*, also known as *Kadensho* (c.1410), has been called "the Bible of Noh". Here he elaborates on the concept of "the flower" (*hana*), which distinguishes superlative acting. Cultivating this was a lifetime's work, and he talks of the performance of an old master as being like the spring blossom on a withered tree.

Now how shall we understand this hana *of Noh in these secret instructions? First of all, you must understand the reason why they have used the symbol of flowers for* hana. *As every kind of plant and flower blooms at its proper time in the four seasons, people think it is beautiful because they feel its blooming as something fresh and rare. In the art of Noh the point at which the audience feels this freshness and rarity will be the interesting part to them.*

Chief among the qualities Zeami promoted was *yugen*, based on the combination of elegance and mystery. It added an element of profundity to the plays. There was a conscious Heian nostalgia in this, for Yoshimitsu wished to emulate the achievements of the past. Thanks to the aesthetic, the theatre form was able to match the refinements of Heian-kyo.

Like others of his time, Zeami was also influenced by Zen. He became a Soto priest in later life, and many of his plays have strong Buddhist themes. It was a characteristic of the age that everything was made into a Way, and like other art-forms Noh was treated as a means of perfection. In this respect the ritualized drama bears comparison with the tea ceremony, which also evolved at this time. Both rely on disciplined, controlled movements to subjugate the self.

The spiritual origins of Noh lay in an older tradition, however, and its Shinto roots are evident in its very architecture. The stage mirrors the independent structures at shrines, which is why it always stands as a separate building even when housed within a modern auditorium. On the back wall is a painted tree, thought to be a reference to the Yogo Pine at Nara's Kasuga Shrine where Kan'ami worked. Legend has it that an old man was once seen dancing beneath the tree, who turned out to be the tree-spirit in human form. It indicates the sacred bond between mankind and the gods that underlies the "mystery plays" of Noh. From this world the action invariably leads to the next, and a magical moment of

transformation is acted out before the sacred pine when spirits stand revealed.

The otherworldliness brought with it a spurning of realism, since Noh's concern is with trapped souls and higher truths. As in Zen, the aim is not outward representation, but spiritual essence. Unworldly movements, masked figures and eerie music are blended to provide what can be a highly charged atmosphere. In the fusion of Shinto and Zen is born "a terrible beauty".

The Repertory

Of the roughly 2,000 texts known to exist, only some 250 remain in the current repertories. Many of these were written by a handful of playwrights in the fifteenth century, and nearly all date from before the mid-seventeenth century. On average, they contain two to three hundred lines and take about an hour to perform. Unlike Western plays, there is little action. The form is more like a recitation. The interest lies not in the narrative, since the stories are well-known, but in the creation of atmosphere.

Tradition divides the plays into five types. First are the god plays, emphasizing harmony between man and deities. Second are the warrior plays, based for the most part on *The Tale of Heike*, in which spirits are plagued by unresolved passions. Thirdly, there are women or wig plays, in which feminine spirits seek release, often from a love obsession. Fourthly comes a large miscellaneous group, featuring mad characters or the encounter of two contemporaries. Finally, there is the category known as Ending Noh, which typically portrays demons. In earlier times, a full programme was made up of a play from each group, performed in proper order. This lasted about ten hours and took the audience through the full range of human-spirit relations. Nowadays, a typical programme consisting of three Noh plays and a Kyogen (comic sketch) might last around three hours.

Many of the plays follow a similar pattern. A wandering priest visits a temple or famous spot, where he engages a local in conversation. This turns out not to be a living person, but a restless spirit with a lingering attachment: love, hatred, revenge, even an over-fondness for cherry blossom. In response, the priest says a prayer for the spirit, which performs a dance before departing. The plays can thus be seen in ritual terms as an intercession for tormented souls.

Performers belong to one of the five schools of Noh. Kanze Noh, by far the biggest of the five, operates out of Tokyo but keeps a theatre in Kyoto, where it puts on regular performances. Kongo Noh is now the only school to be based in the city. It has eighty professionals as well as numerous amateurs. It also has a smart new theatre, next to the former imperial palace. Here, on a Sunday afternoon, the spirits of the past come alive in the comfort of a purpose-built auditorium.

The Art of Noh

More than most art-forms, Noh is an acquired taste. Donald Keene, a long time devotee, writes of "a grandeur of expression fully intelligible only to spectators who have made comparable efforts to understand this endlessly rewarding art." Performers are aware of this, and effort is made on their part to spread awareness through events and demonstrations.

The talks that I have attended usually begin with the stage itself. Made of Japanese cypress, it stands four feet off the ground and is built with all the skill of traditional craftsmen. There is not a single nail. There are four pillars, and the highly polished floorboards allow the actors in their white *tabi* socks to glide across them. No bare feet or ordinary socks are ever allowed to despoil the sacred surface. The stage proper is not the only performance area, for there is also a long covered corridor leading to the dressing area. Here is where the costumed actors make their entrance, as the coloured curtaining is drawn aside. There is a symbolic dimension to this procedure, for the corridor represents the passage between two worlds.

At Nishi Hongan-ji in central Kyoto is a stage dating from 1595, which reminds one of its contemporary in England—The Globe. It stands before a raised hall where the ruling class sat, and in between is an area of open space that was filled by the "groundlings". Unique to Noh are the suspended large jars beneath the stage, which act as acoustic aids. The technique was used here for the first time, and afterwards became common practice.

Performances are characterized by slow and stately movements. The body is held rigid, with the knees slightly bent. Rather than the ball of the foot, the heel takes the actor's weight and the toes lift upwards. The skill rests in gliding over the floor, as if walking on water. The stiff physical posture would not seem to allow for the display of emotion, but this is crucial to the effect and actors work hard to project inner feelings. "Refining the heart is more important than refining skills," Hirata Yukitoshi of the Kongo Noh once told me. An important part of performances is the dance, which expresses the theme of the play in physical form. It holds an important place, and can take up to a third of the performance. Sometimes it hardly seems like a dance at all, but more like a series of poses. Yet it can also be unexpectedly vigorous, with swift motion and sudden jump-turns. Foot stamping, to display anger or power, adds to the effect.

There are few props in Noh, though the simple fan plays a key role. The chorus lay theirs before them when not performing, as if cordoning themselves off. Actors carry a larger type, with coloured designs to match the theme. For gods there are pictures of cranes or tortoise shell; for women there is black lacquered bamboo. During dances it is used as an accompaniment, opening out with the radiance of a butterfly displaying its wings in the sunshine.

Actors are divided into *shite* (lead role), *waki* (literally "side" or support actor), and *kyogen* (who play minor roles and do the interlude speech). It is usually the *waki* who start the play by introducing the context. They then stand at the side, as the *shite* takes centre stage. Unlike Western drama, there is virtually no crossover because the system works on a hereditary principle. Once a *waki*, always a *waki*.

As the representatives of the spirit world, the *shite* wear gorgeous costumes, often in heavy brocades and patterned weaves. Some are five hundred years old and treated as museum pieces. By contrast, the *waki*, representing the human world, wear clothes made of silk, while those of the humble *kyogen* are more ordinary still. The costumes are vital to the effect, for it is these that dazzle the eye and linger in the mind.

The otherworldly quality of Noh derives much of its effect from the masks, and here again the craft has been raised to an art-form. Many have been handed down for centuries, and watching these museum pieces come to life is one of the joys of the aesthetic experience. To the actors, they are much more than just a face covering; they are the spiritual essence of a character. Each has its own individuality, so the choice is a matter of crucial importance. Before going on stage, actors stare at it to absorb its features, and after putting it on they gaze into a mirror as if seeing into its soul. There is a shamanistic element in this, as if they are submitting to its spirit. It explains the great reverence with which the masks are treated. Many of them have a neutral expression, leaving the viewer to imagine the feelings. They can send shivers down the spine, for beneath the wooden shell move human eyes. The high foreheads and small faces, part of the genre's stylized nature, only allow restricted vision. Even breathing is difficult. It makes it all the more remarkable that actors can portray such qualities as grace and elegance.

For some, the essence of Noh lies not in the masks, however, but in the music. The simple orchestra comprises a bamboo flute and two drums (shoulder- and hip-drum), though for certain performances a stick drum is added for extra force. The Noh flute has a haunting quality, which can also be piercingly loud, while the drums have four distinct types of sound made by the placement and shaping of the hand. A handy tip I have found useful during dull passages is to try and differentiate the four sounds. It is these that establish the rhythm of the play, and it is these that control the heartbeat of the audience.

Like a Balinese orchestra, the band has no conductor and works as an ensemble. In this they are helped by the odd cries from the drummers (*kakegoe*). These vary in tone and pitch: some are short groans, others take the form of a long crescendo. They help set the beat and act as a trigger to the next section. They are quite unlike anything a Westerner has ever heard, but once one gets over the strangeness, the combination of shout and drum has a hypnotic effect as a rising "yo-o-o" is followed by a resounding "whop" from the drum.

The final piece of the Noh jigsaw is the script. Opinion differs as to whether this constitutes literature in its own right, or whether, like an opera libretto, it should not be treated in isolation. If Noh is a medieval musical, then the rhythm is integral to the lyrics, and it might be argued that to separate the words from the music is to make a mockery of them. Yet few could deny that there are passages of lyrical beauty in Noh, and many plays borrow from the poetry and prose of past masters. It is in the synthesis of verbal beauty with dramatic mystery and musical accompaniment that lies the appeal of the plays. It is an art-form whose rarefied aesthetics could only have derived from Kyoto.

Past and Future

From its very beginnings Noh enjoyed the patronage of those in power, and Yoshmitsu's enthusiasm was continued by those who succeeded him. A later ruler, Hideyoshi, took a particularly active interest: he not only patronized the Noh schools, but commissioned plays in which he took the starring role—as himself! During Tokugawa times Noh was declared the official art, and like all else in the country it was regulated and codified. It was at this time that, in a process of refinement, performances were slowed down. By the end of the era plays took three times longer than in Zeami's day. The slower the action, ran the thinking, the greater the solemnity.

With the opening-up of Japan after 1868, government support stopped as the country looked to the West for its arts. Noh virtually collapsed, and it was only thanks to the dedication of a few performers that it survived. Ironically, it was around this time that Westerners began to take an interest. Basil Hall Chamberlain provided the first translations in 1880, then the Modernist generation seized on the tradition as an alternative to prevailing realism. Ezra Pound's reworking of Ernest Fenollosa's notes in *The Classic Noh Theatre of Japan* (1917) made quite a splash, and W. B. Yeats even created his own Noh Plays. Oddly, the medieval plays of Japan had become a means of revitalizing modern theatre in the West.

Nowadays in Japan there are 1,540 professional performers, of whom 250 are female. They derive their income from teaching rather than performances, as Noh is very much a minority interest. Yet it is surprising how many spectators are willing to give up a sunny Sunday. Some are practising amateurs and bring the score with them. Others take it as an opportunity for a midday doze, for the event encourages reverie, and the borderline between the dream world and the action on stage is thin indeed. When I queried Hirata Yukitoshi about this, he told me that performers have every sympathy with the slumberers—and even envy them!

That such a spectacle should survive in the modern world is something of a wonder. For over a hundred and thirty years, the Japanese have been pushing Western models onto themselves, and nowhere more so than in the field of music. But things are changing. Only recently has Japanese music been added to the school curriculum, and this should ensure that coming generations have a greater understanding of Noh. A future that once looked bleak now seems brighter, for the stages of Kyoto look set to resound to "yo-ohhh" and "whop" for many years to come.

Comic Interlude

Noh's counterpart, Kyogen, is the bumbling fool that accompanies its elevated brother. In place of stately elegance is rolling buffoonery, and the actors, with their lowered body and bent knees, carry an air of amusement. The humorous sketches, interspersed between Noh plays, serve as relief in similar manner to the comic scenes of Shakespeare's tragedies. The concern is with worldly matters, and the intention is to entertain.

It may seem odd for "low humour" to be sharing the same stage as Noh—from the sublime to the ridiculous, one might say—yet the two traditions are closely related. Both developed out of the *sarugaku* entertainments, which in earlier times were put on at religious festivals. These split into a comic element and a song-dance variant.

The word *kyogen*, meaning "wild words", derives from a Chinese saying that truth can lie in even the utmost folly. The term was first used in the fourteenth century when the priest Genei (1269-1350) created fifty-nine comic plays. These and others were handed down orally until the seventeenth century, when scripts were written down by Okura Tokaaki (1597-1662). He was the Zeami of Kyogen, producing treatises on the art: "The Kyogen makes true things funny, and funny things true," he noted. Much of the humour lies in the stylized manner of the plays, as the guttural delivery and heavy stresses give the dialogue a rhythmical quality. The tone is set by the sing-song style of the typical opening line: *kore wa/kono atari ni/ sumai itasu mono de/gozaru* ("I am a man who lives in these parts"). Many of the plays reverse the social order; servants fool their masters, country bumpkins outwit city types, and husbands are scolded by wives. Irreverence is a stock in trade, and priests are often the target. It is the classic release of tension, an escape valve for the grind of daily reality.

Like Noh, performers are divided into schools. Only two remain, the Izumi and the Okura (a third school, Sagi, dropped out of existence in the 1890s). Izumi used to be known as the "Kyoto school" because of its ties with the Imperial Palace. Now it is the Okura school that is associated with Kyoto through the activities of the Shigeyama family of Kyogen performers.

There are some 260 plays in the current repertory, which is similar in number to Noh. The themes range from the religious to the domestic, and tell of everyday life in medieval times. Human frailty is exposed, though not in a cruel way, for the humour is warm and never vulgar. Of the many sketches set in Kyoto, *Inaba-do* is a popular favourite. It tells of a man who divorces his bad-tempered drunkard of a wife and goes to pray for a new partner. Hearing of this, his wife hurries to the temple where she pretends to be the voice of the gods telling him to go to the city's west gate to meet someone. When he arrives there, he is delighted to find a veiled woman whom he takes home with him. To his surprise she drinks a lot, and when he asks her to unveil he gets the shock of his life. Like a bad penny, his wife has returned...

Wife: *So you say I'm an incorrigible woman? Do you really mean to give me a divorce?*
Man: *The fact of the matter is, it was from a desire to become a monk that I decided to become single again...*
Wife: *In that case, for what purpose did you run off to Inaba Temple?*
Man: *Why, I went to pray for your future health and happiness.*
Wife: *Eeeii! How angry I am, how angry I am. You cowardly rascal! Shall I wring your neck, or shall I bite your head off?*
Man: *Oh, forgive me, please forgive me...*

Another Kyogen play set in Kyoto, *Kuji Zainin* (Lottery Sinner), features the well-known character Taro Kaja, who appears in forty-five Kyogen as well as several Kabuki plays. Like the white-faced circus clown, he is a generic type recognizable by his costume. His role is that of the bumbling servant, who somehow manages to subvert his master. The play takes place just before the Gion Festival, when Taro's master calls a meeting to decide the design of the neighbourhood float. Listening in from the next room, the servant cannot help calling out objections to the suggestions of his master. He even voices his own idea, which is taken up and approved by the committee. The humour lies in the frantic efforts of the master to silence his irrepressible underling.

In recent years Kyogen has won something of a following and is now an entertainment in its own right. The irreverence appeals to a sceptical age. It is by no means the only comic tradition to be found in Kyoto, for there are also medieval skits that are put on at temples in annual performances. Bawdy and satirical, these religious sketches date back to the age of Chaucer.

Moral Skits

The Kamakura era, as we have seen, was a time of famine and cruelty. Out of the gloom Amida shone with a message of salvation, and to spread the word temples organized shows designed to appeal to the lower orders. Buddhism had never wooed the masses in such numbers before.

Three separate groups still maintain the medieval tradition. Of these, that of Mibu Temple is the most celebrated, and even in Edo times the performances were mentioned in guide-books as one of the city's attractions. They are unique in being mimed. Not only are there no scripts, but there are no written guidelines, as the whole tradition has been handed down orally for seven hundred years. The productions were first started by a monk called Enkaku, who rebuilt the temple in 1300. His nickname, Juman (a hundred thousand), was a reference to his reputation for converting 100,000 people to the practice of *nembutsu*. There are thirty-one plays in the repertoire, most of which concern historical topics. Grotesque masks, elaborate costumes, and stylized mannerisms provide the visual appeal, while the repetitive rhythm of drum, gong and flute lulls the audience into a kind of amused reverie.

One of the most popular sketches is a variant of the Noh play, *Dojo-ji*, about a jealous woman who destroys a temple bell under which her priest-lover has hidden himself. The Mibu sketch takes place during the preparations for the consecration of a new bell. It begins with the priest telling two workers to look after things while he is out, but when a beautiful woman appears they eagerly invite her in. She entrances the men—literally—and enters beneath the bell. When the priest returns, he scolds the men for sleeping and together they raise the bell. Underneath is no longer the pretty woman but—in a dramatic change of costume—a fearsome devil.

The Mibu style differs from the Kyogen of Noh. Take the way of laughing, for instance. When Mibu characters are amused, they bend from the waist back and forward, shaking silently with open mouth. When Kyogen characters laugh, they give a series of loud "ha-ha-ha's" in a posed position, leaning forward with the body held stiff from the waist down.

A different tradition can be seen at the temple of Senbon Emmado. This has spoken dialogue and a repertoire of fifty plays. Performances are held in a makeshift courtyard next to the temple and have a friendly community atmosphere. Neighbours can be seen exchanging greetings, and children sit open-mouthed at the costumed creatures. The first play each day is *Emma-cho*, about the temple's deity. It begins with the arrival of a dead man, who is claimed by an eager demon. It is thwarted, however, by the dead man holding up a list of his good works, which has the effect of a crucifix on a vampire. Though the demon tries repeatedly to take his soul, the dead man resists and Emma determines he should pass into heaven. The moral of the play is reinforced by a fearsome statue of Emma in the adjacent building. With his glaring glass eyes, "the king of the underworld" presents a frightening prospect for anyone with no list of worldly virtues to show.

Another type of Nembutsu Kyogen is put on by the Saga Preservation Group, who perform from their base at Seiryo-ji in the west of Kyoto. Oddly for a temple stage, several sketches make pointed fun of priests. One of the most enjoyable depicts a statue of Kannon running off with a beautiful woman who has come to pray. The priest, seeing this, is eager to follow suit and takes the place of the statue. The next woman to visit is spectacularly ugly (thanks to a striking mask), but the priest is undismayed and runs off with her anyway. When I asked afterwards about the moral, the lead actor said that it showed priests would chase any woman, no matter how plain!

Looking around the temple compound with its stalls and jostling crowds, one cannot help imagining that things must have been very similar in medieval times. The clothes might have changed, the lifestyle may be different, but the humour remains the same. This is a tradition that has not really dated, and in a world of mass entertainment one feels lucky to have these "home-made" performances. Now, as during centuries past, the show goes on—and Kyoto is the richer for it.

Chapter Seven
CITY OF UNIFICATION

The Strong Man

The Onin War that devastated Kyoto in the fifteenth century inaugurated a period of Warring Factions, or Sengoku (1467-1568). Power was disputed by provincial warlords, and out of the regional rivalries arose three remarkable men who stamped their authority on the country. These were Oda Nobunaga (1534-82), Toyotomi Hideyoshi (1536-98), and Tokugawa Ieyasu (1543-1616). The men were all from the Tokai region, but each left his mark on the capital. The unifying process in which they were involved has been likened to the making of *mochi* rice cake. Nobunaga prepared the ingredients; Hideyoshi beat them to the right texture; and Ieyasu kneaded them into shape. Or in terms of an omelette, Nobunaga cracked the eggs, Hideyoshi heated them, and Ieyasu ate them.

It was an eventful time in Japan's history, marked by the arrival in 1543 of the first Europeans in the form of Portuguese traders. Six years later the Spaniard Francis Xavier (1506-1562) arrived to begin missionary work. The incomers were named *namban*, or "southern barbarians", because of the direction from which they arrived, and at first they were restricted to Kyushu, where the ports were located. To the curious Japanese, they were the object of much fascination, and *namban* paintings portrayed their fancy clothes and strange faces.

In 1551 Xavier became the first European to set foot in Kyoto. He found the city in confusion and left after two weeks, unable to see either shogun or emperor. "Today much of Kyoto lies in ruins because of the wars; many people have told us that it once had 80,000 houses, and it seems to me this must have been true, to judge from the very large size of the city," he wrote.

Along with Christianity, the Europeans brought the gun. One of the first to seize on the new technology was Nobunaga, which enabled him to gain the upper hand in the struggle with his rivals. Encouraged by the emperor, who saw in him a means of bringing order to the country, he set about subduing factional elements. In a series of brilliant victories he confronted warlords, militant peasants, and temple armies. In 1568 Nobunaga marched into the capital where he established himself as *de facto* leader. He was welcomed by the emperor with a banquet of noodle soup, so impoverished had the imperial household become through the long years of warfare. The new supremo soon exercised his authority. He had little respect for religion and commandeered the heads of Buddhist statues for building material. When the north of the city objected to his taxes, he burned it down. And in 1571, when the great mountain-monastery of Mount Hiei refused to submit, he set about destroying it.

The Tendai temple had long used its warrior-priests to impose its will on the emperor. To Nobunaga, it was simply a nest of corruption. "Go forth and burn it," he ordered his men: "Burn it, the earth must be cleansed." Marching up the sides of the mountain, his army systematically destroyed everything they came upon. Altogether some 3,000 buildings were set on fire. Such was the heat that the waters of Lake Biwa grew warm, and for three days the Kyoto skies were blackened with smoke. In all, 25,000 people perished, including women and children.

In 1573 Nobunaga ousted the Ashikaga and assumed formal charge of the country. Three years later he constructed a massive castle by Lake Biwa at Azuchi, from which the era takes its name. In contrast to the Hiei destruction, he tolerated and even encouraged the activity of missionaries, whom he saw as a counter to the Buddhists. Perhaps, too, he was drawn to their "samurai spirit" of discipline and pride in poverty. In 1576 the first church was established in Kyoto, and by 1613, according to the English trader John Sarris, there were some five to six thousand Christians in the city.

Ironically, the best place to see the Christian legacy of these times is at the Buddhist temple of Daitoku-ji. This houses the grave of Japan's most famous convert, Hosokawa Gracia (1563-1600), in one of its sub-temples, while in Zuiho-in is a modern rock garden in the form of a cross. This honours the founder, a Kyushu lord named Ohtomo Sorin (1530-89) who converted from Zen to Christianity. According to the temple, such was his fervour that he undertook "crusades" against his enemies. Perhaps one gets a clue here as to why this dangerous new religion was later banned.

In 1582 came the dramatic death of Nobunaga. It took place in a Kyoto temple named Honno-ji, where he was resting after dispatching forces to subdue the west of the country. A general named Akechi Mitsuhide (1526-82), father of Hosokawa Gracia, turned traitor and marched his army back to Kyoto where he laid siege to the temple. Mitsuhide was a refined man, who was repeatedly slighted by the rough-mannered Nobunaga and who may have blamed him for the death of his mother. His move caught his opponent unawares, and hopelessly outnumbered, the wounded shogun set fire to the temple and committed *seppuku* (ritual suicide).

Events moved quickly thereafter. As soon as he heard the news, Nobunaga's right-hand man, Hideyoshi, rushed back to the capital, and in the clash of armies Mitsuhide was defeated and killed while fleeing in an ambush of farmers. The "thirteen-day shogun" had enjoyed only the briefest time in power. One of the first things the loyal Hideyoshi did was to offer Mitsuhide's head to Nobunaga's spirit. He also had the temple of Honno-ji rebuilt on a different site, where a tomb was erected to the former leader. Visitors can often be seen here in prayer to the man voted in a NHK poll "the most influential person in Japanese history".

Although Nobunaga had not endeared himself to Kyoto's citizenry, he is nonetheless deified in Kenkun Shrine in the north of the city. Here on 19 October each year—the day on which this Japanese Napoleon first marched into the city—a festival is held in his memory. Its centrepiece is the firing of ancient muskets by men in period clothing. The deafening noise is a reminder of just how awesome this new weaponry must have been. You get the feeling that if opponents were not shot, they would have been half-frightened to death.

The samurai of Nobunaga's time wore dazzling outfits: "dressing to kill" was taken literally. Leather strips pieced together by bright coloured thread were worn together with metal arm-coverings over silk padding. There were layered plates around the neck, and flags of angry devils strapped to the back. The outfit was topped off by broad-brimmed helmets with elaborate carvings and gilded attachments. The more colourful the costume, the greater the glory: by drawing attention on the battlefield, the wearer would make himself the target of attack.

The chief priest of the shrine took the opportunity one year to nominate Nobunaga with two others, Prince Shotoku and Emperor

Meiji, as the "big three" of Japanese history. What did they have in common, he asked? They all imported foreign ways while keeping the Japanese spirit. In this way Nobunaga was championed as forerunner of the current vogue for "internationalization". It may seem strange that a ruthless atheist should be celebrated in this way, but the praise stems from a belief that in unifying the country Nobunaga was acting for the national good. The myth of the noble samurai also plays a part in his fame, which is bolstered by the manner of his death. Bisexual and individualistic, he is in many ways well-suited to the role of modern hero. Betrayed while still in his prime, the provincial warlord remains in the public mind the great hero-martyr of the nation state.

The Second Founder
Only one man in Japanese history ever rose from the peasantry to be supreme leader. That man was Hideyoshi. As if that was not enough, in his sixteen years in power he single-handedly transformed the country and prompted an artistic renaissance. Such was his ambition he even launched invasions of Korea with the aim of capturing China. For Japan, Hideyoshi was a figure of monumental importance. For Kyoto, he amounts to a second founder.

Hideyoshi's humble beginnings taught him of life's hardships. Nicknamed "Monkey" for his looks, he lost his father while young, was mistreated by his stepfather, and left home at fourteen. Later he entered the service of Nobunaga, whom he impressed with his devotion one cold morning when warming his master's slippers by holding them to his chest. In just twelve years he was promoted from errand-boy to commander of his own troops.

Hideyoshi was a man of great vitality, who was full of contradictions. He could be authoritarian, yet he craved approval. He was generous of spirit, yet was also ruthless. He showed great statesmanship, yet was reckless too. And in his love of the arts, he combined the pursuit of refinement with the vulgarity of the *nouveau riche*.

Following Nobunaga's death, Hideyoshi assumed power and set about establishing his authority. Within eight years, he had completed the process of unification, which brought over a century of civil war to an end. Although Osaka Castle served as his military base, it was Kyoto which occupied his attentions. "He never spent much time [in Osaka]," writes Mary Berry; "Kyoto remained his centre, with its courtly diversions, its *daimyo* enclave, and its lively traffic." With his peasant background, he craved acceptance by the aristocracy. To ingratiate himself, he helped restore the fortunes of the imperial family, took lessons in court etiquette, and worked with courtiers on Noh performances. He even succeeded in having himself declared Kampaku (Imperial Regent), a title which was reserved for leading aristocrats, though to the population at large he was simply Taiko (His Highness).

In 1585, three years after seizing power, Hideyoshi gave orders for the reconstruction of Kyoto. It was a massive undertaking, since the city had been devastated by years of neglect. The plan involved the redrawing of boundaries with the addition of new north-south streets. Worn-out wooden bridges were replaced with larger structures on stone supports, and many large temples were restored at great expense. Smaller temples were grouped together on the outer fringes: this helped make them more manageable, as well as serving as a defensive line against attack.

Not content with all this, Hideyoshi added embellishments of his own. In 1586 he built a huge residence called Jurakudai (Palace of the Accumulated Pleasures) on the site of Heian-kyo's imperial enclosure. The location was chosen to lend lustre to the magnificence. Surrounded by a moat, the extensive grounds included tearooms, Noh stages and cherry groves, outside which stood the mansions of supporters. It was Hideyoshi's calling card to the aristocracy, and here in 1588 the peasant's son received Emperor Go-Yozei.

Go-Yozei:
Today is the day
We achieve what we awaited.
In the branches of the pine
I see the promise of our relations
Extending for ages.

Hideyoshi:
As my lord of myriad ages
Has proclaimed here in state,
We may henceforth come closer
Like the green pine

Standing tall by the eaves.

Another of Hideyoshi's projects was the erection of a huge 120-foot Buddha at Hoko-ji, near the present-day National Museum. Completed in 1587, it involved 20,000 labourers. "In the days of Emperor Shomu, it took twenty years to build the Daibutsu-den in Nara. I will build one in five years," he boasted. He was wrong: it took him just three. To offset the costs, he ordered that the swords of non-samurai be donated to the cause. This occasioned the "Taiko's Sword Hunt", a typical piece of Hideyoshi cunning; under the slogan of "Give iron to the Buddha" farmers and warrior-priests were effectively disarmed.

The reconstructed capital was finished in 1591 with earthen embankments and a moat that ran for fourteen miles. The original planners of Heian-kyo had envisaged a city wall, but it had never been completed. Eight hundred years later Hideyoshi fulfilled the dream. The achievements of these years are simply astonishing. In just six years, a city of intermittent ruins had been turned into a national capital worthy of its name. "The city owes much of its present shape and its heritage of beautiful temples to the efforts and vision of Hideyoshi," writes Kyoto expert Judith Clancy.

Sadly, not all of the projects survived. The city wall decayed with age, and the Great Buddha was destroyed by an earthquake. But perhaps the greatest loss was that of Jurakudai, dismantled by Hideyoshi himself only nine years after it was built. He had given the palace to Hidetsugu, his nephew and heir, as he made plans for retirement. But when his mistress Yodogimi (niece of Nobunaga) unexpectedly bore a son, he changed his mind and grew suspicious of his nephew. In 1595 he ordered him to commit suicide, and the residence was disassembled. In the meantime Hideyoshi had built himself a castle at Fushimi-Momoyama, commanding the river route to Osaka. Yet here again, he was unfortunate in his legacy, for it was destroyed soon after his death.

In the 1590s, not content with his achievements, Hideyoshi turned his attention abroad. He dreamed of becoming king of East Asia, and even of taking India. This is usually ascribed to megalomania, although waging war to boost reputations remains common enough, even today. In 1592, and again in 1597, Hideyoshi launched campaigns against

Korea, seen as a stepping-stone to China. The streets of Kyoto filled with the pageant of armies setting out for war. Yet despite early victories, the invasions became bogged down in fighting, and with Hideyoshi's death from illness in 1598 the idea was abandoned.

The city houses a poignant reminder of the Korean adventure in the form of Mimizuka, or Ear Mound. The custom in war was for enemy heads to be collected as proof of victory, but since distance precluded this practice, ears and noses were shipped in brine instead. Like a cat offering its kill to its master, Hideyoshi had them buried in a mound before his Great Buddha. They number in the tens of thousands. In Edo times Korean emissaries used to visit it to mourn the dead, and still today busloads of tearful tourists can be seen paying their respects.

A different side of Hideyoshi is evident at Daigo-ji, where in 1598 he held an extravagant cherry-blossom party. It was a grand occasion, with stops for banquets and poetry reading as his entourage ascended the hillside. The temple had fallen into disrepair in the Sengoku period and at Hideyoshi's bequest it was refurbished. Particular attention was lavished on Sambo-in, a sub-temple that remains a monument to the Taiko's fondness for opulence. The complex resembles not so much a temple as an aristocratic villa. There are teahouses, a Noh stage, paintings by leading artists, and a narrow stream for the floating of saké cups. The gateway for imperial messengers is decorated with Hideyoshi's paulownia and the emperor's chrysanthemum, standing side by side. The declaration says much about its maker's view of things, for Hideyoshi was here placing himself on a par with the descendant of the sun-goddess. The "Monkey" had climbed to the top of the tree.

The centrepiece of Sambo-in is its pond garden. Hideyoshi took a personal interest in its design, though it was not completed until after his death. It shows a taste for the showy, with three islands in place of the usual two, several types of bridge, and a *karesansui* (dry landscape garden) squeezed between building and pond. The variety of shrubbery includes deciduous as well as evergreen plants, while the pond is fed by both stream and waterfall. Most of all, there are rocks—more than 700 in all. Each is carefully positioned, not only for its aesthetic effect but also for the balancing of energy forces. Many are impressive specimens that were presented in homage by far-off lords. Contemplating them, one is reminded of Lafcadio Hearn's claim that "Until you can feel, and keenly feel, that stones have character, that stones have tones and values, the whole artistic meaning of a Japanese garden cannot be revealed to you."

The most famous of the rocks, known as the Fujito Stone, came from the Okayama region. During the Heike wars, a fisherman had been slain on it by a Minamoto general who wanted to preserve the secrecy of a ford there (an incident featured in the Noh play *Fujito*). The death invested the rock with a numinous quality, as if it had absorbed the spirit of the dead man along with his blood. During transportation it was accorded the kind of respect normally reserved for lords, being clothed in silk brocade and accompanied by music. At one time it was owned by Nobunaga, and later by Hideyoshi. Now it sits proud in its garden retreat, lording it over the lesser creatures by which it is surrounded.

When Hideyoshi died, he was buried according to his instructions on the eastern hill of Amidagamine, overlooking the south of the city. The emperor gave orders for him to be deified, and a huge Hokoku Shrine was erected, which became the focus for festivals held each year to commemorate his death. A painting on a six-panel folding screen by Kano Naizen (b. 1570) depicts the crowds at the seventh anniversary. The teeming mass of people and horseback procession show how popular these celebrations once were.

Next door to the shrine, in the temple compound of Hoko-ji, stands a large temple bell that makes an intriguing postscript to Hideyoshi's story. To ensure his succession, he had set up a council of five regents for his young son, Toyotomi Hideyori (1592-1615). One of these was the ambitious Ieyasu, who seized the regency for himself at the battle of Sekigahara in 1600. It was the biggest battle of Japanese history, with 100,000 Tokugawa troops defeating an army of 80,000 led by Ishida Mitsunari. Following this, Ieyasu set up base in Edo (present-day Tokyo); Hideyori was left to grow up in the family stronghold at Osaka.

To weaken the Toyotomi finances, Ieyasu encouraged them to reconstruct the Great Buddha at Hoko-ji, and, on its completion, a large bell was installed on which was written *Kokka Anko* (Peace and Stability to the Country). As fate would have it, an alternative reading for the middle two characters was *ie* and *yasu*. Ieyasu seized on the "breaking up" of his name as a hostile act, which he used as pretext to lay siege to Osaka Castle. In 1615 to escape capture Hideyori killed himself, and the head of his seven-year-old son was displayed at Sanjo Bridge like that of a criminal. With that the Toyotomi line came to an end.

In winning power, Ieyasu had shown himself to be a man of great patience. He had bided his time in waiting to destroy his enemies, and all the time that he served Nobunaga and Hideyoshi he had remained alive to his own interests. Well-known haiku illustrate the difference between the three men. "If the cuckoo won't sing, then I'll kill it," said the ruthless Nobunaga. "If the cuckoo won't sing, then I'll make it," said the resourceful Hideyoshi. "If the cuckoo won't sing, then I'll wait," said Ieyasu.

The defeat of the Toyotomi brought to a close one of the most colourful chapters in Kyoto's history. It was one that after the Heian age most vividly seizes the imagination, for the Momoyama era witnessed a great flowering of art and architecture. With unification had come an upsurge in confidence, reflected in a bold and vigorous aesthetic approach. The values were those of the samurai, and the tone was set by the expansive Hideyoshi. Bright colours, the liberal use of gold and a love of ornamentation characterize the age. Japan had entered its baroque period.

Decorative Art
Momoyama painting can be divided into two types. On the one hand are the large-scale paintings of gnarled pines and animals that decorate temples and castles. On the other is the "genre painting" of city scenes on folding screens. The former had first been used for Nobunaga's Azuchi castle, and the style was taken up by Hideyoshi, after which it spread to temples. The dimensions had never been seen before, as the paintings extended over several walls, sometimes even over a whole suite of rooms. Teams of painters were involved, and special techniques were needed to cope with the horizontal spread. Long-branched trees and winding rivers were, for obvious reasons, popular subjects. The pictures are executed in bold colours, or in black ink on a gold background. Tigers and birds of prey reflect the power of the ruling samurai. A recurring motif is the rugged pine, symbol of fortitude. This was painted to indicate the character of the patron: a solid thick trunk, for example, suggested a strong will and unbreakable resolve.

The full magnificence of Momoyama art can be seen at Nishi Hongan-ji, where parts of Jurakudai were relocated after its dismantling. A suite of spacious chambers built for Hideyoshi reflects his grandeur. This is apparent in the Chamber of Storks, for example, which has 203 *tatami* mats ascending in three levels towards a raised platform. The stork carvings, painted panels, and coffered ceiling give the room an ornate feel despite the vast openness of its flooring. Other rooms speak of the vitality of the age. The Chamber of Fans presents an innovative idea that differed from the conventions of animal and plant. The Chamber of Tigers shows animals never seen live, but drawn from skins and looking like oversized cats. The Chamber of Geese portrays the birds in temporal progression around the room, from flying off at dawn to coming home at dusk.

In the grounds outside is a three-storey pavilion named Hiunkaku (Floating Cloud Pavilion) because of the way its reflection floats on the surface of the pond. It is said to belong, with the Gold and Silver Pavilions, to the "top three pavilions of Japan". There is a tearoom at which guests arrive across a pond, and the upper part is decorated with paintings of the Thirty-Six Immortal Poets though, as the guide jokes, not all are visible since Ariwara no Narihira has run off with Ono no Komachi.

The nearby Chinese-style gate, a splendid piece of Momoyama art, is one with which I happen to be familiar since it stands by the campus where I work. Elaborately carved and brightly coloured, it has an elegant roof supported by pillars. Among the many motifs is a *kirin*, the Chinese mythical creature, said to be the model for the Kirin beer logo. Near it are figures from Chinese legend. One shows a scholar so pure that he had to go and wash his ear out on hearing the suggestion that he take government office. Opposite him is a herdsman who will not let his cow drink in the river—because the other had just washed his ear there! With its gilded decorations the gate speaks of the flamboyance of the age, and the eye-catching design prompted the Lonely Planet series to use it for the cover of their guide to Japan. It is called Higurashimon (Gate of Dusk) because it can be admired all day until it gets dark without the viewer ever tiring. More than just an entrance, I like to think of it as a gateway into Momoyama times and the brash, bold world of its artwork.

Art Schools

The painting of Momoyama times was dominated by the extraordinary Kano School. This was run by the same family for over three centuries, during which time it produced the country's leading artists. It is an achievement unique in world history. The school began in Muromachi times, as we have seen, when Kano Masanobu (1434-1530) established the pattern of working on commission for the ruling samurai. From ink paintings of pine and landscapes, the school style evolved under his son, Motonobu (1476-1559), to a more lifelike and detailed realism. This incorporated elements from the native tradition, known as *yamato-e*, which had roots in the Heian period and used bright, lively colours.

Motonobu's grandson, Kano Eitoku (1543-90), was the great genius of Momoyama art. He injected a sense of vitality into the school style, and he was the first to make extensive use of gold leaf. "Eitoku inherited Motonbou's style, exaggerated its expressionism, and built it up into a kind of baroque style expressing the heroic vigor of his age," writes critic Yoshikawa Itsuji. The artist was a master of "mass production" and responsible for decorating the great castles of the age. He managed this by doing outlines in a thick straw brush, then letting others fill in the details under his supervision. For the Fushimi-Momoyama castle alone, he provided a hundred pairs of screens. Tragically, the pictures perished with the buildings.

The only large-scale paintings of Eitoku to survive are at the Daitoku-ji sub-temple of Juko-in, where in 1566 he worked on a series of wall panels. *Birds and Flowers of the Four Seasons*, done when he was just twenty-four, is his surviving masterpiece. Executed in ink on gold paint, the pictures cover sixteen panels and show the unfurling of the seasons. You can see the vigour in a pine tree from whose twisted trunk a branch reaches down towards a stream before shooting horizontally across. Another section shows waves crashing onto a rock in such lifelike manner that it seems the water is about to splash right into the room.

Following Eitoku, the main branch of the Kano moved to Edo to serve the shogunate. Other branches served local lords, so that the school had a vast national network linked by family ties. From the dynamism of the early masters, a grander style developed, culminating with Kano Tanyu (1602-74). Interestingly, the three geniuses of the family—Motonobu, Eitoku, and Tanyu—were from alternate generations. It seems to bear out the old adage about grandchildren resembling their grandparents. Perhaps, too, the enormity of talent necessitated a generational break.

Mention of Momoyama art would be incomplete without reference to the Tosa School, which is even more closely identified with Kyoto than the Kano. Though less famous, the family were also remarkable in producing artists of note in differing centuries. But whereas the Kano were associated with the samurai, the Tosa were associated with the court. And while the Kano developed out of the Chinese style of ink painting, the Tosa worked in the native *yamato-e* tradition. No idealized landscapes for them, but delicate brightly-coloured nature and literary scenes.

The difference between the schools narrowed during the sixteenth century as the Kano borrowed from the Tosa style. Intermarriage furthered the convergence. Yet the schools retained distinctive styles, and overall the Tosa painting is lighter in tone. I was struck by this once when visiting Shinju-an, a sub-temple of Daitoku-ji, where a Tosa painting on a *fusuma* (sliding door) screen shows an elegant tree trunk, leading the eye towards a sprig of cheerful cherry blossom. It is an

unusually bright note for a temple setting, and noticeably different from the solid Kano style with its sombre tones.

When viewing Momoyama art, it is interesting to note the way artists of the age handled the competing traditions of Chinese ink-painting and Japanese *yamato-e*. It offered them exciting possibilities. One such figure was Hasegawa Tohaku (1539-1610), who was comfortable in both styles. At Konchi-in there is an ink painting of *Monkeys Reaching for the Moon*, which shows the animals with fuzzy outline and black dots for eyes and nose. The arms are made up of perfectly executed cross-strokes, the measured precision of which is all the more astonishing when seen close-up. By contrast, at Chishaku-in is a group of polychrome paintings by Tohaku and his son, which are clearly influenced by *yamato-e*. The *Cherry and Maple* scenes are set on a gold background with lush colours such as verdigris and ultramarine.

A similar versatility marks the other artists of the age, such as Kaiho Yusho (1533-1615) and Unkoku Togan (1547-1618). The latter adopted Sesshu's style to Momoyama opulence by painting *Crows in Plum Tree* in ink on a gold foil background (Kyoto National Museum). The willingness to experiment signifies the confidence of the age, which is also evident in the depictions of common folk found at this time on standing screens. This was a new development, and one that showed a shift in focus towards the secular and demotic. It marks the beginnings of that lively urban intercourse that was to flourish in the vigorous merchant culture of Edo times.

Picturing Kyoto

Portrayals of everyday scenes first emerged in the late Muromachi age and were executed on folding screens, the fashion for which was imported from China. Typical subjects include picnics, festivals, merchant shops, horse-racing, and women of the pleasure quarters. It is as if the pictures are offering snapshots of contemporary life. Early examples are from a distant, elevated perspective; later close-up views offer a more humanistic framework. Replicas of local interest are on display at the partially reconstructed Fushimi-Momoyama castle, and the titles speak for themselves: *Daigo Flower Viewing, Picnic under the Blossoms, Picnic inside the Mansion.*

One of the earliest is *Takao Maple Viewing* by Kano Hideyori (d.1557). It gives a bird's eye view of the area, with a snow-capped Mount Atago in the distance. Large areas of open space suggest the expansiveness of nature, in which are inserted human vignettes. Interestingly, the pine tree and rocks are painted in the Chinese style, while the maple and mountains are in the native tradition.

A popular subgenre is *Rakuchu Rakugai Zu* (Scenes In and Around Kyoto), which provide panoramic overviews of the capital. (*Raku* was a Japanese reading of Lo-yang, the late Han capital to which Kyoto was compared.) The fashion flourished between the 1520s and the 1640s, and there are some eighty screens extant. Taken chronologically, they portray the redevelopment of the city in the aftermath of the Onin War. First come pictures of a bustling city with people going about their work, and later there is a greater emphasis on leisure, as unification brought prosperity to the capital. The screens generally take one of two set forms. The simplest divides the city between the west on the left panel, and the east on the right-hand panel. A more sophisticated approach portrays on one panel the north in autumn or winter, while its counterpart shows the south in spring or summer. In some cases, prominent places are highlighted with names, as if providing an illustrated map of the capital. It must have given patrons a sense of "owning" the city.

The most famous screen is the work of Kano Eitoku, painted on a pair of six-fold screens, known as the Uesugi Screen. It shows a bubbling capital, full of activity and with the Gion Festival in progress. There are 2,485 figures in all, depicted with a lightness of touch. Here a small child is being helped to relieve himself by his mother, and there a streetwalker is propositioning a customer. Elsewhere there are men frolicking almost naked in the Kamo River. Some critics see in the stylized manner a forerunner of the *ukiyo-e* that emerged in Edo times.

One curious feature of the genre is the recurrence of the Gion Festival. Why, it has been asked, did the painters favour that event? The answer lies in the flourishing culture of the merchant-bankers, who sponsored the festival. The mast-like halberds of the festival floats mirrored those of the ships that brought them profits, and they were draped with colourful fabrics imported from countries far away. Since these merchants commissioned the paintings, artists included the festival to please them. It was the biggest of the city's annual events, and today it still remains a potent symbol of Kyoto.

Given the tastes of Momoyama times, it seems strange that one of its great achievements should be the tea ceremony, since it is characterized by simplicity and sparseness. It shows how cultivation of the spirit can go hand-in-hand with a taste for the ornate. Indeed, of all the achievements of the age, it was tea that had the widest impact for it affected the whole range of arts. So central did it become to life in the capital that a study of Kyoto without it would be like leaving the jazz out of New Orleans. At the pure still heart of Momoyama opulence, there stands a modest bowl of whipped green tea.

Chapter Eight
CITY OF TEA

Tea Spirit

A form of ritual. A Zen practice. A training in etiquette. Mindfulness. Seasonal awareness. A social gathering. The Way of Tea is all of these—and more. Spiritual and aesthetic traditions are blended together in a carefully prepared brew designed to enhance the soul and elevate the mind. It is one of the world's great treasures, and its mother-city is Kyoto.

In the coming together of host and guests lies a highly complex set of procedures. Mastery demands years of training as well as expertise in a wide range of fields: ceramics, calligraphy, flower-arranging, hanging scrolls, architecture, history, literature, and food preparation. Like Noh, it is a multifaceted art. The basic principles comprise harmony, respect, purity, and tranquillity. Harmony with others and with nature; respect for self and the surrounding world; purity of mind as well as body; tranquillity in "sitting alone, away from the world, at one with the rhythms of nature, liberated from attachments to the material world and bodily comforts, purified and sensitive to the sacred essence of all that is around," in the words of Sen Soshitsu XV.

Imagine a small room, only four and a half mats in size. The walls are plain. In the *tokonoma* (alcove) hangs a scroll bearing a piece of Zen wisdom, before it a vase of flowers. A handful of guests sit with legs folded beneath them silently listening to the soothing murmur of boiling water. In the doorway appears the host, who on this occasion is a woman in kimono. She kneels on the floor and slowly bows towards the guests, then approaches the kettle, in front of which she sits respectfully. She emanates calm.

With slow, deliberate movement, watched by all, she removes a cloth from her belt and arranges it with practised precision into a series of folds. She symbolically purifies the utensils, removes the top of the kettle, then wipes the tea jar from which she carefully scoops powdered tea into a bowl. To this she adds hot water with a bamboo ladle, before whisking the tea into a bubbly concoction. The bowl is placed out for the first guest. Each movement is calm and measured. The precision is a pleasure.

Before drinking, the main guest bows as if in apology for taking the first drink, then holds the bowl with both hands, placing the left underneath and the right cupping the side. The bowl is raised to the level of the brow in respect and turned twice clockwise so that the decorated "front" faces away and is visible to others. The green frothy liquid has a slightly bitter taste, which offsets the previously digested confection, and the warmth spreads out from the stomach. A slurp of satisfaction signals that the last of the tea has been drunk. The same procedure, methodical and mindful, is carried out for each guest. Afterwards discussion ensues about the wall-hanging and other items of interest. Utensils such as the tea container, scoop and bowls are examined. These are held close to the floor and scrutinized in detail.

The shared communion stimulates the senses. There is heightened awareness of sound in the quiet contemplation; heightened awareness of taste in the bitter-sweet combination; heightened awareness of touch in the hand wrapped round the ceramic bowl; heightened awareness of smell in the hint of incense over the burning charcoal; and heightened awareness visually through the aesthetic display within the narrow confines. There is also a heightened spirituality in the detachment from worldly concerns. "The Way of Tea is a way of salvation through beauty," wrote the philosopher Yanagi Muneyoshi.

There are literally hundreds of ways of serving tea. These range in levels of formality, in styles of presentation, in seasonal variation, in times of day, and in number of participants. A straightforward *chakai* can take thirty minutes. The more formal *chaji*, on the other hand, lasts for about four hours. This typically consists of an elaborate meal followed by "thick tea", then a break before ending with a more relaxed serving of "thin tea". (Thick tea is of a better quality and drunk in a different manner to thin tea. In the past it used to be normal practice, though nowadays it is reserved for more formal occasions.)

Within the room the host will have spent considerable time in preparation. The tea motto *ichigo ichie* translates as "just this one meeting" or "this one time only". Because the occasion is never to be repeated, it is treated as special. The decorations make reference to the time of year. Care is taken, too, to ensure a unifying theme. Typically there is a Zen quotation hanging in the *tokonoma*, the topic of which may be echoed in the motif of a vase or in the flower on display. On special occasions an item of personal significance may be added for the guest of honour.

The choreography is carefully calculated, and consideration is given to energy flows and respectful behaviour. Some of the techniques require remarkable skill, and what looks like mere formality may involve the most subtle of details—bringing the kettle to the boil, for instance, just after guests enter—that are apparent only to those with long experience. In all of this, consideration is given to the aesthetic principle of *shin-gyo-so* (formal, semi-formal, informal). The levels of formality pervade the whole experience, from the architecture of the tearoom to the implements used. Garden paths and fences are also distinguished in this way. The touches that beautify the tearoom are subtle in effect. The ash in the hearth, for instance, is sculpted into shapes such as waves, and pieces of iron are placed in the bottom of the kettle to create a calming sound reminiscent of wind whispering through pine trees. It is details such as these that led Okakura Tenshin to declare tea "a religion of aestheticism".

The idea of slowing down to get in tune with The Way is a fundamental of Taoism, which underlies much of tea practice. The legacy is evident in the concern with energy flows, facilitated by asymmetrical arrangements. There is also a careful balance between *yin* (receiving) and *yang* (giving), and the host is positioned between the water of the refill jar and the fire in the hearth. At the centre of the ceremony is the conjoining of the five elements: wood (charcoal), metal (kettle), earth (pottery), fire, and water. Perhaps it is from such unseen forces that the potency of the occasion derives. "When I am sipping tea in my tearoom," wrote D. T. Suzuki, "I am swallowing the whole universe."

The Taoist elements are blended with Confucian concerns, which can be seen in the emphasis on etiquette and the respect for tradition. Correct behaviour is expected, and the calm assurance of the occasion depends on the orchestrated harmony of the participants. A properly conducted gathering brings with it the sense that all is well with the universe. The idea that the Catholic mass might also have played a part in its formation seems outlandish, yet the theory has recently gained credence. Christian missionaries were in Kyoto when the ceremony was being developed, and tea masters were familiar with converts. Certainly, there are aspects of "thick tea" uncannily like the mass: raising the bowl as if in offering; the passing from hand to hand; the wiping clean with a white cloth. The similarities seem more than just coincidence, and several experts believe that they are deliberate borrowings.

Yet for all this, the key element in the Way of Tea is undoubtedly Zen, for it was born and nurtured in the sect's monasteries. "Tea and Zen are one taste," runs a traditional saying, and the influential Sen no Rikyu, codifier of the ceremony, put the relationship like this:

In Zen, truth is pursued through the discipline of meditation in order to realize enlightenment, while in tea we use training in the procedures to achieve the same end.

The influence of Zen is everywhere apparent. It can be seen most clearly in the *tokonoma* found in every tearoom. This originated as a place of "emptiness" or Buddha-nature, and the hanging scroll it contains often bears a spiritual wisdom. Here are placed flowers as on an altar, and incense is used to perfume the room as in a temple.

Practitioners of tea talk of the deep sense of peace that it brings. The normal busy flow of thought gives way to quiet contemplation, and there is a greater mindfulness as participants focus on the here and now. As always with Zen arts, the goal is the transcendence of self, and the server strives to become one with the serving. "By repeating the same polished actions over and over again, fitting yourself into a pattern, you approach the core of yourself," says Sen Souoku, master of the Musashinokoji School.

Tea Master

Tea first came to Japan with the spread of Buddhism. It was a treasured substance because of its life-enhancing qualities, and ancient sages held that it promoted longevity. They may well have been right, for modern science has since shown that the sort of tea used, *maccha*, is rich in vitamin C with cancer-inhibiting properties. (Ordinary green tea, known as *sencha*, was only introduced to Japan in Edo times.)

To show their respect for the prized substance, Chinese monks had developed a formal manner of drinking tea using bronze utensils. The custom was taken up by Heian aristocrats, who made the fancy goods the focus of social gatherings—much as the European nobility did some six hundred years later. By Kamakura times tea-drinking had died out, and the practice was reintroduced by the Zen priest Eisai on his return from China. Through his friend Myoe, he had seeds planted at Kozan-ji in the north-west of Kyoto. According to tradition, he was aided in his endeavours by the young shogun Sanetomo (1191-1219), whom he converted from alcoholic to "tea-totaller". He wrote a pamphlet entitled *Tea as a Means of Cultivating Health* (1211), and among the benefits he described was one of particular value to Zen: the ability to stay awake during meditation.

Following Eisai, tea "branched out" in differing directions. Aristocrats held tea gatherings at which they wrote and recited poems. There were also tournaments in which guests competed to see who could guess the type of tea, accompanied by extravagant displays of wealth and betting. Some were so riotous that they had to be banned. An influential figure in the refinement of such gatherings was Noami (1397-1481), grandfather of the garden designer Soami. As art advisor to the Ashikaga, he took particular interest in the Chinese utensils. Among the innovations he made was the practice of gliding over the floor as in Noh, rather than just walking. He also brought together the preparation and serving of tea in one room, an important development.

Meanwhile, Zen temples maintained a simpler style, inherited from the Chinese. The influential Ikkyu shared the practice with his disciple, Murata Shuko or Juko (1423-1502), who saw the potential for a Way of Tea in which spiritual development would be furthered through subjugating the ego. It was in keeping with the Muromachi ethos, and represented a major breakthrough. It makes Shuko for many the founder of the modern ceremony.

Shuko was the son of a blind priest from Nara, and he may have studied there under Naomi, who had fled Kyoto to escape the Onin War. This training would have given him important contacts, which enabled him to become tea master to Yoshimasa. As such, he was responsible for the four-and-a-half mat tearoom at the Silver Pavilion, which, as we have seen, became the prototype for later models. He made a number of other important innovations. He introduced Zen calligraphy, and simplified the ceremony by reducing the number of utensils. He also spoke of "harmonizing Japanese and Chinese tastes": in contrast to the opulence of imported tea-ware, he favoured native pottery such as Bizen and Shigaraki, which was made for everyday use and had a rough, coarse-grained surface.

Shuko's ideas were taken up by Takeno Joo (1502-55), not a monk as such but a student of Zen from a Sakai merchant family who moved to Kyoto to study tea. A man of literary tastes, he was drawn to the Heian aesthetic of *wabi* and the appreciation of rustic simplicity. It inspired him to build a thatched tearoom in the manner of a farmer's hut, replacing Shuko's white-papered walls with plain earth. Tea now had its very own building.

One of Joo's pupils was Sen no Rikyu (1522-91), who was also from a wealthy Sakai family. He was to become the greatest of all the tea masters, for he not only brought coherence to the procedures, but regulated with unerring precision the dimensions and proportions. It is to his genius that we owe the Way of Tea as we know it today. Rikyu showed an interest in tea from an early age. He studied for some fifteen years with Joo, and realizing the vital connection with Zen, took religious instruction at Daitoku-ji. He also travelled widely to improve his knowledge of ceramics, receiving instruction from the head of the kilns he visited. By middle age he was acknowledged for his all-round expertise.

When he was fifty-eight, Rikyu was appointed tea master to Nobunaga. It was a prestigious position, which brought him substantial estates. By this time tea was closely associated with the ruling samurai and had an important political function. It was used as a means to settle disputes, and expensive tea items were exchanged to cement alliances. As master of ceremonies, Rikkyu became privy to the innermost concerns of state.

Following Nobunaga's death, Rikkyu was taken on by Hideyoshi, who had already built himself a reputation as a tea man. It was common for warriors to take tea to steady nerves before battle; Hideyoshi once did so in full sight of his enemies to impress them with his strength of spirit. He looked up to his tea master and often sought his counsel. Once when he was laying siege to Odawara Castle, he asked Rikyu to provide a vase for a tea ceremony. With nothing to hand, the tea master fashioned one out of a piece of bamboo, making a diagonal slice for the opening. It is an instance of tea's ability to improvise.

One of Rikyu's beliefs was that in the tearoom all should be equal. To this end, he devised a small square opening that could only be entered on one's knees. This "crawling entrance" not only enforced humility but was so designed that samurai could not bring in their swords. It was a revolutionary idea, which stripped the warriors of their weapon and promoted the tearoom as a place of peace.

Under Rikyu's influence, tea aesthetics developed in the direction of *wabi-sabi*. The term is notoriously difficult to translate: it involves appreciation of the natural and simple, together with a feeling of melancholy at the transience of beauty. It prefers irregularity and understatement to the showy and pretentious, and favours the patina of age over the perfection of the new. In short, spiritual wealth is found in rustic simplicity.

Another of Rikyu's amendments was to the *kaiseki* food course, which was a basic component of tea in Momoyama times. (The name *kaiseki*, meaning "warm stones", referred to the Zen monks' practice of staving off hunger pangs by placing the stones on their stomachs.) The standard fare was soup, rice, pickles and side dishes. Rikyu adapted this menu to the aesthetics of tea, and drew up rules about the order and content. Carefully chosen ceramics complemented the food, which was prepared so as to be pleasing both to the taste-buds and to the eye. Rather than gratifying the desire to eat, the small mouthfuls showed how each precious moment should be savoured.

The sophistication of Rikyu's taste can be seen in the anecdotes told about him. One concerns the sweeping of a garden. Cleanliness is a key component of tea culture, as it is in Zen, and the garden should be kept free of leaves. Once when asked if a garden was clean enough, Rikyu took hold of a young tree and, giving it a vigorous shake, scattered autumn leaves over the ground. The resulting pattern, irregular and natural, added the perfect finishing touch for the day's gathering.

As tea master to Hideyoshi, Rikyu's life was uncomfortably bound up with his paymaster. Between them lay a yawning gap in temperament, and the difference in character had tragic consequences. Rikyu was calm, dispassionate, and a man of considered judgement; Hideyoshi, by contrast, was mercurial, ambitious, and strong-willed. Yet he was no fool, as stories about him attest. On one occasion, he tried to catch his teacher out by presenting him with a gold basin and a sprig of plum blossom to arrange. Without hesitation Rikyu poured water into the bowl and scraped off the blossom so that it floated on the surface. The petals floating on the water had a poignant beauty that the pupil was forced to admire. On another occasion, Rikyu had grown a magnificent crop of morning-glories, which were rare at the time. News of their beauty reached Hideyoshi, who was eager to see them. But when he arrived to take tea, he found the crop had been cut down. At a loss, he entered the tearoom where stood a single dazzling flower. The tea master had picked out the best of the crop to teach his pupil a lesson: in terms of *wabi*, less is more.

The difference between the two men is evident in the tearooms they favoured. At Yamazaki just outside Kyoto is Rikyu's only surviving tearoom. It is a two-mat room built in 1582 at a time of fighting, so that warriors could remain composed in the face of death. Built in the style of a peasant's hut, it has rough-textured earthen walls, unpolished beams and papered windows. Irregular and asymmetrical, it is a prime example of *wabi*. Hideyoshi, by contrast, had a tearoom whose walls were covered in gold leaf and whose utensils were made of gold. It could be dismantled and transported around the country on his travels. There is a replica at Fushimi Momoyama that is so glaringly garish as to make one feel almost sick.

In 1587 the two men came together for the largest tea gathering in history, when Hideyoshi invited all and sundry to a Kitano Tea Party. The glorified country fair with its 800 pavilions was intended to promote social harmony. Some lucky folk were served personally by the ruler, and Rikyu, too, participated in the event as a way to promote awareness among the wider population. It was the talk of the time, and is commemorated in an annual event at Kitano Tenmangu Shrine, where geisha serve tea to the general public.

In 1591, Rikyu was ordered by Hideyoshi to commit suicide. It was a shock to contemporaries, and the reason still remains unclear.

Several factors may have been involved, including Hideyoshi's rejection by the widowed daughter of Rikyu and his unease at the profits his teacher was making from tea goods. There could also have been friction over the planned invasion of Korea, and military men, jealous of the tea master's influence, may have intrigued against him. The situation came to a head when Hideyoshi learned of a life-size statue of Rikyu, which had been placed in the main gate of Daitoku-ji. This was in celebration of its reconstruction, which the tea master had funded. It meant that visitors to the temple, including Hideyoshi who took his lessons there, would have to pass beneath the statue as if lower in status. It was taken as a sign of arrogance and a deliberate insult.

Hearing of Hideyoshi's displeasure, Rikyu made no effort to save himself, but prepared calmly for death. He wrote two farewell poems, one in Chinese and one in Japanese, then committed *seppuku* (ritual suicide) in the tearoom of Juko-in. The manner of his death had a nobility in keeping with the Way of Tea. Despite the disgrace, his teachings survived in direct transmission, as his family was soon pardoned by a repentant Hideyoshi. Today there are three Sen estates, all run by a direct descendant, and each constitutes a school of tea in its own right. The split happened at the time of Rikyu's grandson, Sotan (1578-1658). He passed the estate he had inherited on to one of his sons, while setting up in an adjacent house with another of his sons. The former is known as Omotesenke (literally, the front Sen house), and the latter as Urasenke (the back Sen house). Later, a third son established a separate school in nearby Mushanokoji.

The three schools developed different characteristics. Omotesenke became associated with aristocrats, Mushanokoji with *wabi* (aesthetics of simplicity), and Urasenke with commoners. It was the latter that emerged as the most popular of the tea schools, and by some estimates it now claims up to eighty per cent of tea practitioners. It benefited from an explosion of interest among women in the early twentieth century, when the study of tea was seen as part of a proper education for a "lady". Now the overwhelming majority of practitioners are women—quite a contrast with Rikyu's time when the ceremony was dominated by warriors and women were not allowed to take part.

Along with the feminization of tea has come its inter-nationalization. Again, the Urasenke school played the dominant role in this process, and it claims a presence in some hundred different countries. At the same time, it runs a course in Kyoto for a select group of foreigners, as a result of which there are presently several licensed "gaijin" teaching in the city.

In 1989, in one of those cinematic coincidences, there appeared two different films on the life of Rikyu. The more acclaimed, with Mikuni Rentaro in the lead, portrayed his relationship with Hideyoshi and blamed his death on the intrigue of powerful lords. It was directed by Teshigawara Hiroshi, head of the Sogetsu school of *ikebana*. Slow and stately, it has the pace of a tea gathering and the visual appeal of a flower arrangement. The film appeared during the "bubble economy" of the late 1980s and is interesting for what it has to say about the state of the nation. It was a time when values were badly skewed by material wealth, and the *nouveau riche* extravagance of Hideyoshi is contrasted with the restraint shown by his tea master. The decorum and refinement Rikyu displays are shown to be in every way superior to those around him. He is here held up as role model for the nation, not so much a tea master as a "man for all seasons".

Tea Garden

The traditional tearoom stands as an independent building in its own garden, and Kyoto boasts the finest collection in the world. Some are at temples, some on large estates, and some in private gardens. Students of tea have field trips to study their finer aspects, but visiting them is enjoyable in itself because of the concern with aesthetics. The approach begins with a garden whose purpose is to prepare the visitor mentally for the occasion. It comprises a symbolic journey, leading from the outside world to that of a "rustic sanctuary". The word for tea garden is *roji*, which translates as "dewy path", and for Rikyu it was "six-tenths transition and four-tenths landscape". The components are few and plain: a moss floor; evergreen shrubs; bamboo; a few trees; a stone lantern; and a wash-basin. There is no gaudy display, nor fancy ornamentation. "The garden serves the human soul," writes author and practitioner Preston Houser. "It is a secular stage whereupon our spirituality is brought into play and reflected back to us."

Progress through the garden is marked by a series of thresholds. Visitors first arrive at the outer garden, often rocky or sandy, which contains the waiting-area. Here guests have time to "acclimatize" to the surroundings. After a while, the host appears to greet the guests, who then proceed through the middle gateway into an "inner garden". Bamboo shrubs or small trees rising above the head give a sense of entering deeper into nature. Undisturbed moss and boulders provide an unspoilt atmosphere, as if in remote countryside. Added to the natural elements are man-made features, such as a stone lantern. This was introduced by Rikyu, following the example of votive lanterns at Buddhist temples.

One essential item is the wash-basin, where guests stop to clean their hands in a symbolic act of purification. As much as a physical rite, it is a washing away of the "dust of the world". This is done in the same way as at Shinto shrines: taking the ladle, one washes first the left hand, then the right, then cupping the left hand one washes out the mouth.

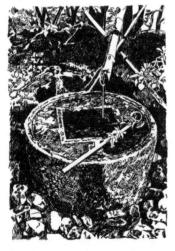

The basins are made out of natural stone and set low down, so that washing enforces a posture of humility.

In the passage through the garden the guiding agent is the path, the most common form of which comprises stepping stones placed close together for the shortened gait of those wearing kimono. Since tea culture dislikes the sterilizing effect of uniformity, the stones are irregular in shape and vary in size and colour. The height at which they protrude is a matter of delicate judgement: different tea schools have different standards. The subtlety of tea manners is further encapsulated in the *sekimori*, a small stone neatly tied around with rope, which is placed on paths to indicate the way is barred. Another sensitive touch is the sprinkling of water over the path to the tearoom. It shows the host's solicitousness, providing freshness and in the summer relief from the oppressive heat.

Visitors have now arrived at the tearoom. Ideally, this is set on higher ground and has a rustic appearance, like a mountain hermitage. The materials blend in with the surroundings: straw roof, wooden posts, *tatami* floor, and earthen walls covering a bamboo frame. The environment exudes a sense of peacefulness and ease; the mind has settled, the spirit is stilled. The visitor is ready to take tea.

Tea Room

Not every tearoom is blessed with a garden approach, but nonetheless all generally conform to a common pattern. There is a preparation area and a main room, in the centre of which is a sunken hearth for the heating of water. In the summer this is covered over and a brazier used instead. Utmost care is taken with the construction, and the craftsmanship is of the highest order. The ceiling is low—five foot nine is the standard—which is suited to an occasion in which participants sit on the floor. The portion over the host's head is generally lower to signify humility and respect for the guests. The windows are small openings, which sometimes expose the grid of supports holding up the wall. Many are covered with *shoji* (paper screens) to create a soft, suffused atmosphere that enhances spirituality. The positioning of the windows is a crucial design item, as it affects the play of light. Rikyu favoured a darkened atmosphere, though his successors preferred to open up the tearoom to the garden outside.

The pursuit of the rustic does not necessarily come cheap, for the materials are often the choicest of their type. Take the pillar for the *tokonoma* (alcove), for example. A highly prized wood is *Kitayama sugi*, a type of cedar from the north of Kyoto. This alone can be as expensive as a luxury car. Putting together a simple "hut" can end up costing more than a residence seven times its size!

Anyone with an interest in tea or Japanese culture will gravitate to Daitoku-ji, known as *chazura* or "the face of tea". It has been associated with tea since before the days of Ikkyu, and not surprisingly contains some famous tearooms. There is even the Hut of Leisure in which Rikyu killed himself, though it has since been rebuilt and relocated. (According to tradition, a tearoom survives as an entity as long as it keeps the same *tokonoma* pillar.)

Here perhaps I should make a belated confession. Though fond of the spiritual profundity of tea and aware of its centrality to Kyoto's culture, I have felt myself debarred from pursuing it by an inability to kneel in the *seiza* position due to a damaged knee. Though it is possible instead to use a small stool to help deal with the problem, self-consciousness and bodily stiffness make one reluctant to spoil the elegant orderliness. Nothing is as pleasing as the way Japanese "pack themselves" into neat, tightly-arranged units with feet neatly folded beneath bottom. Nothing, conversely, is as disturbing as a sprawling *gaijin* unable to stand up without staggering.

Yet lack of tea study does not preclude my enjoyment of the practice, and I take an amateur's delight in the opportunities on offer. These include the monthly meetings at the Heian Shrine, where each time a different school of tea hosts the event. This allows one to see the (often negligible) differences between the schools. It also allows one to savour the seasonal changes, which are highlighted by references in the tea gathering: white snow-like flecks on a February kimono; pink cherry blossom cakes in spring; an incense holder decorated with June swallows; a single bell-flower in the October vase.

Another way in which an amateur interest can find outlet is in visiting some of the outstanding tearooms around the city. Some are in famous tourist spots and easy to see. Others are closely guarded secrets. In this respect I have been fortunate in having had contacts that allowed me to visit the three Sen estates in north Kyoto. These are each named after a representative tearoom, the most famous being the Konnichian of Urasenke. Here is the Vatican of the tea world, with "ambassadors" in distant countries and important connections in high places. Royalty and heads of state come to pay respects, and in the street outside dignified figures come and go. Getting permission to visit is no simple matter, and you really do get the feel that you are entering tea's "holy of holies".

The tearoom after which the estate is named translates as "Hut of this Day". It was named by Sotan, who had invited his Zen master from Daitoku-ji to celebrate its completion. The monk was delayed, so Sotan went out leaving a note asking him to come again the next day. When he returned, he found a note saying, "A negligent monk expects no tomorrow." It brought him to a realization of life's priorities, and he named his tearoom accordingly. It is a tiny one-and-a-half mat affair, which exemplifies the *wabi* style. There is even a clay floor for the *tokonoma* instead of the usual *tatami*. The guest's area has a crawl-through doorway at one end, and opposite it a space for a hanging scroll. For anyone with claustrophobic tendencies, the prospect of entering the cramped dark space is unsettling, though the Urasenke representative is quick to counter that the half-light intimacy is not only comfortable but promotes shared communion.

Despite its aristocratic connections, the Omotesenke estate is more relaxed in atmosphere. A special feature is the "middle gateway", which contains a window-like opening through which the host greets guests. Here is a real sense of threshold, like Alice passing through the small doorway that leads into the secret garden. Beyond the gateway lies Fushin'an, the teahouse after which the estate takes its name. It dates from the mid-seventeenth century and is typical of the "grass hut style". Outside is a hanging shelf for samurai to leave their swords, and inside the slim central post is made of red pine still bearing its bark.

The third of the estates, and the most homely, is that of Mushanokoji Senke. The garden is squeezed into a small compound, where a cleverly laid path expands the sense of space by its meandering. It leads through an Edo-era gateway of airy grace that typifies the symbolic role of the feature, for there is no physical barrier but an archway that acts as symbolic threshold. The tearoom, which was designed by the founder in the mid-seventeenth century, has only two mats with a board inserted in between. It is flanked by a fence that epitomizes tea aesthetics. Made of tightly bundled strips, it is functional yet pleasing with posts that are spaced so as to enable tantalizing glimpses of what lies beyond.

Beyond the Sen estates lie other tearooms, too numerous to mention. One place of note is Kodai-ji, which has two unique examples brought from Hideyoshi's Fushimi castle. Shiguretei (Pavilion of Autumn Rain) is the only two-storey tearoom in Japan and was designed by a disciple of Rikyu for the Kitano Tea Party of 1587. Karakasatei (Pavilion of the Open Umbrella) has a roof with spokes radiating outwards from a high central point. The effect is as the name suggests, and one can imagine the joy this must have given Hideyoshi as he took his tea with the rain coming down.

Another place of note is the Katsura estate, which contains a thatched tearoom called Shokintei (Pine-tree Harp Pavilion). Light and airy, it stands by a landscaped lake and offers superlative views. House and garden come together here in utter perfection, and it brings to mind the words of Sen Soshitsu XV: "Taking a bowl of green tea in your hands and drinking it, you feel one with nature, and there is peace."

Katsura is associated with the great designer of the age, Kobori Enshu (1579-1647). A multi-talented figure, he was a tea master who also excelled in calligraphy and poetry. In terms of design, his great forte lay in the integration of samurai tastes with the graceful court style. The "eight-window teahouse" is an example, opening up the stark samurai hut to its landscaped surroundings. Kyoto boasts many examples of his work, including "the top three classic teahouses of Japan"—those at Koho-an, Manshu-in and Konchi-in. Japanese love to rank things in this way, though on whose authority is unclear and one often suspects, as in this case, a healthy dose of self-promotion. Nonetheless, there is no doubting the quality of the creations. The clay walls and plain wood speak of an age of refined austerity so unlike the brash consumerism of modern Japan that even without taking tea, the visitor is "refreshed" by the natural aesthetics and simplicity of form. One can see how the tea principles of harmony, respect, purity, and tranquillity are written into the very fabric of the buildings. Here, one feels, is the spirit of tea in physical form.

Tea Art

The number of Kyoto shops related to the Way of Tea is extraordinary, and many embody its finest qualities. Take those selling tea, for instance, which even when venerably old are always spotlessly clean. A famous example is the 280-year old Ippodo (literally, "Keeps Just One Thing"), which has a black wood ceiling, exposed beams, and antique storage jars spaced along its shelves. Samples are neatly laid out in the glass counter, with prices mounting towards the eye-popping end of the range.

The confections used to sweeten the mouth also have their own specialist stores. Some are part of a longer tradition, and can trace their roots back as far as Kamakura times. There are coloured pieces made of sugar, as well as cakes in which dough covers a mix of sweet beans. The material and design are carefully chosen, with seasonal relevance as much a concern as taste. Shape and texture are vital to the effect, for they are meant to be visually appetizing too. The care taken in the preparation should be reciprocated by the mindfulness with which they are consumed.

Other shops cater for the utensils: kettles, bowls, whisks, caddies, water containers, standing shelves, scoops, ladles and incense holders. Each has been made into an object of aesthetic concern. Indicative of the care taken is the employment by the Sen family of Ten Craft Families, who for generations have been perfecting the specially made goods. Taste in such goods can be highly individual. This is nowhere better seen than in the works of Furata Oribe (1544-1615), a one-time military commander who became tea master to the second Tokugawa

shogun, Hidetada. His ceramics, bold and adventuresome, bear a distinctive stamp: twisted handles, oddly angled curves, and a sense of the dramatic make him an avant-garde artist of visionary power even by today's standards.

Appreciation of the utensils is a vital element in the Way of Tea, and just as performing as host requires years of practice, so does learning the aesthetics. Anyone who has attended a tea gathering will have noticed the way participants pore over the items involved as they are passed around. Eyes are brought close and utensils examined from all angles. What on earth are they looking at? Each of the items has its own aesthetic peculiarities. Take the tea scoop, for example, which is typically a thin piece of bamboo with a joint in the middle. To the uninitiated it looks uninteresting, but to a trained eye the narrowness of the neck and the angle of the curve are crucial to its elegance. Tea containers are also treated with special respect, since they hold the precious central substance. There are two types, those for thin tea and those for thick. The former are made of wood and decorated with lacquer, the most common type being named *natsume* (jujube) after its shape. The thick tea containers, called tea caddies, are usually made of ceramic with an ivory lid. These are kept in beautiful bags of woven silk (often of Chinese origin) and tied with coloured cords.

By contrast, vases for flowers tend to be modest, plain, and free of decoration. They come in three types: standing vases; those that hook into the wall or pillar; and those that are suspended from the ceiling. Materials include pottery, metal, basketware and bamboo. Like other tea goods, they are divided into the formal, semi-formal, and informal. The lotus, for instance, being a symbol of Buddha, is considered a high-class flower and is paired with a formal bronze container.

The flower-arranging of tea, known as *chabana*, has its origins in the practice of altar offerings. This developed into the art form of *ikebana*, which stressed asymmetry and respect for nature. For Rikyu, however, it was too ostentatious, and he simplified the arrangement. One or two modest flowers, offset perhaps by a thin budding branch, suffice to represent the time of year. Loud combinations, thorns, and strong fragrances are avoided. Buds are preferred to full blossom. The intention is not to impress, but to place the flowers, in the words of Rikyu, "as they are in the field".

Of all the artefacts, it is the bowls that have the widest reputation. These are highly prized and can reach astronomical prices, difficult for an outsider to understand. When the first Westerners reached Japan, they were so astounded that they ascribed the custom to barbarism. Even today many find the fascination baffling. For those with an understanding of pottery, however, there is a deep satisfaction in the details. These include the grain, texture, shape, feel, glaze, pattern and markings. The very best bowls not only embody the qualities of tea, but have a spiritual quality as if in their inwardness they offer an opportunity to contemplate the preciousness of the moment. They contain not just tea, but tea spirit.

Though tea-ware can be drawn from any ceramic style, it is Kyoto's very own Raku that is the most celebrated. "Raku first, Hagi second, Karatsu third", runs a traditional saying. The pottery was developed by a tile-maker named Chojiro (1516-92), and the style is continued to this day by his descendants. The son of a Korean immigrant, Chojiro was approached by Rikyu to create a purpose-made tea bowl. The design the two of them produced had tall sides with a relatively flat bottom to accommodate the motion of the whisk. It took its name from a seal inscribed *raku* (pleasure) presented by an appreciative Hideyoshi.

Unlike most pottery, Raku is shaped by hand and low-fired in simple kilns. The result is soft-bodied and irregular. The colours divide between a rich black, a warm red and a creamy off-white: these are thought ideal to offset the dark green of the tea. The black is particularly striking—alluring, mysterious, profound. Since the colour contains within it all others, the unifying quality lends it spiritual significance. It is as if in emptying the bowl, one comes face to face with the dark emptiness of the universe.

Raku is not the only Kyoto pottery associated with tea; there is also Kyo-yaki. Dating from the seventeenth century, it is an elegant young dandy compared with its older brother. The typical design has brightly coloured vignettes of pine, bamboo or cranes. That Raku is made for tea there can be no doubt, as its rough shape and texture are designed for the hand. Kyo-yaki, by contrast, demands attention by its visual brilliance. The delicate artwork surely ranks among the finest brushwork ever executed on pottery.

During the Edo era Kyo-yaki set the standard for pottery, and its artists were recognized among the best in the land. Chief among them were Nonomura Ninsei (fl. mid-seventeenth century), his pupil Ogata Kenzan (1663-1743), Aoki Mokubei (1767-1843) and Hozen Eiraku (1795-1854). As the "father of Kyo-yaki", Ninsei deserves special mention. He moved to Kyoto in the 1640s to set up a kiln at Ninna-ji. His favoured base was black enamel, over which were painted small, highly decorated motifs. As well as bowls, he created tea jars and incense containers highly praised for their refinement. For the first time pottery was recognized as an art instead of a craft.

Ninsei's pottery was part of a wider process in Edo times by which tea spread from being an elite pursuit to one practised by the wider population. As we shall see in the next chapter, the influence of tea played a vital part in the culture of the age, and on Kyoto crafts in particular. The seeds Eisai brought back from China were planted in fertile ground indeed.

Chapter Nine
CITY OF TRADITION

A Military Touch

The Edo period (1600-1868) was a time when the Tokugawa dynasty held power, society was tightly controlled, and Japan was cut off from the rest of the world. The country was parcelled out among *daimyo* (lords), beneath whom the citizenry were divided into four classes: samurai, peasants, artisans and merchants. Rules governed every aspect of life, dictating even the type of clothing worn. Punishments were draconian, and the samurai carried a licence to kill. There was a national network of spies, and the enforcement of collective responsibility created peer pressure to conform. The system was underpinned by an ideology of neo-Confucianism that emphasized birth rather than merit. Loyalty to one's superior was the paramount virtue, valued even over filial duty. For some, the period represents the world's most successful example of totalitarianism.

The *daimyo*, who numbered some 250 in all, were tied to the Tokugawa by the practice of "alternate residence". This meant that they had to spend every other year in the city of Edo (now Tokyo), leaving their wife and eldest son as hostage when they returned to their region. The financial burden of keeping two residences, plus the funding of processions to the capital, weakened their ability to build independent power bases.

The period is known for its isolationism. Christianity was banned from 1612, and from 1638 contact with the outside world was forbidden (with the exception of some Chinese and a small Dutch mission on the island of Dejima at Nagasaki). Seclusion brought stability, though there was a price to be paid in the Tokugawa stranglehold.

Kyoto in this age was still the country's capital, but more in name than in substance. With political patronage centred in Edo, it was not long before the cultural mainstream moved there too. The Kano family is an example. Another is Hishikawa Moronobu (1618-94), one of the originators of *ukiyo-e*. The son of a Kyoto embroiderer, he moved to Edo in the 1660s where he developed the art of black-and-white woodblocks.

Yet, despite its losses, Kyoto remained a thriving centre, particularly in the first half of the era. Not only was it still the aristocratic centre, but it was also the country's second largest city with a population of just over half a million. Edo was a robust city of samurai where the future was being forged; Kyoto, by contrast, was steeped in the past and a city of feminine arts.

The pathway linking the cities—the Tokaido—was upgraded in 1604 into a highway wide enough for horses to pass. It ran between Sanjo Bridge in Kyoto and Nihonbashi in Edo. On average it took twelve days to walk, though teams of couriers could rush through a message in under three days. Along the way were "barriers" where travel-papers were checked, as well as fifty-three way-stations (famously painted by Hiroshige). It was not only the busiest route in the country, but possibly in the world. Pack horses, palanquins, and pilgrims thronged the path, and there were grand processions of *daimyo* and noblemen. The highest priority of all went to the annual transport of new tea from Uji, before which even the most powerful of lords had to give way. Guidebooks detailed accommodation and points of interest along the route. There were ditches for drainage, stone guideposts, distance markers and even embankments planted for shade. The handful of Westerners to see it (those based at Dejima) were astonished by the route's efficiency.

For Kyoto the great symbol of the age was Nijo Castle, built by Ieyasu shortly after his victory at Sekigahara in 1600. The architecture, with its heavy gates, double moats, and fortified walls, speaks of military power, and its location in the heart of the city was a clear statement of intent. From the fortress a governor kept a wary eye on the city, particularly the activities at court. It served, too, as a base for the Kansai area, and it was from here that the 1615 siege of Osaka Castle was masterminded.

In 1603 Tokugawa Ieyasu had himself proclaimed shogun in Nijo. Thereafter he made only occasional visits to Kyoto, marching into the city at the head of an army in an impressive show of force. Over time such visits came to be seen as no longer necessary, and after 1634 not a single shogun went to Kyoto for 220 years.

Within the castle is the highly decorated Ninomaru Palace. It was fitted out in 1626 for an imperial visit, and the lavish decorations speak of a desire to impress. There are thirty-three rooms in five buildings, which are divided by rank in ascending order. Each is built on a slightly higher level, leading from reception rooms for imperial messengers to those for trusted allies and ending with the private rooms of the shogun. In the Confucian world of the Tokugawas, status was all-important: even the *daimyo* were divided into inner and outer lords according to who had been allies at the battle of Sekigahara.

The decoration was entrusted to Tanyu, the young genius of the Kano family. He was only twenty-five at the time, and was helped by his even younger brother, Naonobu. Between them they were responsible for over 900 panels, each of which was carefully crafted to the purpose of the room. The allegorical import is best seen in the weapon room, where on a sturdy pine with horizontal branches sits a beady-eyed hawk. The tree represents Tokugawa power extending through the land, over which the authorities keep watch, and the intimidating scale is exemplified by a branch that is thirty-three feet long. It is the mythic force of painting like this that led Okakura Tenshin to call Tanyu "the Ieyasu of the painting world".

The outer waiting rooms, where former enemies were received, contain pictures designed to deter subversion. Massive pines, birds of prey and carnivorous animals sent the message that the shogun was robust and quick to pounce. By contrast, the inner waiting rooms had more friendly images. There were pheasants, egrets and flowers. Gold leaf reflected the glory of the Tokugawa on those present. And in the private quarters, where only the shogun and his womenfolk were allowed, was a *sumi-e* landscape with idealized features that invited the viewer to relax and gaze into the distance.

Nijo Castle says much about the insecurities of the age. The halls are constructed to prevent access from one to another, and there is a hidden bodyguard room next to where the shogun held audience. Most famously, there is a "nightingale veranda" whose floorboards squeak when trodden on. It was a simple alarm system that would soon detect any intruder.

The early part of the Edo era was a time when dangerous *ronin* (masterless samurai) roamed the land, disaffected by the loss at Sekigahara. One such was master swordsman, Miyamoto Musashi (1584-1645), author of *The Book of the Five Rings* (1645). Determined to make a name for himself, he went to Kyoto to challenge representatives of the leading sword school. It was astonishing cheek, all the more so since the unknown provincial fought with a wooden sword. His victories upset the school so much that they set up a duel at which they planned to ambush him. The resulting encounter, The Duel at Ichijo-ji, is one of the most famous incidents in sword-fighting. The episode is retold in Yoshikawa Eiji's popular *Musashi*, a fictional biography first serialized in the 1930s. Filled with insight and Zen wisdom, it shows the development of a headstrong youth into an enlightened swordsman under the guidance of the Daitoku-ji priest, Takuan Soho (1573-1645). The young swordsman is a shrewd strategist, full of clever tricks, and on this occasion he climbs the hill behind the duelling site so as to descend unexpectedly on his opponent. On the way he stops to pray, but then wonders to himself:

> *What need have I of the help of the gods? Am I not already one with the universe? Haven't I always said that I must be prepared to face death at any time?*

In the event, Musashi is himself surprised when instead of a single dueller he is set upon by the whole school. Amazingly, he manages to fight them off. For those who have seen the Oscar-winning Samurai Trilogy (filmed in the 1950s), it is impossible not to think of the swashbuckling Mifune Toshiro, a lethal model of concentration, fighting a rearguard action through the ricefields in the early dawn.

Like other samurai, Musashi practised Zen arts and was skilled in calligraphy and carving. He also painted under the name of Niten, and two of his paintings can be seen at the To-ji sub-temple of Kanchi-in. *Eagles* captures the majesty of the bird as it is about to swoop and is set above an official seat for the emperor, guarding the imperial back as it were. The other, named *Bamboo*, suggests that the artist could paint with both hands, which is significant as Musashi became famous for his two-sword fighting technique.

The samurai ethos of the early Edo period is evident in a safehouse not far from Nijo Castle. Named Nijo Jinya, or Nijo Inn, it was started in the 1670s and took over thirty years to complete. From the outside it seems a simple one-storey building, but inside there are three floors and twenty-four rooms. For lovers of ninja, it is a delight. The inn was built by a rice merchant whose father had fought on the wrong side at Sekigahara and who decided to set up business providing accommodation for high-ranking visitors to the capital. Although the regulations for merchant houses were severe, he managed to subvert them with some unique arrangements. The corridors, for example, are covered in *tatami*, so that by removing the wall panels it was possible to extend the room size beyond that permitted by the regulations.

It is the defensive measures, however, that make the building so special. The ceilings are low to prevent the raising of swords. There are hidden stairways, removable flooring, and a secret half-storey invisible from the outside. There is also a false plank at the top of a stairwell to send intruders tumbling, and above the reception area is a soundproofed guard post so that anyone concealed there could leap onto the person below. Outside in the garden are wells for fire-fighting purposes that also double as places of concealment.

It would be wrong to assume, however, that Edo-era Kyoto was military in nature, for the instability of the early years soon gave way to an age of regulated law and order. It was in this climate that the merchant class rose to prominence and their prosperity prompted a boom in traditional crafts. But before this, surprisingly, the old court culture enjoyed a remarkable Indian summer in which arose some of the most admired villas of Japan. It can be seen as a late final flourish for the aristocratic tradition of Heian-kyo.

Heian Revival

For most of the Edo period, the emperor was reduced to a symbolic role, dispossessed of power and hidden from view. The nobility was restricted to some 200 families and herded together into the imperial park. Together, emperor and court were allotted the income of a lower *daimyo*. Unable to compete in material terms, the aristocrats sought consolation in tradition. It was a way of coping with their impotence, for it provided a means of affirming superiority in other ways.

The years between 1624 and 1650 saw the establishment of a number of outstanding estates in and around Kyoto. These include the imperial villas of Katsura and Shugakuin as well as the palace garden of Sento Gosho. Though they date from a similar period to that of Nijo Castle, they could hardly be more different. In place of brute power are simplicity and naturalness. Refinement is their guiding principle.

For many critics, the Katsura estate marks a highpoint of Japan's architectural arts. It also offers the earliest known example of the Edo Stroll Garden in which traditional techniques are used to create a fixed route around landscaped grounds. The central feature is a large pond, around which are created special "scenes", with carefully sited bridges transporting the eye from one area to the next. The effect is heightened by a "conceal and reveal" technique, by which views are kept hidden from sight until a turn in the path displays them to the visitor.

The founder was Prince Toshihito (1571-1629), who wished to create a meeting-place for poets and artists. Drawn to the glamour of the past, he chose a site close to where the Fujiwara family had once lived. Katsura had been famous in Heian times as a moon-viewing spot; Genji himself had gone there to gaze dreamily at the moon while listening to music. Toshihito was a devotee of tea, and the garden reflects its principles. The paths are laid out in formal, semi-formal and informal styles. Water-basins and stone lanterns are used as garden decoration. Tea pavilions are integrated into the landscape; one seems to float on the water, while another built on a small incline mimics a mountain retreat. The main buildings, which appear towards the end of the walk, are simple in appearance but exquisite in execution. Straight lines and undecorated wood leave the eye free to dwell on the details. There are specially created fastenings, doorbells in the shape of flower arrangements, and a set of shelves with eighteen different kinds of wood. Even the clasps have won admiration.

The estate was completed by Toshihito's son forty years after work had first started, but one senses the founder's spirit in the atmosphere. Such was his sensitivity that he only visited rarely, not wishing to spoil the effect by over-familiarity. Boating on the pond was restricted to autumn when moon-viewing was at its best, and only then did the family permit itself the rare pleasure of staying overnight.

It was long thought that the estate was designed by the great landscaper of the age, Kobori Enshu. Though that now seems doubtful, it is clear that his ideas shaped its layout. He was not only the major theorist of the age, but responsible for many of the most prestigious projects. These include the stern military-style garden at Nijo Castle with its rugged rocks and stark boulders. By contrast, the garden he laid out at Sento Gosho evokes a sense of ease and leisure. It was built in 1630 for the retirement of Emperor Go-Mizunoo, and there is a strong Heian nostalgia evident in the references to Genji, Komachi, and the poet Ki no Tsurayuki who once lived on the same site. In later centuries the garden was modified with a shoreline of 110,000 carefully laid oval stones. These were presented by an Odawara *daimyo*, and for the journey to the capital each stone was individually wrapped in silk. It shows just how much care was taken to make the garden into a work of excellence.

Go-Mizunoo (1596-1680), for whom the estate was built, had become emperor at fifteen and was pressured into marrying the shogun's daughter. Though he tried to resist Tokugawa control, he found himself powerless and in 1628 resigned in favour of his five-year-old daughter. She was the first "reigning empress" since the eighth century. The former emperor took a keen interest in architectural arts, and he put the knowledge he gained from his collaboration with Enshu into the creation of Shugakuin Villa. This was funded by the Tokugawa to keep him harmlessly occupied. Set on an incline on the eastern hills, it contains a lower, middle and upper pavilion, each with its own enclosure. As at Katsura, the materials are humble for an imperial estate—earthen walls, wooden pillars, paper panels, and cypress bark roofs. It was a demonstration of how to live in "genteel poverty".

Compared with its peers, Shugakuin is a sprawling affair, containing rice and vegetable fields. Its chief glory is the use of borrowed scenery, which constitutes surely the most spectacular example of this technique anywhere. To view it in autumn is an unforgettable experience. The Taj Mahal, the Forbidden City, the Himalayas: these are magnificent, in keeping with expectations. The dramatic effect of Shugakuin is altogether unexpected. A pathway up the incline leads first past the lower garden to reveal the Hiei foothills, then over farm fields to where Kyoto opens up in the valley below. Beyond the middle pavilion, it becomes steeper and begins to zigzag with a hedge on either side to block the view. At one of the bends, the hedge line stops all of a sudden and gives way to a vast openness to north and west. Even the phlegmatic Japanese in our party let out gasps of astonishment at this point.

In the panoramic view that presents itself, rolling mountains ablaze with autumnal hues stretch the length of the horizon. Down below a landscaped lake is fringed by the fiery colours of maple trees, the effect of which is doubled in intensity by their reflection in the still waters of a lake (it is kept purposely shallow—a mere twenty inches—to maximize its reflecting quality). Beyond it, in the middle distance, lies a forested incline, and to its right the green slopes of a mountain side are planted with evergreen. It takes some moments to absorb all this.

Further uphill stands the Upper Villa where Go-Mizunoo liked to enjoy the setting sun. Sitting there gives one a sense of majesty with the picture-perfect scene displayed down below. No wonder the former emperor enjoyed visiting so often, for he came two or three times a year accompanied on the short excursions by a grand entourage. He liked to hold poetry and moon-viewing parties, while on the lake he went boating accompanied by music. Here, in this wistful revival of Heian culture, he must surely have felt he had escaped altogether from the stranglehold of the Tokugawa.

Art Sublime

Between the seventeenth and the nineteenth century, there flourished a number of artists known collectively as the Rimpa School. They excelled in decorative arts and were drawn from the upper levels of the merchant class—what might be termed "old money". Like the nobles, they drew inspiration from the past. Their work, which makes much use of gold and silver, is typically found on screens, fans, and album pages. They were long forgotten, but were "rediscovered" by the American art critic, Ernest Fenellosa (1853-1908), whose championing of them led to their exposure abroad. Now they are seen as important influences on Art Nouveau and the likes of Klimt and Matisse.

The two geniuses of the first generation were the calligrapher Honami Koetsu (1558-1637) and the painter Tawaraya Sotatsu (d.1643). The former was something of a Renaissance man. The son of a sword-maker, he was brought up to appreciate craftsmanship and studied tea with Furuta Oribe. He was an outstanding calligrapher, as well as a master of lacquerware and pottery. He also published Heian literature in woodblock decorated editions, known as Saga books.

In 1615 Koetsu was given land by Ieyasu at Takagamine, in the north-west of Kyoto. Here he established a colony of artists that included some of the most talented men of the age, including Sotatsu. The son of a fan-painter, the artist painted in the *yamato-e* tradition and his pictures are unusual for having no contemporary references. Nature and literary scenes were his forte, with *Genji* and *The Tales of Ise* his favourites. "It was Koetsu who focused attention on the classical past; but its recreation was Sotatsu's achievement," writes the art critic Mizuo Hiroshi.

Together Koetsu and Sotatsu produced beautiful picture scrolls, combining the former's calligraphy with the latter's painting. *Poems of the Thirty-Six Immortal Poets*, for example, has fluid running calligraphy inscribed over a flock of silver cranes against a gold background. This was executed with materials of the highest quality, and the stylish effect makes it even today a popular design for stationery and other goods.

Among Sotatsu's paintings the most famous is his screen rendition of the *Gods of Wind and Thunder*, belonging to Kennin-ji. The two popular deities are depicted in colour on gold foil: Fujin (God of Wind) is shown with a narrow bag of wind blowing in a graceful ark like a silk scarf, while Raijin (God of Thunder) holds a circle of hand drums. There is also a touch of caricature, for Fujin has a Botticelli-type grin while Raijin happily bangs the drums like a young child. The figures are placed so far apart that they spill off the edges of the screen, yet they are held together by the balance of the composition. The result is a work that resonates with energy and humour.

Towards the end of the century, the Ogata brothers, Korin (1658-1716) and Kenzan (1663-1743), revived the Rimpa style in triumphant fashion. They had a personal connection, for their grandfather had been a member of Koetsu's community. The offspring of a leading textile-merchant, the brothers were raised in the appreciation of fine designs. Korin showed early promise, but he dissipated his energies in the pleasure quarters. After getting into debt, he turned to his younger brother who had set up a pottery business. Together they produced some stunning ceramics.

Kenzan's pottery was one of the sensations of the time, and it is said his workshop was the first brand name in Japan. The products are startlingly bold and original, even by today's standards. No less striking is the variety: dazzling bellflowers on a yellow background; square-shaped dishes with *sumi-e* in underglaze brown; chessboard-patterned black-and-white saké cups. Much of the work consists of food dishes for the *kaiseki* food used during the tea ceremony. It was designed to present a feast for the eyes. Tsuji Kaito, second head of the Tsujitome *kaiseki* masters, said that he was overwhelmed by how the beauty of the plates was brought out by the food, as if Kenzan had foreseen the effect in his design. "I bowed my head to the greatness of the man," he declared.

Korin later achieved fame in his own right. He had trained himself by making copies of Sotatsu's works, and he excelled in decorative designs and flowering plants. One of his most famous works is *Iris*, inspired by an episode from *The Tales of Ise*. It is painted on a gold background so that the silhouettes of the flowers stand out in a dancing line along the margin of unseen waters. Korin's lavish style appealed to the merchant class, and he often painted their patron deities, Ebisu and Daikoku. He also did kimono designs, which formed an important part of Tokugawa art. The flat surfaces provided scope for imaginative designs, and specialist skill was needed in coordinating the picture to the shape of the folds.

The Ogata brothers worked at a time when the country was experiencing a "gilded age" known as Genroku (1680-1710). It saw the rise to prominence of the new *chonin* class (townsmen), who differed in taste from the aristocracy and the samurai. Excellence emerged in a number of fields. In painting the Kano and Tosa schools flourished; *ukiyo-e* woodblock prints evolved; in theatre Noh and Kabuki enjoyed popularity; and in literature Saikaku's prose, Basho's poetry, and Chikamatsu's plays marked a historical highpoint.

The age is characterized by its extravagance. Clothes were showy, and crafts were sumptuous. An anecdote about Korin typifies the times. At a fashionable picnic he attended, his companions all brought gold-lacquered lunch boxes. To show them up, he unwrapped food in bamboo skins decorated on the inside with gold leaf, which he nonchalantly tossed into the nearby stream. The incident brought him trouble with the authorities, for displays of wealth were forbidden by law.

The Ogata brothers represented the last of Kyoto's *machishu* culture, which was led by powerful merchants and artists with links to the aristocracy. With the rise of the Tokugawa, the economic rug was pulled from under their feet and the centre of patronage shifted to Edo. Kenzan himself moved there at the end of his life, and Korin also went between 1704 and 1710. It shows in which direction the cultural current was flowing. Nonetheless, the Rimpa School rank among the greatest artists ever to have come out of Kyoto. "Koetsu, Sotatsu, Korin and Kenzan," writes Mizuo Hiroshi:

> *four masters of decorative art, four reasons one feels fortunate to have been born in Japan. This is not only because of the tremendous artistic value of their many works, but also because these embody the very essence of what is Japanese in Japanese art.*

The Floating World

Near Shijo Bridge stands a striking statue of a figure in a bravura pose. Closer inspection reveals it to be a woman mimicking the manner of a samurai, with a sword thrown nonchalantly over her shoulder. This is Izumo no Okuni (d. c.1640), the founder of Kabuki. Though the drama is no longer associated with the city, it was in Kyoto that this vigorous art form had its origins.

Okuni had once been a shrine maiden at Izumo Taisha, where she performed sacred dance. In Kyoto she entertained crowds on the dry riverbed at Shijo. This was a popular place for performance, for the land was not subject to tax. Okuni mixed humorous sketches into her act, and the style she developed became something of a sensation. It was dubbed *kabuki*, or crazy. (Later the word was given Chinese characters which altered its meaning; *ka* for song, *bu* for dance and *ki* for skill.) The shows became so renowned that Okuni's troupe was invited to perform before both emperor and shogun. The Okuni Kabuki Screen (c.1603) shows them performing at Kitano Shrine, accompanied by flute and drums. On stage can be seen an actor holding a sword, a teahouse woman, and a clown with a towel over his head. It would seem, then, to be the group's most famous sketch, *Fun at the Teahouse*, a bawdy piece of cross-dressing in which Okuni played a samurai picking up a prostitute, acted by a man.

The new entertainment proved a popular alternative to the elevated style of Noh, and at one time there were as many as seventeen Kabuki stages along the Kamogawa. As in Restoration England, actresses used the theatre to advertise their "wares", and the excitement this generated led to outbreaks of disorder. As a result, in 1629 women were banned and replaced by boys. For some of the audience, however, the young boys were no less enticing than the women. In 1652 they too were banned. Thus, in a complete reversal of Okuni's military strutting, men came to play women's roles. It was in this way that the tradition of the *onnagata* (female impersonators) was born. Their ability to represent "femininity" was held to be greater than that of females, because of the distance involved. It was a stylization that epitomized the real thing, similar to the way that Japanese gardens "out-nature" nature.

The clampdown on Kabuki was symptomatic of the Tokugawa regime; in their Confucian world fun-loving spontaneity was regarded with suspicion. In 1617 "entertainment women" were restricted to specific areas, where pleasure-seeking could be safely overseen. Here were herded together all kinds of entertainers from jugglers to courtesans, so that the revelry could be contained within set parameters.

It was in such areas that the culture of the "floating world" (*ukiyo*) evolved. The phrase had long been used in a Buddhist sense to indicate the illusory nature of life: "In this floating world, does anything endure?" asked the narrator of *Tales of Ise*. Now, however, the phrase took on a secular meaning of transient pleasures. The originator, Asai Ryoi (1612-91), was a masterless samurai who took orders at Kyoto's Honjo-ji and became a prolific writer. In *Tales of the Floating World* (1661), he gave a satirical account of a worldly monk named Ukibo and included this famous passage:

Living only for the moment, turning our attention to the pleasures of the moon, the snow, the cherry blossoms, and the maple leaves; singing songs, drinking wine, diverting ourselves in just floating, floating, caring not at all for the poverty staring us in the face, refusing to be disheartened, like a gourd floating down the river; this is what we call the floating world.

Not surprisingly, the floating world looms large in the arts of the period, for the *demi-monde* offered an appealing alternative to the strait-jacketed world of the Tokugawa. Among those drawn to it was the author Saikaku Ihara (1642-93). The son of an Osaka merchant, Saikaku had turned to writing after the death of his wife. He became the great chronicler of Genroku times and the diarist of its private secrets. To read him is to be transported on a rollicking and fast-moving trip through Edo times. His style was the picaresque, and his themes were love and money. No one better captured the spirit of the age.

Saikaku started out as a haiku poet, but turned to prose in 1682 with *The Life of an Amorous Man*. Comical in tone, the novel pitches its hero from wealth to poverty and back again. Each chapter illustrates an aspect of the age, and the miniature portraits have been compared to the "genre paintings" of Momoyama times. For Donald Keene, it is "the first novel of significance for almost five hundred years". Such, indeed, was its success that it initiated a genre of *ukiyo-zoshi* (Tales of the Floating World).

The novel parodies *The Tale of Genji* by having 54 chapters hung around the life and loves of a central character. But unlike the Shining Prince, the hero, Yonosuke, is a worldly merchant whose love life is erotic in nature: by the end of the book the indefatigable bisexual has slept with 3,742 women and 725 boys. In his restless quest for novelty is embedded all the consumerism of Genroku. The novel's irreverent tone is evident in a "feast of abstinence" held at To-ji. Though meat is forbidden, the group seizes on the fact that drink is allowed. "As the sun rises and sets," runs their Buddhist text, "so does human life. No one can escape this law." To this a drunken Yonosuke responds, "Let's make the best of it then before our sunset comes," and off goes the group to the nearby pleasure quarters. It is the *carpe diem* philosophy of the floating world.

The playful fun of the men in Saikaku's world contrasts with the plight of the women, who are the victims of fate—one of the author's main themes. In the third of his *Five Amorous Women* (1686), he tells of a true-life incident involving the wife of a rich Kyoto merchant who falls for one of her husband's employees. Since adultery was punishable by death, the pair run off to Lake Biwa where they pretend to stage a double suicide. This allows them nine months together before they are caught and executed. The story had a resonance for Edo citizens, and the playwright Chikamatsu made a *joruri* (puppet drama) version in 1715.

The episode exemplifies the clash of *giri* (duty) and *ninjo* (feelings), which was the great preoccupation of the age. Samurai were associated with the former, merchants with the latter, and finding the right balance was a concern for all. It was an issue, too, in marriage, which was seen in terms of social obligation. A bride entered a household rather than a relationship, and her duty was to maintain the family line. The volatile nature of passion made it suspect to a regime for which stability was the main concern: "Keep love in the brothels," ran one of the official slogans. It was in such a climate that the pleasure quarters flourished. "Floating, floating, caring not at all for the poverty staring us in the face"—such was their guiding maxim.

Haiku Master

Matsuo Basho (1644-94) is hardly associated with Kyoto. He is linked with the Deep North and with Edo, where he had his home. Indeed, he

took his pen-name from the banana-tree (*basho*) which stood outside his hut there. Yet the poet-wanderer also had close connections with the imperial capital. He was born not far away, in Iga Province, and may even have studied in Kyoto for a while. He was fond of the city, often visited on his wanderings, and it was in Otsu by Lake Biwa that he chose to have his grave.

The poet had started life as a low-level samurai, but dropped out of a promising career and in 1672 moved to Edo. He studied Zen and came to see in haiku not an artistic diversion but a means to a meaningful life. This prompted his wanderings, and aware of the profound loneliness of existence, he sought solace in the ego-less world of nature. He visited the Kyoto area on at least five occasions. He cherished the historical associations and identified with predecessors such as Saigyo, Sesshu and Rikyu, to whom he felt bound by "the spirit of the artist who follows nature and befriends the four seasons." One of his haiku, soaked in nostalgia, tells of how the sound of a cuckoo drew him to the past, prompted perhaps by Sei Shonagon's fruitless expedition to the woods for a cuckoo-inspired poem:

Even in Kyoto,
I long for Kyoto,
When the cuckoo sings.

The poet was particularly fond of Lake Biwa and its environs. The lake is thought to be five million years old, making it the third oldest on earth, and it is surrounded by dramatic mountains like Mount Hiei and Mount Hira. In the days before jet-skis and concrete, it was a haven of unspoilt nature with ancient woodland teeming with wildlife. It had long been known as Omi, but during the seventeenth century the name changed to Biwako because its shape resembled the *biwa*, or lute. Following the Chinese custom, special scenes around the lake were selected for Eight Famous Views (later painted by Hiroshige). When Basho was challenged to include them all in a haiku, he cleverly came up with this:

Seven Views obscured—
But then in the mist I heard
The bell of Mie.

In 1690 Basho spent the summer in the Unreal Hut (Genju-an) by Lake Biwa. It was on the side of a small hill, from the top of which he could view the lake, and for a while he relaxed after his long wanderings. He wrote a *haibun* (haiku essay) about his life of seclusion, telling of the simple pleasures he enjoyed: the views, the wildlife and the nearby places of interest.

During the day an old guardman or villager from the foot of the nearby hill comes to talk with me about unusual happenings, such as a wild boar foraging in the rice fields or a hare lurking around the barn yards. When the sun sets behind the hill and light comes, I sit quietly and wait for the moon. By the light of the moon, I walk around and my shadow follows me. When it gets late, I return to the hut to meditate on good and bad, gazing at the shadow's edge cast by the lamplight.

The next year Basho stayed in Saga at The Hut of the Fallen Persimmons (Rakushisha). It belonged to one of his most important followers, Mukai Kyorai (1651-1704), the son of a wealthy physician from Nagasaki. It was Basho's second visit (he was to come again in 1694, a few months before his death), and he described the stay in his *Saga Diary* (1691). Unlike his other accounts, it is a real diary with exact dates. It tells of a relaxed time: "I forget my poverty, and enjoy a serene, leisurely life here," he wrote. The final haiku speaks of his departure:

Ah, the summer rain—
On the walls are traces of
Peeling poem cards.

There is a strong seasonal atmosphere to the poem, for the high humidity of the rainy season is causing the cardboard pieces to come unstuck. Looking at them, the poet fondly remembers the poetry sessions with his friends. It also conveys a sense of the poet himself "peeling away" as he prepares to depart from the hut.

The visit brought Basho into contact with another of his followers, Nozawa Boncho (d. 1714), and together with Kyorai the three men compiled *Sarumino* (The Monkey's Cloak, 1691). Arranged by season, it is considered one of the finest anthologies in Japanese literature. It showed that the short verse could be a serious art form capable of expressing profound ideas about the nature of human existence.

Three years later came Basho's death at the age of fifty-one. It happened near Osaka while he was on another long journey. He had asked to be buried at Gichu-ji, a small temple at Otsu next to his beloved Biwako. It contains the grave of the Minamoto warrior, Kiso Yoshinaka, to whom the poet was attracted, prompted perhaps by the description of his battlefield death in *The Tale of Heike*. Basho had once visited the graveyard with his friend Yugen, who wrote a haiku about the occasion:

Back to back
With Kiso Yoshinaka—
How cold it is.

The poet was seated with his back to Yoshinaka's grave, and the "cold" of the last line seems to embrace not just the wintry day, but a sense of loss, the gulf between humans and the icy finger of death. It contains all the suggestive resonance that characterizes good haiku. It was in this marriage of brevity and profundity that lay Basho's gift to posterity.

The Literati

A hundred years after Basho, an artist living in Kyoto came across a hut in the grounds of Kompoku-ji where the poet had once stayed. It was in dilapidated state, and in tribute to his predecessor he decided to restore it. His name was Yosa Buson (1716-84), and he is recognized now as second only to Basho in terms of haiku. The hut he repaired, Basho-an, stands on an incline and is surrounded by woods with views over Kyoto. Buson loved the area and often held haiku sessions there. He also wrote an essay expressing his commitment to nurturing the seeds Basho had planted. It was here also that he chose to be buried:

When I come to die
I shall be near his stone—
The withered pampas grass.

Born in a village near Osaka, Buson moved to Edo before becoming a monk and wandering the country for ten years. From the 1750s he based himself in Kyoto, delighting in the city's literary associations. Unlike the samurai tastes of his predecessor, he was fond of Heian literature and enjoyed the spirit of place.

Slow days passing—
In a corner of Kyoto
Echoings are heard.

In his time Buson was known more as a painter than a poet, and he was a leading figure in the Literati Movement. This had originated in China where mandarins retired to take up a life of art and study, in keeping with the Confucian tradition of cultivating virtue through studying the past. Practitioners saw themselves as amateurs, freed from professional ties and conventions. Rather than pleasing patrons, the literati pleased themselves. There was a playful feel to their art, typified by paintings of sages in the woods enjoying themselves.

An early practitioner was Ishikawa Jozan (1583-1672), creator of a splendid small villa called Shisendo (Hall of the Immortal Poets) in north-east Kyoto. Jozan had been a samurai in the service of Ieyasu, but fell out of favour when he broke ranks during the siege of Osaka Castle. He took orders at Myoshin-ji, and it was not until he was fifty-eight that he built his hermitage, which was the first of its kind. It contains a study lined with portraits of Thirty-six Chinese Poets, a small moon-viewing room and an attractive garden, which many rate among the best in Kyoto. Tradition holds that Jozan enjoyed his retreat so much that when Go-Mizunoo came to visit, he was too engrossed to even go and receive the former emperor.

By Buson's time, a hundred years later, the literati lifestyle had become more established, thanks in part to the state sponsorship of Confucianism. Prominent among the arts they practised were calligraphy and painting, the latter tending to the softer "southern style" of idealized landscapes. The delicate brushwork was in stark contrast to the dominant style of the age, represented by the vigorous lines of the Kano school.

Buson only came to painting late in life and was self-taught. "For my paintings I had no human teacher," he wrote, "my teachers are the masterpieces of Japanese art." One of his specialities was *haiga*, which combined calligraphic haiku with an illustrative picture. He also specialized in horses, and in the Kyoto National Museum is a dramatic ink-painting showing a herd of *Wild Horses* (1763) in a craggy valley, where a pony, rather endearingly, is rubbing its side against a rock face.

Another of the literati active in Kyoto at this time was Buson's contemporary, Ike no Taiga (1723-76). Born into a peasant family on the outskirts of the city, he started his career at fourteen by painting fans. He was patronized by a teahouse owner who pressured him to marry her daughter. He gave his consent, but only if she waited seven years. In the meantime he went travelling, climbed Fuji, inspected Western art in Edo and experimented in painting styles.

Taiga was an eccentric figure, who could paint with fingernails in lieu of a brush and loved nothing better than painting outdoors. He was much influenced by the artwork at Manpuku-ji, a temple at Uji which had been established in 1661 by the Chinese immigrant Ingen (1592-1643). The temple became a vital centre of Chinese arts, and provided a strong impetus for the Literati Movement. Taiga first visited it as a precocious six-year-old, when he gave a calligraphy demonstration, and he remained a lifelong friend of the monks there. The Chinese influence is evident in his painting at Ginkaku-ji called *Men of Letters*. It shows Taoist sages enjoying activities such as chess and lute-playing. The pinkish faces are done in a liquid calligraphic style that looks surprisingly modern, and there is a bamboo trunk broken up into overlapping parallel sections like the fragmented pieces of a Picasso painting.

As with the other movements we have seen, the literati art drew inspiration from the past. A similar impulse lay behind the boom in the city's crafts during this age. The driving force behind this was the great social phenomenon of the age—the rise of the merchant class. It led to an explosion of finely made goods and a cultural flourishing whose legacy is still evident in the profusion of traditional craft shops that enrich modern Kyoto.

Capital Crafts

With the stability of Tokugawa times leading to increased harvests, there was greater prosperity among the population at large. Business thrived as luxury items that were once the preserve of the ruling class became affordable by ordinary townsfolk. Goods from the capital had high prestige because of their reputation for excellence. Anything that had "come down" from the capital (*kudarimono*) automatically had high value. It meant boom times for Kyoto's craftsmen.

The city's mercantile spirit had been given an early boost by the building of the Takase Canal in 1611. It was the project of a prominent merchant, Suminokura Ryoi (1554-1614), and represented advanced engineering for its time. Branching out from the Kamo River, it ran in one direction towards Nijo and in the other to Fushimi, where it connected with the river to Osaka. Over nine miles in length, it was constructed so that in times of flood the surplus water would run back into the Kamo. It remained in use throughout Edo times, and at one time up to two hundred flat-bottomed boats plied its length.

One of the main water-borne items was lumber, for Kyoto was being rebuilt after the devastation of the Warring States period (1467-1568). The wood was brought from the forests to the west of the city and unloaded in Marutamachi (Log Town) and then transported to the middle of town to be cut up in Kiyamachi (Wood Shop Town). Along the wharf there merchants dealt in goods from Osaka like soya sauce, rice and charcoal.

By Genroku times, the capital's artisans had difficulty keeping up with demand. Two brands to profit were Kenzan pottery and Yuzen fabrics. The latter was named after Yuzensai Miyazaki (d.1758), a painter of fans who applied his skills to a method of dyeing involving the use of rice starch to separate areas to be dyed. These were "fixed" by being washed in the Horikawa, where the long rolls staining the waters became one of the city's sights. The breakthrough allowed for the application of large-scale pictures to kimono, and Yuzen's landscapes became a rival to Korin's hand-painted flowers and plants.

Genroku Japan was described in Engelbert Kaempfer's *History of Japan* (1693). The author was a German physician who worked for the Dutch at Dejima and accompanied their annual mission across the country to pay respects to the shogun. His book long constituted the West's best resource on Japan and informed Jonathan Swift's *Gulliver's Travels* (1726), in which the eponymous hero briefly visits Nippon and its imperial capital, which he calls Miyako. In the passage below Kaempfer tells of its bustling merchant life:

> *Miyako is the great magazine of all Japanese manufactures and commodities, and the chief mercantile town in the empire. There is scarce a house in this large capital, where there is not something made or sold. Here they refine copper, coin money, print books, weave the richest stuff with gold and silver flowers. The best and*

*scarcest dyes, the most artful carvings, all sorts of musical instru-
ments, pictures, japan'd cabinets, all sorts of things wrought in gold
and other metals, particularly in steel, as the best tempered blades,
and other arms are made here in the utmost perfection, as are also
the richest dresses, and the best fashion, all sorts of toys, puppets,
moving their heads of themselves, and numberless other things, too
many to be here mentioned. In short, there is nothing can be thought
of, but what may be found at Miyako, and nothing from abroad
however neatly wrought that some artist or other in this capital will
not undertake to imitate.*

Much of the boom in crafts owed itself to the spread of the tea
ceremony. Metal workers, for instance, benefited from the demand for
kettles, and at one time there were up to seventy smiths around Sanjo
Bridge. They also cast a wide range of other goods including pans and
bells with gold and silver inlay, or enamel on copper. Kyoto
lacquerware, noted for its black sheen, also enjoyed an upturn. The
technique had been introduced from China in the ninth century, and
was used to cover almost every object, from ornamental boxes to swords
and tableware. The process involved up to fifteen coats, each of which
was rubbed down to a smooth base in order to achieve the glass-like
finish. Inlaid pictures completed the effect. A variant was Kodai-ji
lacquerware, which involved the sprinkling of silver and gold on the
still wet surface, resulting in a slightly raised surface.

Bamboo products were another popular item, and not just for tea
goods such as whisks and vases. The bamboo grown around Kyoto is
tough and glossy, suitable for high-quality fencing. The elegant bamboo
umbrella, still used by geisha, took its present form in Edo times and
became a much-loved fashion accessory. It forms the backdrop for
many *ukiyo-e* portraits of women, where its circular form offsets the
sensuous curves of the kimono.

Ceramics also came into their own. The forced influx of Korean
potters after Hideyoshi's invasions of the 1590s had helped to raise
standards, and Kyoto was known for its colourful Kiyomizu-yaki,
popular with pilgrims. The pottery developed from around 1615
among a group of potters clustered around the slope leading to the
temple. Still today the area is filled with pottery shops—and bargain
hunters.

Production of saké saw a dramatic upturn at this time. The trade had a long history, and by 1400 there were already some four hundred small brewers in the city. In Edo times came the establishment of larger companies, including Gekkeikan, which remains a brand name known for its "thin" taste, in keeping with the Kyoto tradition. Similarly the city's "famous products" of tofu and *yuba* (skimmed tofu) are light in taste, showing a sophistication that derives from the aristocratic heritage. By contrast, Edo as a city of samurai, was known for its thicker, less subtle, tastes.

The religious reforms of the early Edo period proved good for business too, since they stipulated that every household had to register with a Buddhist sect. This led to a sharp increase in the demand for religious artefacts, such as rosaries, statues, bells, candle and incense holders. Kyoto altars were particularly sumptuous, with meticulous craftsmanship covered in gold foil.

The architectural expression of this booming merchant culture was a shop-residence known as *machiya*. This is unique to the Kyoto-Osaka

area and was restricted by law to two storeys. Since the property tax was calculated according to the width of the frontage, the premises were kept narrow but extended long and deep (hence their nickname of *unagi no nedoko*, or eel-beds). The distinctive features make them easily recognizable. The walls are made of scorched wood, which seals it from disease and reduces the risk of fire. Inside is a shop area where customers can be received and goods set out. Family rooms are towards the rear of the house, and at the back is a place for entertaining guests where works of art were once displayed. The small gardens, or *tsubo niwa*, in the middle and at the back of the houses contained elements from the tea garden—a lantern or water basin, rocks and one or two plants. Because of the regulations governing the house's exterior, merchants poured their resources into the gardens instead. It gave them a touch of the upper-class elegance they envied.

The accumulation of valuable possessions led to the construction of *kura*, or storehouses. These were purpose-built to protect goods from damage, and the walls are about two feet thick. This solidity not only kept out fire, but ensured a moisture-free interior where perishable items like scrolls, kimono and screens could be stored in safety. Squat but attractive, the whitewashed buildings are still dotted around the city and speak of the mercantile prosperity of the past.

Another sign of the times was the establishment of a number of "small Kyotos" around Japan. With the prolonged stability, provincial *daimyo* had turned from warfare to the pursuit of arts, and several sought to emulate the culture of the capital. As well as inviting leading figures to their domain, they sent local artisans to Kyoto to learn from the masters. A noted example is Kanazawa, where the Maeda family patronized artist-craftsmen pursuing pottery, Noh and Yuzen dyeing. When Sen Soshitsu (founder of Urasenke) was invited in 1666, he took along the head of the Raku school and the visit gave birth to the highly regarded Ohi pottery.

But of all the developments of the age, it is the weaving centre of Nishijin that best typifies Kyoto's mercantile vigour. The area had been first settled by weavers after the Onin War in the late fifteenth century, and by 1700 there were some 5,000 craftsmen. The trademark product was the *obi*, the long ornate strips that are wrapped round the middle of the kimono. These can be amazingly decorative, and even more expensive than the kimono itself.

Nishijin came to dominate the country's woven goods. In 1781 there were 2,500 looms; by 1877 the number had risen to 7,839. The city's textile dealers became rich on the back of this boom, and many acted as bankers to impoverished samurai and aristocrats. It was from such families that emerged some of the powerful dynasties of modern Japan. The precursor of the Mitsukoshi department store was a small family business in Kyoto that ran the city's first fixed-price emporium. And Mitsui Takatoshi (1622-94) opened a store in 1673, which expanded to Edo and became the foundation of the Mitsui trading empire.

Something of the merchant ethos of Edo times can be sensed in the lively festivals held each year at the city's Ebisu Shrine. These take place on 10 January (Toka Ebisu) and 20 October (Hatsuka Ebisu). They originated in the custom of merchants returning from business in Edo to give thanks for a successful trip. Over the course of three days something like 100,000 people pass through the narrow shrine gate to pray for success in their business ventures. Here is all the chaos and jollity of a medieval fair. Jostling crowds stand ten deep before the shrine, tossing coins over the heads of those in front towards the offering box. The altar is piled high with over 200 huge saké bottles, and along the sides is a busy trade in amulets and keepsakes. *Gagaku* music provides an other-worldly atmosphere as *miko* (shrine maidens) perform sacred dances, and smiling festival-goers carry off bamboo branches bearing trinkets and treasure-boats to bring them prosperity. It does not take much imagination to substitute topknots and kimonos for the modern clothes and to see here the figures of another age. Here in this good-natured throng, the old merchant bustle of Kaempfer's Miyako seems to come alive before one's very eyes.

Edo Ends

Near modern-day Sanjo Bridge is a curiously large bronze statue of a samurai on all fours. It is a striking monument, yet even among Japanese few know whom it represents. It was put up in an age when imperialist sentiment ran high to honour a man who had revered the emperor in earlier times. His name was Takayama Hikokuro (1747-93). He had come on a visit to Kyoto in 1783, and on first entering the city he prostrated himself towards the imperial estate.

When Hikokuro discovered that the palace had been left in ruins following a fire, he angrily blamed the shogunate for neglecting its "sacred duty" to repair it. Storming off to Toji-in, in the north-west, he vented his feelings by slicing off the wooden heads from three Ashikaga shogun and exhibiting them at Sanjo like common criminals. The display won popular support, which goaded the shogunate into action. It was an early indicator of the shift in loyalties from shogun to emperor that was to culminate in the Restoration of 1868.

By the start of the nineteenth century, the shogunate was increasingly ineffective. National finances were in disarray following a widespread failure of crops, and there had been famine in the countryside. The Tokugawa were no longer the force they once were, and rather than ruling they had come to rely on a balance of power among the *daimyo*. The samurai were enfeebled by the long years of peace, and disaffection was rife among the lower ranks, many of whom were in debt to powerful merchants.

At the same time the legitimacy of the shogun was being undermined by the work of scholars. Studying the past was important to Confucians for the maintenance of good governance, and in delving into the past historians explored the roots of national culture. The influential Motoori Norinaga (1730-1801) stressed the centrality of Shinto, of which the emperor was head. And Rai Sanyo (1781-1832), who lived in Kyoto by the Kamo River, wrote a long historical work entitled *Nihon Gaishi* (1844), which suggested that the role of military commander belonged by right to the emperor but had been usurped by political dynasties.

In 1853 came the sudden appearance of Commodore Perry and his "black ships". The steamships were the most advanced of the time, and the show of force was intended to back up the American demand for open ports. As well as the opportunity to trade, the US wanted re-supply facilities for their ships *en route* to China. They also demanded the safety of sailors, for shipwrecked survivors had been maltreated by the xenophobic regime. Isolationism had served the Tokugawa well, however, and they were loathe to allow outside interference. Yet they knew they were outmatched, so when Perry returned a year later they reluctantly agreed to open two ports to the US, though there were many who objected. In 1858 the Harris Treaty ceded more rights, allowing trade and the principle of extraterritoriality in six Japanese ports. This was seen by many as capitulation and caused widespread anger with the shogunate.

From the confinement of his Gosho palace, Emperor Komei (1831-67) expressed opposition to the idea of foreigners tainting the country's sacred soil. For a while anti-shogun elements rallied round the popular slogan of *Sonno Joi* (Revere the Emperor, Expel the Barbarian), and Kyoto became the focus for disaffected samurai. By the 1860s, tensions were running high in the city.

From 1862 to 1868, Kyoto stood at the epicentre of a storm that ripped the Tokugawa edifice to pieces. It was a tumultuous six years, which threw up one hero after another, and many of the events have taken hold of the popular imagination. Leading the cause of imperial restoration were two western domains: Choshu (modern-day Yamaguchi) and Satsuma (Kagoshima). They were bitter rivals: whereas Choshu favoured violent overthrow, Satsuma was more accommodating. The split between them seriously weakened the opposition.

In 1863 the shogun went to consult the emperor. It showed the direction in which power was shifting. The visit is notable for occasioning the formation of a special police force, which was recruited from the sword-schools of Edo. Their role was to counter anti-shogunate forces in Kyoto, but it turned out that many sympathized with the opposition. The group was disbanded and a nucleus left behind to continue the work. Out of this emerged the now legendary Shinsengumi.

At first the group was based around Mibu Temple, where its members had such a bad reputation that they were called *Mibu-ro* (Mibu wolves), a wordplay on *Mibu roshi* (masterless samurai). The most prominent member was the arrogant Serizawa Kamo (1830-63), who took advantage of his position by running up debts, abusing women, and picking fights. He was assassinated in an internal plot, probably carried out by his rivals, Kondo Isami (1834-68) and Hijikata Toshizo (1835-69). The two men were followers of *bushido* (the Way of the Warrior) and ran the group with iron discipline. They restricted membership to top swordsmen, and enforced a code of conduct called *Gohatto*, which stipulated that members could never leave once they had joined. Brotherhood took precedence over private matters. It was all for one and one for all, with any breach of the rules ending in the enforcement of *hara-kiri*.

The most famous episode in which the group was involved was the Ikedaya Incident of 1864. Realizing that anti-shogun conspirators were plotting assassinations, the Shinsengumi rushed to the inn where they were meeting. The numbers involved were small—around thirty on each side—but the outcome was crucial. In the two-hour battle, eight of the plotters were killed and twenty-three arrested. Outstanding in this conflict was master swordsman, Okita Soji (1844-68), a young friend of the leaders and afflicted with tuberculosis. It was only during the fight that his cough alerted them to his condition.

A month later the group took part in the Hamaguri Gomon Incident, when Choshu samurai attempted a coup d'état by forcing their way into the imperial palace. Though they were repelled, the fighting caused a fire that lasted three days and destroyed half the city. Following these events, the fame of the Shinsengumi spread and recruits flocked to join them. In all, they had some 240 members.

At this point the charismatic figure of Sakamoto Ryoma (1836-67) enters the story. The young *ronin* was an energetic figure with strong self-belief. "Although I was born a mere potato digger in Tosa, a nobody, I'm destined to bring about big changes in the nation," he once wrote to his sister. In 1865 his involvement in politics brought him to Kyoto, where he set up a secret pact between the Choshu and Satsuma groups. It is seen as the single most important development in the collapse of the Tokugawa, an astonishing achievement for a young man acting on his own.

The night after the signing of the pact, a shogunate police squad raided the Teradaya Inn where Ryoma was staying. Hearing the intruders, the landlord's daughter, Oryo, rushed out of her bath stark naked to warn the guests upstairs. In the fight that followed, Ryoma held off the attackers with a revolver while his bodyguard wielded a spear. Soon after his escape, Ryoma married Oryo and took her off to Kyushu on a trip celebrated as the first ever Western-style honeymoon.

The next year Ryoma established a large-scale corporation called the Kaientai, a forerunner of Mitsubishi. Based in Nagasaki, it consisted of armed merchant boats and ran guns for anti-shogunate forces. He still hoped to avoid bloody civil war, and while at sea drew up the Eight On-Board Policies that called for a return of the emperor system together with a form of parliament. This was presented by the Tosa *daimyo* to the new shogun, Tokugawa Yoshinobu (1837-1913). Knowing that his forces were outmatched, Yoshinobu accepted the terms and formally resigned in a ceremony at Nijo Castle on 13

October 1867. It was a historic moment, which marked the end of seven hundred years of military rule. It was a poignant moment for the Tokugawa, as their ancestor Ieyasu had become shogun in the very same castle 265 years earlier.

A month later, Ryoma was dead. Together with his friend Nakaoka Shintaro (1838-67), he was at Omiya, in the shop of a wealthy soy dealer, when members of a shogunate group stormed in and killed the pair. The murders showed that the Tokugawa still retained support. Shortly afterwards, when the emperor was declared head of a new government, pro-shogunate forces from Osaka moved on Kyoto where they were joined by the Shinsengumi. It marked the beginning of the Boshin Civil War (1868-9).

The opening battle took place at Toba Fushimi, on the edge of Kyoto. Though the small imperial army, comprising Choshu and Satsuma troops, was outnumbered, it won the battle. Three months later came the fall of the Tokugawa stronghold of Edo, following a negotiated settlement. Even then the loyal Shinsengumi fought on, knowing that defeat was certain. Kondo was killed near Tokyo; Okita died of tuberculosis; and Hijikata fought a rearguard action all the way up to Hokkaido, where he died in the final battle of the war.

The dramatic events of these years have been the subject of numerous novels and films. An early interpreter was Shimozawa Ken, whose *The Legend of Shinsengumi* (1928) was made into a film in 1963. Even more influential was the novelist Shiba Ryotaro (1923-96). Little known in the West, he was not only his country's top historical novelist but a leading thinker in the debate about "Japaneseness". His books show how determined people can bring about decisive change, two notable examples being *Moeyo Ken* (serialized 1962-64) about the Shinsengumi, and *Ryoma ga Yuku* (serialized 1962-66) which lionizes Sakomoto Ryoma.

Among the films that have brought the period to life, two in particular deserve special mention. One is *Ryoma Ansatsu* (Ryoma's Assassination, 1974), which portrays the last three days in the life of the revolutionary. It shows him as a playful, wilful sort of character having fun in the chaotic events that have overtaken the city. A radical free-thinker, he calls to mind the time the film was made, during the heady days of 1970s student riots when calls for liberation also led to violence. One of the film's actors, Matsuda Yusaku, was father to the star of a later

film about the same period, called *Gohatto* (1999). Based on stories by
Shiba Ryotaro, it was directed by Oshima Nagisa (*In the Realm of the
Senses*) and features the Shinsengumi. Lyrical and elusive, the picture
contrasts the strict code of the samurai band with their ready acceptance
of homosexuality. The story centres around the arrival of an aloof
eighteen-year-old into the troupe, leading to an outbreak of lust and
resulting in murder. As in other Oshima films, the erotic obsession
serves to disrupt the patterns of everyday life.

Interestingly, the age's heroes fought on opposite sides and
represent differing values. In the case of Ryoma, the status is not
difficult to understand because he speaks to modern values both as an
individualist and an internationalist. To the young who flock to his
grave in east Kyoto, he stands for vision and purpose: "I want to have
my dream and follow my path like you," says one of the hundreds of
messages left there. In the NHK poll of 1998, he was voted second only
to Nobunaga as the most influential Japanese of all time.

The case for the Shinsengumi is less clear. As hitmen for the
Tokugawa, they were not only on the wrong side of history, but were
also known for their excessive violence. Their methods were brutal,
their code repressive, and their behaviour fanatical. For many years they
were remembered in Kyoto with disgust, and in early fiction they were
depicted as villains. Yet all that has since changed, and the
"repackaging" of the group has much to do with the appeal of samurai
movies, where they are depicted as master swordsmen sworn to defend
their cause with their lives. The leading triumvirate has all the glamour
of The Three Musketeers, enhanced by the mystique of early death:
Kondo and Hijikata died in their mid-thirties, Okita even younger.

The saga calls to mind that other group story, The Forty-Seven
Ronin, and there are similar elements in the secret bonds and tragic
end. Even the mass suicide is echoed in the forty or so Shinsengumi
who killed themselves. In both cases the story serves to champion
samurai values. "Loyalty and Patriotism" was Shinsengumi's recruiting
slogan, and other qualities held up for admiration include duty, self-
sacrifice, sincerity and the acceptance of authority. (Japan's modern
army of *salarymen* marches to a similar tune.)

With the demise of the Shinsengumi, the Tokugawa cause came to
an end as the new government was joined in Tokyo by the teenage
Emperor Meiji. For Kyoto, too, it marked the end of an era. Within the

明治時代の
帝王様.

isolated world of Tokugawa Japan, the city had been able to capitalize on its heritage of arts and crafts. The Imperial Renaissance, the Rimpa School, the literati, even the courtesans of the pleasure quarters were all underpinned by a sense of tradition. Now, however, Kyoto was to face the biggest challenge in its history, as a city that had thrived in the sheltered climate of national seclusion faced survival in an age when the country looked for its models not to the past, but to the West.

Chapter Ten
CITY OF GEISHA

A Work of Art

Four million copies sold in the US; translated into 34 languages; a multi-million dollar lawsuit; optioned by Steven Spielberg, then filmed by Rod Marshall. *Memoirs of a Geisha* (1997) caused as much interest in the exotic east as *Japonisme* a century before, when a craze for all things Japanese had swept through Europe. Once again, it seemed that geisha were "in". Perhaps they have never really been out.

Geisha may have originated in Tokyo, but it is Kyoto with which they are most associated. For over two hundred years the city's *geiko* (the local name for geisha) have had the reputation of being the most sophisticated in the country. Uniquely, too, Kyoto retains the custom of teenage trainees called *maiko*. They feature in tourist posters for the city, something that brash modern-minded Tokyo would never think of doing.

The *maiko* typifies the popular image of geisha as a doll-like figure decorated from head to foot. Her face is a painted white mask with eyebrows underscored in red and small scarlet mouth. Her kimono is bright and eye-catching, with long dangling sleeves at the side and trailing *obi* at the back. She walks on dauntingly high wooden clogs, some four inches high. The white face is arresting; much of the fascination lies in its ambiguity, for like skin-tight clothing it reveals as much as it conceals. The thick paste stops short of the hairline to leave a strip of naked skin, as if in a facial striptease. It continues round the back of the ear before plunging down the neck where the nape is decorated with two points in the shape of the letter W (for formal occasions there are three prongs). These extend suggestively downwards, leading the eye down the back which is part-exposed by the low-hung kimono collar. The back of the neck, with the hair tied up to reveal its elegantly tapered shape, was traditionally considered erotic.

Given the ensemble, it is remarkable that the *maiko* can move about freely, let alone walk gracefully. The silk kimono they wear is tight-fitting, like a corset, and requires special care as it is worth a fortune. The cloth is made from a strip twelve yards long and is hand-painted with dyes from natural sources such as berry or bark. Together with the accessories, it can weigh as much as forty pounds, which is not far short of half the weight of the young females who wear them. Crowning the outfit is an elaborate hairstyle in which waves of waxed black hair are folded over and decorated with hairpins and silk flowers. The style differs as the *maiko* makes progress through the ranks, and once it is set it is kept for a week at a time. To preserve its shape, the *maiko* sleeps with her head on a block of padded wood so that her neck is raised off the ground. Getting used to this (no tossing and turning) is part of the rigorous training.

By contrast, the costume of the geisha becomes plainer as they age. Wigs are worn until around thirty, then largely dispensed with, as are the white faces. *Zori* slippers replace the wooden clogs, *obi* become less resplendent, and kimonos tend towards single colours. The bright butterfly of spring fades gracefully towards the autumn of her life.

Much of the fascination with geisha has to do with their remoteness. Like royalty, they inhabit a special world, hidden from view. They not only dress differently, but they live differently from ordinary people. Their whole culture can be seen as a series of distancing devices that include the special style of talking, the refusal to accept first-time customers, and objectification through the beautiful accessories. In her book on the subject, Lesley Downer wrote of the difficulty of penetrating the geisha world. Fluent in Japanese and armed with connections, she was met everywhere with polite evasion. "No matter how long you are here, you will never understand the intricacies of our system," she was told. It was as if the "flower and willow" world was so delicate that it needed to protect itself in an enveloping cocoon ("flower" represents beauty and "willow" grace).

Yet mystique alone is insufficient to explain the appeal, for the exoticism is only skin-deep. It was brought home to me once when the faculty at my university were entertained by geisha at a banquet, and after the dance performance one of the *maiko* was seated next to me. White face, red tinted eyebrows, exotic hairstyle, bright-coloured kimono: here was a cultural thrill indeed. People were flying around the world for just such an experience. *Sakura dosu* ("I'm Sakura"), she told me in her lilting Kyoto accent. In between smiles and plying drinks, she patiently answered questions she had been asked a thousand times before. How long had she been a *maiko*? (Two years) Where was she from? (Hiroshima) What did her parents think about her choice of job? (They were worried) Why did she want to become a geisha? (She liked traditional arts) What was the hardest part for her? (Getting up to study) What did she think of her job? (She liked it) Why? (She could meet interesting people).

Since none of my colleagues showed any desire to join us—no doubt it looked unprofessorial—the conversation moved on to her interests: rock music, action movies, and manga. When she learned I was from Britain, she told me how much she liked Beckham and the Beatles. The conversation had entered familiar territory, for it was one I had had many times with my students. By now I was no longer relating to a *maiko* as such: I was talking to an eighteen-year old in fancy dress.

Clearly then, there is something other than mystique that keeps customers going back—and at such great expense. (A party of five being entertained for a couple of hours by two geisha and a *maiko* might expect to pay $400 each.) Those who have seen elderly geisha will know that sex is not the issue. It concerns an altogether different kind of appeal, which has to do with geisha "art" in the broadest sense of the word. This includes the mastery of dance and music that first gave the profession its name (geisha means "arts person"). Added to this are the skills of companionship and comportment. Every detail of behaviour, every utterance of speech is chiselled and polished towards perfection. The Kyoto geisha, Fumicho, puts it this way:

> Before everything else, a young woman must learn the subtleties and perfection of proper posture and refined etiquette. These include such fundamentals as how to sit or stand or bow properly as well as more difficult things such as how the hands should be used to gesture, or placed in the proper position when sitting or standing. Correct and controlled use of language is of great importance.

If individuals are "constructs", as postmodernists claim, the geisha are the ultimate examples, for these self-made creations are committed to artifice. "To polish one's life into a work of art, however high-flown it

may sound, is the idea behind the discipline of a geisha," writes Liza Dolby, the only foreigner to have done the job. It requires total dedication and an almost Zen-like subjugation of the will.

Picasso was once asked why one of his scribbled pen-portraits should be worth so much when it took him so little time to produce. "It took me all my life," he responded. Geisha might answer similarly to questions about their high charges, for their finely-tuned performances result from long hours of training. Their ethos embraces a love of fine kimono; self-discipline in grace; and mastery of traditional skills. When you pay for a geisha, you pay for a work of art.

Pleasure Quarters

Imagine a walled and moated fortress dedicated to pleasure. Inside are performers, procurers and prostitutes. Here the normal rules of society no longer apply, and classes mix easily. It is a male paradise of saké, song and sex, freely available to those with money. In contrast to the regulated world outside, here there is a licence to do as one pleases.

Such was the nature of the great pleasure quarters of Edo times. They were places to let off steam, a safety-valve for the highly regimented society. Edo had Yoshiwara; Osaka had Shinmachi; and Kyoto had Shimabara. It was set up in 1641 among open land on the western edge of the city, and the name means "island in the fields". It was a tongue-in-cheek reference to the Shimabara Uprising of 1637, when a Christian stronghold in Kyushu had been bloodily suppressed. Some said the pleasure quarters looked like the castle fortress, others claimed its establishment was so chaotic that it resembled the uprising.

It had all begun with a brothel area near the imperial palace. This was licensed by Hideyoshi in 1589 on the basis that it was better to have such places officially supervised. The enlightened policy (predating that of modern Holland by some four hundred years) was continued by the Tokugawa. As Ieyasu said, "These are necessary evils, and if they be forcibly abolished, men of unrighteous principles will become like ravelled thread." By 1641 the proximity of the red-light district to the imperial palace was unsettling the court, and a new location was found just to the west of Nishi Hongan-ji. Like the nearby temple, it was a walled compound with moat and gate. To the locals, it must have been a jolly spectacle to see the floating world of Buddhism joined by that of hedonism. Sex and religion, those two great preoccupations, enjoyed the thrill of proximity.

Within the compound women were divided into a hierarchy according to beauty and accomplishment. The elite were the *tayu*, a type of courtesan whose favours were reserved for the rich. Their world was modelled after that of the nobility; they were given names similar to those of princesses, and their "ladies-in-waiting" addressed them in the deferential language of court. When they went on assignments, they were accompanied by parasol bearers in the kind of processions enjoyed by the aristocracy.

The *tayu* were trained as entertainers, and among their skills were arts that had previously been restricted to the nobility, but were now being spread among the merchant class. The instrument they favoured was the *shamisen*, a kind of three-stringed banjo imported from Okinawa during the fifteenth century. It was made of cat-skin and plucked with a large plectrum of wood or ivory. Later they turned to the *kokyu*, a three-stringed instrument which is held upright and bowed.

In *Tales of an Amorous Man*, Yonosuke samples the courtesans of the country and declares those of Kyoto to be superior. On one occasion he is invited by a Shimabara *tayu* on her day off for a tea ceremony, and the sophistication suggests that it might well have taken place at court:

At the tea brewer's seat sat the courtesan Takahashi as hostess, her hair in bangs, brilliant with a golden ornament. Her inner garment was of plum-red sheer, her robe of white satin embroidered with the crest of the Sambaso, a symbolic theatrical design. Her overrobe displayed an irregularly spread pattern of a long-tailed fowl and vermilion tassels.

Presently an attendant brought word from the kitchen: "Kyujiro has returned from Uji."

That meant, Yonosuke knew, that Kyujiro had been sent all the way to the Uji brook to fetch pure water for the tea. Although it seemed to be a mere trifle, the thought behind it—the desire of the courtesan to obtain the purest water possible for the tea, for his pleasure—was no trifling matter.

When the rites were over, Takahashi began to wet a number of ink slabs. "All this beauty of the snow spread outside before us," she said, "should not be wasted by our just looking at it. We should all compose verses and preserve the impressions forever."

As is evident, the *tayu* dressed to impress. In fact, they wore probably the most elaborate costumes in Japanese history, grander even than those of Heian aristocrats. Layers of bright undergarments were topped by a heavily embroidered over-kimono with padded hem. The huge hair creations, like a parody of a Paris fashion display, were stuck through with more than twenty hair-pieces weighing almost seven pounds. When they walked, it was with the majestic motion of an Elizabethan galleon under full sail. Of all the peculiarities of the clothing, the most striking was the *obi* being tied at the front rather than at the back. This was at one time the fashion for married women, and the *tayu* mimicked it to show they were "tied" for the night. It carried, too, the suggestion of availability, as if with a pull of the sash the whole outfit would fall apart like some well-wrapped Christmas present.

Like the courtesans of Restoration England, the *tayu* were fabled creatures whose reputations spread throughout the land. They were mentioned in guidebooks, and Saikaku describes how men captivated by the descriptions travelled huge distances to experience their charms. *Ukiyo-e* prints helped to publicize them further. *Portrait of a Courtesan Smoking Her Pipe* by Kitagawa Utamaro (c.1753-1806) shows one such beauty with criss-cross "chopsticks" through her hair, tiny rosebud mouth, and provocatively turned head.

Of all the courtesans, none was as celebrated as Yoshino Tayu of the early seventeenth century. She was noted not only for her beauty, but for her skill as a *raconteuse*. Requests for her portrait came from as far away as China, and among her lovers was supposedly Miyamoto Musashi. It is believed that the emperor's chief advisor made her an offer she could hardly refuse—but she did, for love of an ordinary man four years her junior. She was a friend of the aesthete Honami Koetsu, and funded the temple gate of Josho-ji built by his son. It is here that her grave lies, and every year there is a festival in her honour. It offers a rare chance to see the remaining *tayu*, currently only four in number and in a sense play-actors since they no longer function as courtesans. Here one can see close-up the astonishing clothing as well as the peculiar formal walk, dubbed "figure of eight" for its great circular sweeps of the foot.

Shimabara was closed down in 1958, following the introduction of anti-prostitution laws. The surviving banquet rooms are in a richly appointed building called Sumiya, which was once an important salon. Sakamoto Ryoma and Saigo Takamori brought merchants here to solicit funds for their cause. Here, too, the opposition Shinsengumi partied, and there are sword marks in the pillar of the *tokonoma* made by an enraged Serizawa Kamo when he was refused service for not paying his bills. The entertainment area is decorated with superb woodwork and paintings by the likes of Yosa Buson and Maruyama Okyo. There is also a concealed stage, to which the *tayu* could make their way along a secret passageway. It must have made for a dramatic effect when the sliding panels were suddenly thrown back, and there before the guests stood a *tayu* poised and ready to perform.

Life in the pleasure quarters could be anything but pleasurable for the women who worked there, and there are stories of them trying to escape or making desperate attempts at suicide. Their position was insecure, their work unsavoury, and their future uncertain. Yet most had no choice in the matter, for they were bound by financial ties as tight as the *obi* that restricted their body movements.

The heyday of the *tayu* was in the seventeenth and eighteenth centuries. Their skills declined with their success, and they began to call on others trained in dance and music to perform for their guests. These belonged to a new profession, called geisha. Lower in status, they evolved from the entertainment put on by tearooms at a time when Shimabara held a monopoly on prostitution. It was not long, however, before they came to dominate the entertainment business. Like cuckoos in the nest, they were to outgrow and eclipse the older profession.

A New Profession

In early Edo times, as peace returned to the country, there was a sharp upturn in the number of pilgrims visiting Kyoto. For most people, religion was the only officially sanctioned purpose for travel, and people took advantage of this pretext to see the wonders of the country, leading in 1658 to the publication of the first guidebooks of Kyoto. To cater to the pilgrims, teahouses were set up around popular destinations. They offered entertainment by young girls (*odoriko*), who gave Kabuki-like performances. There were waitresses, too, who offered extras not necessarily on the menu.

The teahouses became important meeting places, and some functioned as male clubs. It is interesting to note a similar development at this time on the other side of the world, where a coffee house culture was taking place in England. The first coffee shop was set up in Oxford in the 1650s, and the fashion spread to London where it provided a focus for social and political gatherings. It was out of these that the first English newspapers emerged in the form of broadsheets. The Kyoto teahouses filled a similar function, as can be seen in the great *cause célèbre* of the seventeenth century involving the so-called Forty-Seven Ronin. The incident was sparked by a *daimyo* named Asano who wounded a shogunate official called Kira Yoshinaka in Edo Castle. Since the use of weapons there was strictly forbidden, Asano was ordered to commit suicide. His followers, led by Oishi Kuranosuke (1659-1703), believed that the sentence was unjust, since the man who had insulted him went unpunished. Though it was expressly prohibited by law, they dedicated themselves to revenge.

To give himself time, Kuranosuke set up house in Yamashina, to the east of the city, and for nearly two years pretended to be living a life of dissolution. He frequented a teahouse where he gave himself up to drink and women—or so it seemed. In fact, all the while he was secretly meeting with his fellow conspirators. The result was that on 14 December 1702, Kira was murdered in Edo. Following the act of revenge, the forty-seven men who took part in the plot were in their turn ordered to commit suicide. They ranged in age from seventy-five to fifteen, and their action won widespread admiration.

The story is among the best-known in Japanese history and has been retold countless times. It was turned into a Kabuki cycle called *Chushingura*, which takes some eight hours in all to perform. It contains a famous scene with Kuranosuke in a Kyoto teahouse, where he seems to insult his dead master in order to deceive government spies. Though not historical, it is set in Ichiriki, the most illustrious of Kyoto's teahouses.

It was not until some time after this episode that the word "geisha" came into use. It was first applied in 1750 to a type of male companion; yes, "male", for these were *shamisen*-playing men with an entertaining line in banter. By 1779, when the new profession was officially regulated, women had caught on to the opportunity it offered them. The "female geisha" proved so popular that within a generation they had all but driven the men out of business (a handful of "male geisha" remain, even today, in Tokyo). The usurpation mirrored that of Kabuki, where men had taken over from women, and the two professions have much in common. Both emerged out of the "floating world"; both thrive on artifice; both inhabit the *demi-monde*; and both have the whiff of scandal.

By the nineteenth century geisha had become modish figures who were celebrated by admirers of *iki*, a sort of "daring chic" that combined casual elegance with worldly nonchalance. Although the geisha of Edo were the most celebrated of the age, it was those of Kyoto who stole the limelight in the Meiji Restoration. It was even said that the whole event was plotted in the city's tearooms, as the samurai who flocked to the imperial capital spent their evenings in the city's geisha districts. The imperial faction favoured Gion, the Shinsengumi frequented Pontocho, and both sides patronized Shimabara.

One of the most famous affairs of this time concerns a geisha of Gion named Ikumatsu (1843-86). She became the lover of Kido Takayoshi (1833-77), a.k.a. Katsura Kogaro and one of "the three heroes of the Restoration". Though he paid off her debts to the teahouse, she continued working in order to supply him with information—a geisha Mata Hari. She saved his life once by cajoling him out of attending the meeting at Ikedaya, and not long afterwards the pair were forced into hiding. Later they married and went to Tokyo, where he became a leading member of the government and she a pillar of society. The story illustrates the opportunities the career of geisha offered women. It not only gave young girls an education, but access to influential and wealthy men. Several were the daughters of impoverished nobility, unable to give them the kind of upbringing they wished. In a sense, it was a substitute for sending them to court.

The "Meiji geisha" proved something of a sensation, and those who had helped the imperial cause were feted as heroes. Novelists like Izumi Kyoka (1873-1939) and Ozaki Koyo (1867-1903) celebrated their virtues, and the government discussed matters of state in geisha teahouses (known as *machiai* politics). One reason for their prominence was that they were the only women at this time able to converse with men on equal terms. With the opening of the country to the West, their fame soon spread abroad, thanks to the interest in all things Japanese. Gilbert and Sullivan's *Mikado* (1885), Pierre Loti's *Madame Chrysanthème* (*Madam Chrysanthemum*, 1888), and Puccini's *Madame Butterfly* (1904) spurred interest in the exotic female. Riding the wave was Sadayakko (1871-1946), an Edo geisha whose tour through the US and Europe in 1899-1900 generated huge publicity.

Numerically, the peak for the geisha came in the 1920s when there were 80,000 in all. There was no shortage of candidates, as the rural poor were forced to sell off their daughters. By the 1930s, though, the tide was beginning to turn and articles appeared in the Japanese press suggesting that the whole idea was out of date. The fashion setters of one age were becoming the dinosaurs of the next.

The Second World War almost sunk the floating world altogether as Kyoto's entertainment areas were temporarily suspended. Although they opened up again afterwards, it was not with the same vigour as before. The orientation of post-war Japan was so completely at odds with geisha traditions that it is something of a wonder that they have survived at all. Yet here they still are, shedding a little bit of Edo-era magic as they walk the streets of the twenty-first century. Like an endangered species, their charm lies as much in the rarity as the finery.

The Flower Districts

Modern Kyoto boasts five geisha areas, known as *hanamachi* or "flower districts". They first developed in the eighteenth century, when collections of tearooms were licensed for entertainment. In order of size, the figures for 2004 were as follows: Gion Kobu (82 *geiko*, 24 *maiko*); Pontocho (43 *geiko*, 5 *maiko*); Miyagawa-cho (39 *geiko*, 23 *maiko*); Kamishichiken (15 *geiko*, 8 *maiko*); and Gion Higashi (11 *geiko*, 5 *maiko*). The flower districts lend the city a special character, though they are but a pale shadow of the thriving enclaves they once were. The areas constituted a huge support system for the teahouses that stood at their heart. There were teachers to train the geisha in their arts, and skilled craftsmen for the specialized goods: fans, fabric, kimono, wigs, hair decorations and all the other accessories. Food and saké merchants grew rich from the entertaining. The geisha were not so much individuals, as an industry.

Kamishichiken in the north of the city has claims to the oldest pedigree, for it traces its origins to the time of Yoshimitsu, the Ashikaga shogun. In 1444 he had shops set up from wood left over from rebuilding Kitano Shrine (the name of the district means Northern Seven Shops). A century later the area was boosted by Hideyoshi's Great Tea Party, though it was not until the eighteenth century that the teashops were formally licensed. They benefited from the patronage of nearby Nishijin, whose merchants in prosperous times liked to indulge in lavish entertaining.

The other flower districts are situated around the Shijo area, at the heart of which is the dry river bed where informal performances were once held. Miyagawa-cho emerged around the 1660s as a spin-off from the Kabuki world. Its name, meaning "pure river", was a reference to the purification of Yasaka Shrine floats in the river just south of Shijo. It was along here that many of the Kabuki stages were located, and teahouses were set up to entertain the theatre-goers. On the other side of the river, Pontocho catered to businesses along the Takase canal. ("Ponto" is thought to derive from the Portuguese for "point" in reference to a prominent spur of land once visible in the river.) The area had been made safe from flooding in 1670, after which teashops sprang up in a narrow passageway along the Kamo River. In 1813 the district was given formal recognition, and became one of the city's liveliest areas. Set in tiny alleyways, it has a distinctive feel that makes it unique among flower districts. It is even said that the phrase "the water trade", the popular term for the entertainment business, arose from the geisha's practice here of attracting boatmen on the river.

The largest of the geisha areas, Gion, grew out of stalls set up around Yasaka Shrine. This was a popular destination for pilgrims, as the shrine was said to prevent illness and promote prosperity. It benefited from the backing of wealthy merchants, and in early Edo times was extensively rebuilt. Shortly afterwards the area between the shrine and the river was secured by flood control, opening it up to development. It became such a sprawling district that in 1886, for administrative reasons, it was split by the prefectural government into Gion Kobu and Gion Higashi.

The five flower districts put on annual dance performances, which offer a chance to sample the differences between them. Each area has its own theatre, with its own distinctive character. These are grand occasions, popular with citizens and tourists alike. For the flower district, it is a community event: local businesses offer sponsorship, residents make a point of turning out, and a network of supporters helps by selling tickets. The performances date back to 1872, when Gion put on "Miyako Odori" (Dance of the Capital) and Pontocho put on "Kamogamo Odori" (The Kamogawa Dance). They were part of a campaign to promote the city and provide a focus for the influx of spring tourists. Later, other geisha districts followed suit, and an autumn programme was also introduced.

The performances were a daring innovation, because geisha art was a private affair and the dance style (*Kyo mai*) was not intended for public display. Its origins lay in court dance, and it had developed for privileged patrons familiar with the stories on which the dances were based. Since it took place in small rooms, it dispensed with large gestures in favour of subtle movement. As with other Japanese traditions, the dance is not a form of self-expression but a matter of "absorbing" fixed patterns by constant repetition. It demands patience and self-control. Here is how former geisha, Iwasaki Mineko, describes it:

> *Traditional Japanese dance looks very different from its Western coun-*
> *terparts. It is done in white cotton* tabi *socks rather than special shoes.*
> *The movements, unlike ballet, for instance, are slow and focus on one's*
> *relationship to the ground rather than the sky. Like ballet, however,*
> *the movements require highly trained muscles to perform and are*

taught as fixed patterns (kata) *that are strung together to form an individual piece.*

Many of the dances are like mimed drama, telling melancholy stories of lost love. Elements are drawn from traditional theatre, and one recognizes the components. As in Noh, there are rapid short steps done while twirling a fan. As in Bunraku (puppet theatre) there are doll-like movements. And as in Kabuki, there are set poses with cute head gestures.

The Inoue school of dance, based in Gion, is the most prestigious in Kyoto. It was established in 1781 and has only had five heads, all of whom assume the name of Yachiyo. When Japan introduced the system of "living national treasures" in 1955, the first to be honoured was Yachiyo IV (1905-2004). Her marriage to a Noh actor indicates the close links of the two art-forms, and like the drama the school is noted for its ability to express powerful emotions through controlled movements.

For the annual performances, geisha dances are adapted to the big stage and given an air of theatricality. Instead of a single dancer, small groups perform in unison. Rows of elderly geisha are ranged along the side playing *shamisen*, flute and drums. Exquisite sets and lighting add to the visual appeal, while themes such as "The Four Seasons of Kyoto" provide a simple framework into which can be fitted folk dances and other adapted pieces. Gion Kobu presents the classic version, and its "Miyako Odori" enjoys the highest status. It is said that while other flower districts dance for the audience, Gion Kobu dances to please the gods—a reminder of its Noh connections. Other districts have a more popular appeal, and their theatres are more intimate. The "Kamogawa Odori", for instance, includes a revue sketch in which geisha act as sword-swirling samurai in the manner of Takarazuka musicals. Admirers have included Charlie Chaplin:

> *We Occidentals cannot stage a sword fight without a touch of the absurd, for no matter how fierce the fighting, one detects a modicum of caution. The Japanese, on the other hand, make no pretense at realism.*
>
> *They fight at a distance, apart from each other, making sweeping gestures with their swords, one attempting to cut off the head of*

*the opponent, the other slashing at the opponent's legs. It is like a
ballet. The combat is impressionistic, terminating in a posture of
victor and vanquished.*

Was it the precise choreography or the young girls in costume that
appealed to the dainty perfectionist?

The performances come to a rousing end when a grand finale
brings all together in a dazzling display of brightly coloured kimono.
The designs can be overwhelming. On one occasion when I attended,
there were purple kimono, the upper half of which was decorated with
flowers of pink and orange, while the lower portion was embroidered
with gold over a thick red inner lining. This was complemented by
white *obi* bearing a design of multi-coloured leaves. Weaving round the
stage in swirling patterns, twirling fans in one hand and flower
bouquets in the other, the geisha filled the stage with a riot of colour
that brought gasps from the audience. The sinuous bends of the body
and the sensuous curves of the kimono created a kaleidoscopic effect of
constantly changing shapes. The result was stunning. In a city filled
with seasonal splendours, this is one of its finest flowerings.

Gion Walking

In all Japan, there is only one geisha district licensed to entertain
visiting heads of state: Gion Kobu. It is a measure of the prestige it
enjoys. Though it no longer retains the splendour of its past, if one
walks around in the late afternoon one can still get a sense of how things
once were. It has the feel of another age, as if cordoned off from the
modernity which surrounds it. "For Japanese themselves, going to Gion
is like travelling to a foreign country," writes Irie Atsuhiko.

The two types of building that characterize the flower district are
the *ochaya* (teahouses for entertaining) and the *okiya* (geisha boarding
house). It is the former that is the geisha's public space. The teahouses
are two-storey wooden buildings with latticed windows and *noren*
(hanging cloth) at the entrance carrying their name. Inside,
entertainment rooms have *tatami* floors and a *tokonoma*, just as in the
traditional teahouse.

There is an *ukiyo-e* picture of *The Gion District* by Tsukioka
Yoshitoshi (1839-92), which shows a youth going to a tearoom where
his father is one of those involved with The Forty-Seven Ronin. It is an

almost rural scene with the young samurai making his way along a garden path against a backdrop of trees. There is a stone lantern on one side and a rustic house on the other. It looks for all the world as if he is going to a tea ceremony, and is a reminder of the geisha's origins. The influence of tea remains strong, evident above all in the strong seasonal awareness, for kimono and accessories always reflect the time of year.

The most famous of the teahouses is Ichiriki, and photographers often gather outside to snap visiting celebrities. General MacArthur was entertained here after the Second World War, and heads of state such as US President Gerald Ford have come to visit. So exclusive is it that even top-ranking figures have been turned away, including in recent times one of Japan's most successful pop singers.

The *okiya* is the geisha's private space where geisha live in a family of women. It will be familiar to readers of *Memoirs of a Geisha*. The owner takes the role of "mother", and under her may be one or two young *geiko*, referred to as "older sisters", and a *maiko* who is known as "younger sister". There may also be a pre-apprentice (*shikomi*), who acts as a kind of maid; she is in training to be a trainee, and the eagerness with which she carries out her chores shows her suitability. The house is off-limits to men, except perhaps for a fitter who comes in the afternoons to assist the women in donning their kimono. The job, like much else in the traditional world, is hereditary. Folding, wrapping, and tucking in the yards of cloth can take up to an hour for the unskilled. A fitter can manage the operation in under ten minutes.

It is in the *okiya* that young girls go through the butterfly-like evolution from raw teenager to radiant geisha. The training, which lasts up to five years, still remains rigorous though not as harsh as formerly. The girls receive no salary, but all their expenses are paid for by their "mother", so that, like royalty, they need carry no money. Custom dictates that *maiko* wear a different kimono each month, and special occasions require special kimono. The cost can be staggering. Some are provided by the *okiya*, but those that have to be bought are debited to the *maiko*, together with the fees for her lessons and training. In the past the debts meant a lifetime of servitude, and even these days the amount can run up to half a million dollars—enough to put off all but the most determined.

At the start of their careers, *maiko* are bound to a mentor in a ceremony that mimics part of the Shinto wedding ceremony called *san-san-kudo* (three-three-nine). It consists of the two women taking three sips each from three cups. As in a marriage, the *maiko* then takes a new name that makes reference to her "partner". It signifies the close bond of the pair.

When debuting, *maiko* do the rounds of the teahouses, giving greetings to all those with whom they may have future dealings. In this the individual is accompanied by her "older sister" or other house employees. It is one of the grand occasions of the flower district, with local journalists and well-wishers thronging round to watch her "launch". If she is of special note, the coming-out may even make the national news.

Life for the *maiko* is a never-ending round of classes and learning. Morning lessons include traditional arts such as dance, *shamisen*, Japanese drum, flute, flower arrangement, tea and calligraphy. Of these dance has the highest prestige (*maiko* literally means "dance person"). Afternoons are given over to dressing and make-up: it takes 45 minutes alone to apply the white make-up properly. In the evenings come the parties, where she learns by *minarai* (looking and learning). The parties, called *ozashiki*, are the heart of the geisha's job and take place from six in the evening. Here small groups are entertained while they eat and drink. The tearoom in which the parties are held may not even have a kitchen, but will order in food from outside caterers. A typical session lasts two to three hours, with up to five guests entertained by two geisha. Iwasaki describes the attraction:

> *Men come to them for beauty, for art, for conversations. Our "play" involves everything from the tea ceremony to flower arrangements, to arts, to talking about the book you are reading, conversation never seems to end. Forty or fifty minutes into the "party", we perform our dance and then talk about various things or explain the dance. And soon the party is over.*

For entertainment purposes, geisha are divided into two kinds: those who specialize in dance, and those who play *shamisen* and sing. Geisha songs are known as *kouta* (short) or *nagauta* (long), and the novelist Nagata Mikihito (1887-1964) wrote one telling of his love for the area:

> *There is a dim moon over Higashiyama:*
> *In the bonfires of the hazy nights*
> *A dream lingers round the red cherries;*
> *My thoughts are on the long hanging sleeves,*
> *My dear Gion, and your dangling obi.*

The cost of being entertained by geisha is such that, by and large, customers are limited to those with expense accounts, and walking around Gion in the evening one often sees inebriated dignitaries being seen off into their waiting limousines. In the past, the evenings did not necessarily end that way, for there was a custom of *zakone*, or sleeping over. The writer Tanizaki was fond of the practice:

> *It was, indeed, one of the most entertaining characteristics of Kyoto. A number of customers and a number of geisha and maiko all slept together in one room. Spreading their bedding over the floor, they all jumped in together. It was as simple as that. I do recall it was rather distracting at times, and one would often wake up the next morning with a splitting headache. But it was a jolly custom.*

Tanizaki frequented the teahouses near the Shirakawa, where along the river stands an attractive row of wooden houses with woven bamboo blinds. It is a reminder of how the whole area would have looked in former times. A nearby monument bears lines by the poet Yoshii Isamu (1886-1960), which conflate the flowing water of the Shirakawa with the floating world of pleasure:

> *No matter what they say*
> *I love Gion*
> *Even in my sleep*
> *The sound of water*
> *Flows beneath my pillow.*

Dreams, illusions and fantasy—such is the nature of the "water trade". It is a topsy-turvy world where geisha greet each other every evening with a cheery "good morning" as they start work. There is much of Wonderland about it. Filtered through the mind of Lewis Carroll, Oxford was transmogrified into a playground for Alice of bizarre happenings and absurd conversations. What, one wonders, would the lover of whimsy have made of Gion, with its winding passages and strange customs? Here a room is full of drunken giggling, there a plaintive voice sings an *enka* (Japanese blues), down the side-street echoes the clip-clop of wooden clogs. Then, all of a sudden, from out of a mysterious opening, appear the white-faced creatures of the night, propping up their red-faced companions.

Bordering Gion's southern flank is the Zen temple of Kennin-ji, and around the corner stands a popular love hotel where couples rent rooms by the hour. Religion and sex, a potent mix, is a reminder that many of Gion's most treasured customers are priests from the wealthier temples. Even the name Gion hints at the connection, derived as it is from the Japanese reading of an Indian temple, Jetavana-vihara, famous for its gardens. Was the intention to suggest a paradise on earth? Well, it may not be that, but you can be sure that by the end of the evening there will be many who think it is.

Fact and Fiction
Representations of the geisha have taken many and various forms: down-trodden victim; paragon of the arts; symbol of beauty; sex object;

champion of Japaneseness. The imagery often says more about the observer than the observed. For some the geisha is a fetishized male fantasy, for others the ultimate expression of the feminine. The representations tend to hover between extremes, as if there is a need to deal with this exception to the norm by pigeon-holing her.

The outmoded notion of geisha as dolled-up prostitute stems from an age of impoverishment. The misunderstanding has been furthered by "hot-spring geishas", known as much for their bedroom skills as for their traditional arts. These pale imitations of Kyoto's polished creations are referred to humorously as *daruma* or "knock-down" geisha for the ease with which they fall on their backs. The idea of the sexually available geisha was perpetuated by Hollywood in films such *The Teahouse of the August Moon* (1956), memorable for Marlon Brando playing a Japanese character, and *The Barbarian and the Geisha* (1958), in which a miscast John Wayne portrays Townsend Harris, America's first consul, who in the 1850s was presented with a geisha for his comfort.

Being nice to men with large pockets was part and parcel of a geisha's job, and in the past it was difficult to survive without a patron. "To my mind," says Arthur Golden, author of *Memoirs of a Geisha*, "a first-class geisha is more analogous to a kept mistress." Nowadays, the rules are strict. "Nobody sleeps with any client," says the *geiko* Kimina: "That's not allowed. If anyone touches me, I tell my 'mother' and she comes in and says 'Oh, please sit next to me.'" Having to sit next to a doughty *mama-san* is apparently enough to sober up even the most lascivious businessman!

The watershed year for the geisha came in 1958, with the passing of an anti-prostitution law. No longer could there be any suggestion of trading sex for money, and the whole system was modified so that geisha could live off their entertaining. In effect, the law was only confirming an economic reality, for the kind of poverty that forced women to sell themselves no longer existed. One aspect of geisha life that has nonetheless won much attention is the custom of *mizuage* (the auctioning of a girl's virginity). In a sense, this was the formalized equivalent of the arranged marriage, by which virginal young girls were sent into "good families" in exchange for a dowry. Though such practices no longer play a part in the geisha's job, fictional representations still continue to perpetuate the image.

One person drawn to geisha stories was the director Mizoguchi Kenji (1898-1956). He had a vested interest: his own sister had become a geisha and paid for his education. Identification with her shaped his view of the world, and in two celebrated films he turned his camera on Gion. Mizoguchi's *Gion no Shimai* (*Gion Sisters*, 1936) is widely considered Japan's best pre-war film. It concerns two sisters, one of whom is traditional and self-sacrificing, the other modern and self-seeking. In the clash between them neither emerges a winner, for both end up broken-hearted. It seems that true love has no place in their exploited world. Here can be found all the themes that feminism only took up forty years later. "Why are we made to suffer so?" says one of the sisters, "I wish there weren't any geisha. I wish they never existed."

Ironically, Mizoguchi was a frequent visitor to Kyoto's flower districts, and he returned to the subject in the post-war *Gion Bayashi* (*A Geisha*, 1953). It is a tale of innocence corrupted, as a sixteen-year-old who joins a geisha house is pressured into sex to save her *okiya* from bankruptcy. Winding passages and confined spaces project a sense of restricted freedom. The ending sees the young *maiko* setting off on her debut, accompanied by the "elder sister" who sacrificed herself in her stead. It is a statement of sisterly solidarity, and among those impressed was Penelope Gilliatt, who described it in *The New Yorker* as "not only one of Mizoguchi's masterpieces, but also one of the few perfectly tuned works of sensibility in the twentieth-century visual arts."

A later film, *Omocha* (*The Geisha House*, 1998), also bears a Mizoguchi connection in that its scriptwriter, Shindo Kaneto, was a friend and collaborator. It tells of Tokiko from a poor Nishijin family who wants to be a *maiko* to help pay for her sister's education. The director, Fukakusa Kinji of *Battle Royale* fame, had waited thirty years to film the story and the warm lavish colours in which he shoots it tell of his fondness for the subject matter. The film is set in 1958, in the twilight of the "bad old days". This is evident when a seventy-eight-year-old man is lined up for the young girl's deflowering, and though horrified at first, the *maiko* submits to her duty. Two women remain in the room, kneeling discretely behind drapes, to confirm the act. It is a token of the money involved. Yet contrary to expectations, the scene ends with Tokiko smiling, for in the loss of her virginity she has sacrificed all for her sister. Like a samurai unflinching in the face of death, the young *maiko* has proved herself worthy.

The similarity to *Memoirs of a Geisha* is striking, for both focus on the trials of a young trainee and the suffocating web of relationships that surround her. No doubt every geisha of a certain age had a similar story to tell. It was one that fascinated Arthur Golden when he happened to meet the son of such a woman in Tokyo. It took him fifteen years to capture it all on paper, and his book has been celebrated for its "ventriloquism". Every author has to enter imaginatively into a fictional world, but here a writer was crossing a divide of unusual dimensions. The degree to which he succeeded can be seen in a review by the British novelist, Margaret Forster:

> *Memoirs of a Geisha is the sort of novel that novel-lovers yearn for, which is to say, so convincing that while reading it you become transported to another time, another place, and feel you're listening and seeing with someone else's ears and eyes.*

Golden's book tells of Sayuri, daughter of a poor fisherman, who is sold at nine to a Gion geisha house. The hardships she undergoes are heart-wrenching, yet at the end she emerges successful. Part of the fascination of the Cinderella story is the interweaving of fact and fiction. "Although the character of Sayuri and the story are completely invented, the historical facts of a geisha's day-to-day life in the 1930s and 1940s are not," wrote the author.

Golden had been helped in his research for the book by a one-time Kyoto geisha named Iwasaki Mineko. She not only told him her life story, but arranged for him to see behind the scenes. He even managed to see the way that geisha were fitted into their kimono. "I am indebted to one individual above all others... To Mineko, thank you for everything," he had written. After the book was translated into Japanese, Iwasaki read it and was stunned. "I thought of killing myself, of committing *hara-kiri*," she claimed. In interviews she spoke of being upset by the misrepresentation and the way the book perpetuated the connection with sex. "Geisha are not prostitutes," she said, "they are performance artists, improvised one-woman shows... He wrote that book on the theme of women selling their bodies. It was not that way at all."

To set the record straight, Iwasaki launched a libel suit and wrote an autobiography. It also became an international bestseller, and *Geisha of Gion* (2002) tells a remarkable story. As a young child, Iwaskai was talent-spotted by the eighty-year-old head of a geisha house, and her formal training, in keeping with tradition, started on the sixth day of the sixth month of her sixth year. Like the Jesuits, geisha believed that habits learnt before adolescence lasted a lifetime. Although Iwasaki suffered years of humiliation, she survived to become the top earner in Gion for six years running. By twenty-nine she was burnt out and retired. "I had given Gion Kobu everything I had and it was no longer giving me what I needed," she writes.

One of the most extraordinary incidents is the revelation of her affair with the married actor Katsu Shintaro, famous for playing the blind swordsman Zatoichi. The romance began when he demanded a date. In a deliberate echo of Ono no Komachi, Iwasaki agreed—on condition that he attend Gion every night for three years. Amazingly, he did.

"Kiss and tell" is one thing that geisha never do, for confidentiality is an iron rule of business. That Iwasaki would reveal everything about the geisha world was bad enough. To spill all about an adulterous affair while the wife in question was still alive seemed to many the height of bad taste. Some of Iwasaki's other anecdotes give pause for thought, too. She did not care for Queen Elizabeth's attitude to Japanese food, so flirted with the Duke of Edinburgh out of spite. She allowed Prince Charles to sign her fan, then threw it away because it had been ruined. She writes of her obsessive drive to be top, even at the expense of her health, and her attitude to her former enemies is unforgiving. By the time she writes of being ostracized in Gion, one begins to wonder whether there might not be good reason.

Like Golden, Iwasaki ends her book on an elegiac note, as if the world of which she writes may not exist much longer. Concern about the future is widespread, for the flower districts are wilting. At its peak Gion had over 1,000 geisha. Now in the whole of Kyoto—all the flower districts combined—there are just 190 geisha and 65 *maiko*. Small wonder that Lesley Downer subtitled her book, *The Secret History of a Vanishing World*. The decline is an inevitable result of modernization. For the post-war generation, reared on a diet of Western films and television, the subtle delicacies of the "flower and willow world" have little appeal. As Fumicho, a *geiko* of Miyagawa-cho, comments:

> *The writing seems to be on the wall. It seems that young Japanese are not at all interested in the traditions and wonders of their own culture. To say this makes me sad is an understatement in the extreme.*

In response, the normally conservative geisha world is striving to make changes. There is less rigidity about refusing first-time customers. Geisha are "rented out" to hotels and restaurants. *Maiko* are sent on promotional tours abroad. And bars run by former geisha offer a cheaper alternative to the real thing.

The crisis has led to much discussion about the future. Some believe the flower districts will be preserved as a tourist attraction. Others see them closing down, like Shimabara. But for the moment, geisha still adorn the streets of Kyoto, and wherever they walk they are treated like film stars. Heads turn, and cameras flash.

And so we come back to the pretty picture postcard of a young teenager who represents Kyoto to the outside world. Some take exception to the marketing, seeing in the cuteness a misrepresentation of modern Kyoto. Geisha, after all, play no part in the lives of the vast majority, and what they represent is anathema to some. Yet it is possible to see in the *maiko* much more than just a pretty face. Here, in the guise of a young female, is the embodiment of a heritage, and many of her attributes can be traced back to the court customs of Heian-kyo. The elegant comportment for example, with its web of politeness, connects to the delicate sensitivities of Heian courtiers. The white face, too, for it is thought this originated with aristocrats highlighting their faces when visiting the emperor so that he could make out their features in the gloom that surrounded him.

"Geisha remain the last bastion of traditional accomplishments," writes Tanaka Yuko, "including *shamisen* playing, the singing of traditional songs and narratives, Japanese classical dance, the *taiko* drum, the Japanese flute, formal etiquette and deportment, the art of donning a kimono, and more." Once denigrated as a glorified prostitute, the geisha now finds herself lauded as cultural icon. Everything about her, from the decorations in her hair to the slippers she wears, speaks of Kyoto's heritage of fine craftsmanship. Nothing exemplifies this more than her crowning glory, the kimono, in which is displayed all the brilliance of Nishijin. Put together the whole ensemble—the clothes, the skills and the comportment—and there stands over 1,000 years of history. Not so much a living doll, as a living tradition.

Chapter Eleven
CITY OF JAPANESENESS

Reinvention

Meiji Japan (1868-1912) is synonymous with modernization and a rapid process of reform. A country that for centuries had been cosily wrapped in isolation was suddenly exposed to the harsh realities of international politics. The challenge was met in remarkable fashion: within decades a feudal country of separate fiefdoms was transformed into a unified state with industrial clout. *Fukoku Kyohei* (Enrich the Country, Strengthen the Military) became the national slogan.

The desire to catch up with the West, which spurred the Meiji government, was driven by a fear of colonization. It was an age when 85 per cent of the world was controlled by foreign powers, and "ambitious Japan" wanted to join the rulers rather than the ruled. The measures taken were swift and radical: samurai were stripped of their powers, feudalism dismantled, and industrialization introduced. To mark the new era off from that of the Tokugawa, the capital was moved to Edo and renamed Tokyo (Eastern Capital).

In 1904-5, just forty years after the sway of the samurai's sword, the country beat Russia in modern warfare. It was an astonishing victory, which marked the first time that an Asian country had defeated a powerful European colonizer. The clash had developed out of the rivalry between the two countries for dominance in Korea and Manchuria. The issue was settled in the Treaty of Portsmouth (1905), which recognized Japan's control of Port Arthur, the South Manchurian railroad, and Korea. The country had forced itself onto the world stage to take its place among the leading powers.

What was Kyoto's part in the new order? When the sixteen-year-old Emperor Meiji left the city in May 1869 to take up residence in Tokyo, tearful citizens lined the streets to see him go. For a city that had been the imperial seat for over a thousand years, it was a traumatic moment. The transfer left it with an empty heart—literally. The imperial estate at Gosho lay vacant, for together with the emperor went his court. That was not all; the new era marked the end of the line, too, for the *daimyo* who had kept estates in the city to bolster the shogunate. There were many who lost their jobs—attendants, craftsmen, artists. The city lost more than its confidence; it lost its very *raison d'être*.

By way of reaction, Kyoto sought to reinvent itself. Almost overnight, it transformed itself from a city of tradition into the country's leading modernizer. A string of firsts came pouring out: the first state schools, the first water-power station, the first large-scale works, the first trams, the first town hall, the first film projection, and the first symphony orchestra.

One notable area in which Kyoto led the way was education. The country's first elementary school was established in 1869, the country's first middle school in 1870, the first girls' school in 1871, and the first kindergarten in 1875. To complement the investment, there was the country's first public library in 1871. It was in keeping with the city's tradition of scholarship, and Kyoto was in time to become a magnet for higher education, second only to Tokyo in its number of universities.

The reinvigoration embraced far more than education, however, and the city also undertook substantial construction projects. The great achievement of the age was the building of the Biwako Canal (1885-90). Nothing quite like it had been seen before. It was an enormous undertaking, which cost ten times the city's annual budget, and meant channelling the water from Lake Biwa over twelve miles through mountainous terrain. As well as transportation, the water was to be used for industry, irrigation and a hydro-electric station (only the second of its kind in the world). Incredibly, the project was entrusted to a newly graduated student named Tanabe Sakuro (1861-1944). It took him five years to complete, and involved Japan's first large-scale dynamite blasting and its largest tunnel. When the canal was ready, the governor declared three days of festivities. Seventeen workers had died, and a stone monument to them declares, "For every victim, a million benefited."

The canal was a forerunner of the large-scale works that have defaced modern Japan, but unlike later projects it was carried out with sensitivity. At Nanzen-ji an aqueduct runs through the grounds of the ancient Zen temple, yet the Victorian brickwork is unintrusive and makes an unusual "feature". The neighbouring incline, where goods were unloaded from boats onto a small railway, has since become something of an attraction. And the landscaped canal along the Philosopher's Walk is now one of the city's chief jewels, famous for its avenue of cherry trees and as a place to promenade.

The drive to modernize led in the 1870s to the erection of Western-style buildings, first in wood and later in red brick. The Imperial Kyoto Museum, built in 1895, is a fine example of the latter. Built in the style of the French Renaissance, it has a classical façade that makes one sole concession to the spirit of place: follow the columns upwards and you find not ancient Greeks, but Buddhist deities.

An area particularly rich in Western architecture is that around Doshisha University in the north of the city. Herein lies an interesting story. Niijima Shimeta (1843-90) was a samurai with an interest in "Dutch learning" (this was European science, transmitted in Edo times through the Dutch at Dejima, the island off Nagasaki). The young man was so eager to learn from the West that in 1864, even before the Meiji Restoration took place, he stowed away on a boat to America. This was at a time when people could still be put to death for foreign travel, and he was lucky to be befriended by the captain, who sponsored him to study at Amherst College. During the nine years he spent in the US, the samurai metamorphosed into Joseph Hardy Neeshima, ordained priest. Two years after returning to Japan, he set up the first church in Kyoto since Momoyama times. He also started an English school, which with funds from American missionary groups he built up into the flourishing Doshisha educational group. The organization bought land from the once mighty Shokoku-ji and set up a centre of learning containing gothic-style administrative buildings, chapel and library, including the oldest red-brick building in Kyoto (1884).

The transfer of land from a Zen to a Christian institution was a sign of the times, as the new government with its Shinto ideology was hostile to Buddhism while being eager to learn from the West. The mania for Westernization reached a peak in the 1880s with the glittering balls at Tokyo's Rokumeikan, a huge Western-style pavilion where the cream of Japanese society donned Western dress and aped foreign manners. The reaction against this trend led to a greater appreciation of the national heritage, and in Kyoto the authorities became more concerned with the preservation of traditions.

The Janus City

Just as Japan became fascinated with Western ways, Europe was infatuated with *Japonisme*. Imports from the Far East became fashion items, and *ukiyo-e* was all the rage in artistic circles. Goods like kimono, bamboo umbrellas and lacquered goods were in demand, and most of the artefacts originated in Kyoto. To promote its products, the city hosted trade fairs and took part in industrial exhibitions. At the same time, there was a strong promotion drive to tap the new market for internal tourism, and the establishment of the geisha dances was part of a campaign to make Kyoto a prime cherry blossom destination.

For the city's 1100th anniversary in 1894, the Kyoto authorities constructed the huge Heian Shrine as a memorial to its heritage. It is dedicated to the first and last emperors to reside in the city: Kammu and Komei. The shrine is a scaled-down copy of the original state hall of Heian-kyo: in contrast to the Western buildings going up all over town, here was a strikingly Chinese piece of architecture. It exemplifies the Janus-nature of post-Restoration Kyoto, as the city looked with one face back to its Heian heritage and with the other towards modernization. Even now, the city remains a baffling mix of progressive tendencies mixed with ultra-conservatism.

As part of the anniversary celebrations, a new annual festival was launched. Named the Jidai Matsuri, or Festival of Ages, it was set for 22 October, the day on which Kammu founded the city. The intention was to restore pride to the old capital by displaying the glory of its history. Here, before the eyes of the world, passed all the famous figures of the city's past, starting with the imperial supporters of the Meiji Restoration and going back all the way to the time of Kammu. There were originally 500 people in the parade (nowadays there are 2,000), and the costumes and props were all made in traditional manner—a hugely expensive undertaking. Take the silk kimono for Murasaki Shikibu, for example, which has cloud patterns woven into a russet fabric and is worth some $8,000. Yet it is hardly even seen during the parade since it is worn under a court robe.

The garden of the Heian Shrine is an extensive affair, surrounding it on three sides. It was constructed by Ogawa Jihei (1860-1933), who sought to capture the spirit of Heian times in a traditional pond-garden. But he also gave the grounds a contemporary feel through a profusion of shrubs, some of which were imported from Europe. The garden is known for its weeping cherry-trees, which in early April make the Western section a fantasy in pink.

Ogawa was one of the top gardeners of the age. He had been adopted into a family of gardeners whose lineage stretches back to 1751, and he was the seventh to bear the name. He helped restore many of the city's gardens, and was known for exploiting the water provided by the Biwako Canal. "I want to be known as a person who returned the city to 'the purple mountains and crystal streams' capital of old," he once said. The "lively waterflow" that characterizes Ogawa's garden can be seen in Maruyama Park, which he restored in 1913. Here he built a central pond, fed by an energetic stream. A waterfall and strategically placed rocks enhance the sound effects. It gives the park something of the joyful freshness of clear water running through old Heian-kyo. Another example of his work can be seen at Murin-an, an end-of-the-century villa belonging to the Meiji statesman, Yamagata Aritomo (1838-1922). It was here that an important conference was held just before the Russo-Japanese war that determined the country's foreign policy. The garden was executed by Ogawa to Yamagata's design, and its main feature is a gentle slope and stream, behind which the eastern hills are "borrowed" as a backdrop. It is an interesting example of experimentation, as the Western-style buildings act as a foil to a garden that mixes traditional elements with a lawn and imported plants. Here in the interplay of water and nature one sees a fusion of East and West.

There are many private estates from this time, and it is interesting to compare the leanings of their owners. Some inclined to traditional retreats, others strove to be modern and Western. One of the old-style estates, Hakusasonso, belonged to an artist called Hashimoto Kansetsu (1883-1945). He was a lover of Chinese art and a tea master, and in literati style he set about creating a suitable retreat. The estate he created in 1916, close to the Silver Pavilion, has a historical feel, as he was a collector of garden items. One of the most intriguing is a group of sad-faced statues he assembled from around the country lamenting the death of Buddha.

Another artist active in pre-war Kyoto was Kawai Kanjiro (1890-1966), a friend of the English potter, Bernard Leech, and one of the originators of the folk art movement (*mingei*) in the 1920s. For hand-made crafts to compete with cheap mass-produced goods was a monumental challenge, and in response Kawai came up with some inspired pottery. Robert Yellin of *The Japan Times* describes the effect:

> *Kawai's output is so tremendous that it almost seems as if some supernatural force was guiding him. "When you become so absorbed in your work that beauty flows naturally then your work truly becomes a work of art," he wrote in an essay titled "We Do Not Work Alone." The somewhat eccentric Kawai was an extraordinary being, like an elf working alone late into the night; many of his pieces are full of a beauty and mystery that one can only describe as otherworldliness.*

Kawai's house, not far from the Kiyomizu pottery area, is preserved as a museum and shows simple rustic tastes with a kiln at the back. He had acquired the land in 1921, and his work there formed an oasis of busy creativity amidst the gathering storm clouds of the 1930s. Even as the potter was shaping his ethereal masterpieces, the country was donning military garb and girding itself for war. It led to defeat, occupation and a fresh wave of Westernization.

War Survivor

The Second World War proved traumatic for Japan, as the pain of defeat was accompanied by the flattening of its large cities. In six months of blanket bombing in 1945 some 300,000 people were killed and over eight million rendered homeless. The nuclear explosions over Hiroshima and Nagasaki added to the devastation. Yet Kyoto survived almost intact: incredibly, just ninety-one houses were destroyed (19,000 were torn down as fire prevention measures). The city had every reason to be fearful, for it was an important manufacturing centre with a population of around a million. Yet it was spared by the intervention of a single man—the US Secretary of War, Henry Stimson.

By good fortune, Stimson happened to be familiar with Japan. He had visited in 1926 and was aware of Kyoto's centrality to the nation's culture. Accordingly, he gave instructions for the B-29s to spare the city. Nonetheless, Kyoto was then selected as the number one choice for the Atomic Bomb Target Committee, but again Stimson came to the rescue. "I struck off the list of suggested targets the city of Kyoto," he wrote: "Although it was a target of considerable military importance, it had been the ancient capital of Japan and was a shrine of Japanese art and architecture."

Following the war, as Japan set about the business of recovery, workers flocked to the large-scale rebuilding in the big cities. This post-war reconstruction helps to explain Kyoto's relative lack of growth. In 1940, the city stood in third place in terms of population, behind Tokyo and Osaka. By 1960, it was in fifth place behind Nagoya and Yokohama. By 2004 it was in seventh place, just behind Sapporo and Kobe. While the younger cities expanded, Kyoto was constrained by its heritage and geography, as the traditional industries and enclosing hills restricted its expansion.

For a while, the old capital remained relatively untouched by post-war developments. Films of the 1950s show a traditional cityscape of wooden houses and towering pagodas. All was to change, however, with the rapid growth of the 1960s as large-scale construction transformed the city centre into one of ferro-concrete. Immodest high rises thrust their way to prominence, and brash American-style shops asserted their neon presence.

Japan's "economic miracle" can be attributed to a number of factors. Demilitarization and migration from the countryside meant the availability of a large pool of labour, while the ban on rearmament enabled capital to be directed towards priority industries such as coal and steel. At the same time, redistribution of land boosted rural production, and the high rate of Japanese savings meant that surplus money could be invested in new equipment. The well-educated urban population was driven by a strong work ethic, and government policies ensured that manufacturers were aided by protection of the home market. As a result the country witnessed a take-off in economic terms, with an average annual growth rate through the 1960s of eleven per cent.

With the increase in affluence, traditional mores gave way to modernity. While Tokyo embraced progress with open arms, Kyoto as the old capital was seen as a stronghold of qualities that were being sacrificed in the rush to economic success. Representations of the city focussed with nostalgic fondness on the ties with the past that were fast disappearing. Many of the portrayals were literary in nature, but others were the product of a vigorous new artform that had taken root in Kyoto—the cinema.

The Japanese Hollywood

It all started with Lumière. Literally. Inabata Katsutaro (1862-1953) was a Nishijin businessman who happened to study in Paris in the same class as Auguste Lumière. Together with his brother, Louis, the Frenchman had invented a machine to project film, and when he offered his former classmate the chance to acquire it, Inabata jumped at the chance:

> I believed that this would be the most appropriate device for intro-
> ducing contemporary Western culture to our country, and so I asked
> the doctor [Lumière] for a monopoly right in Japan, and came back
> with one engineer and a few pieces of equipment.

Back in Kyoto, Inabata managed a successful projection for the first time in January 1897. A public showing followed in Osaka. He then sold out to Yokota Einosuke, whose company was the precursor of Nikkatsu. One of his teams made a documentary of the Russo-Japanese War (1904-5). More importantly, in 1907 he recruited the man who was to become "the father of Japanese cinema"—Makino Shozo (1878-1929). Makino had been the manager of Kyoto's Senbon-za Theatre, and his first film as director, *The Battle of Honno-ji* (1908), successfully exploited the city's historical associations and set the pattern for the future. Makino went on to make over 300 silent movies and, almost single-handedly, created the genre of *jidaigeki* (historical drama).

In 1908 Makino hired a young Kabuki actor called Onoe Matsunosuke (1875-1926), whom he turned into the country's first movie star. The actor made over 1,000 silent movies in all, and at his peak was churning out nine a month. His flamboyant style, derived from Kabuki, featured acrobatic stunts and rolling eyes, giving rise to his nickname "Eyeball Matchan". These early films were anything but silent, since they were accompanied by a narrator called *benshi* who not only delivered lines but provided a running commentary. This was done in theatrical manner, and some performers even became famous in their own right. Rather than the film, audiences went to see their favourite narrator.

In 1912, Makino's success led Nikkatsu to make Kyoto its base for historical movies. Thus was formalized a split by which Tokyo studios took charge of contemporary films and Kyoto the period films. The framing of Japaneseness thus became a bipolar venture, with the city of the eternal present set off from the city with a past. By the 1920s, Makino had moved away from the stylized choreography of Kabuki towards greater realism, particularly in terms of sword-fighting. Emphasis was put on action rather than atmosphere, and his success enabled him to build his own studio in 1925. It coincided with a Golden Age for Kyoto in cinema terms.

The Great Kanto Earthquake of 1923, which devastated Tokyo and Yokohama, destroyed half a million homes and forced the relocation of several major studios to Kyoto. The heart of the film-making area was at Uzumasa, and the production rate was staggering: by the 1930s over 500 films a year were being made in the city. This was a time when Japanese cinema was second in output only to that of the US, though tragically fewer than two per cent of these pre-war films still exist.

Kyoto's *jidaigeki* were a huge favourite with the nation, and by one estimate they made up some forty per cent of Japan's pre-war output. The majority were samurai movies, and these make an interesting parallel with the Western, which before the 1960s made up nearly a quarter of all US films. It was as if in both countries, after a period of rapid modernization, the populace needed to digest social changes through a return to the past. It gave rise in both cases to a mythic version of history; on one side stood a heroic cowboy spreading civilization through the power of his gun, on the other a samurai dispensing justice in the slash of a sword. The images clashed in the Pacific War, but afterwards came together in the person of Kurosawa Akira, whose love of Westerns led him to create *Seven Samurai* (1954) and *Yojimbo* (1961). These inspired in turn *The Magnificent Seven* (1960) and *A Fistful of Dollars* (1964). It was like a game of cultural give-and-take.

With film stars and studios based in Kyoto, this was the heyday of "the Japanese Hollywood". The glamour of the period is typified by the villa of Okochi Denjiro (1898-1962), up on the western hills. An actor with a long and successful career, Okochi made his name in *Tange Sazen* (1935) as a samurai with scarred eye and missing arm—a kind of Nelson in warrior uniform. The actor used his money to set up house on a hilltop in Arashiyama. The setting is very much the stuff of dreams: on one side it overlooks a river gorge, while on the other it looks over Kyoto's northern fringes. A lifelong Buddhist, Okochi sought communion with nature, and the promenade garden he created with its tasteful paths and borrowed scenery combines austerity with elegance. It is a star's home, with a Zen feel—a physical reminder of Kyoto's glory days as a thriving cinema centre.

By the 1960s the bubble was bursting, as the studio system began to break down. The rise of television, the return of production to Tokyo, a downturn in demand for *jidaigeki*, outsourcing and location shooting dealt one blow after another. Now there only remains the Toei Movie Land, a mini-version of Universal's theme park, where samurai movies are still occasionally shot for television. For Kyoto's time as the Japanese Hollywood, it was a decisive call of "Cut!"

Kurosawa's Gate

During the 1930s, samurai films had been used to promote nationalist values such as self-sacrifice and the acceptance of authority. This led the US Occupation Forces to issue a ban on all films "favoring or approving feudal loyalty and direct or indirect approval of suicide". It was not until 1950 that the *jidaigeki* recovered, and it did so in the most stunning manner. The breakthrough came with a Kyoto film that in 1951 won the coveted Golden Lion at Venice. The director was Kurosawa Akira (1910-98), and the film was *Rashomon*.

The story concerns a twelfth-century rape told from differing points of view, and the conflicting versions suggest the impossibility of ever knowing the "truth". To the baffled studio executives who questioned his purpose, Kurosawa explained it like this:

Human beings are unable to be honest with themselves about them-selves. They cannot talk about things without embellishing. This script portrays such human beings, the kind who cannot survive without lies to make them feel they are better people than they really are. Egoism is a sin the human being carries with him from birth; it is the most difficult to redeem.

The result was a film that spoke to the despair of post-war Japan as it struggled to come to terms with the new realities. It seemed to capture the way that pre-war simplicities had been replaced by conflicting "truths".

The film script was adapted from two short stories by Akutagawa Ryunosuke (1892-1927): "In a Grove" supplied the plot, while "Rashomon" provided little more than the titular gate. Kurosawa made several changes, including the addition of a cynical commoner who counters the priest's belief in human salvation:

> Commoner: *If men don't trust each other, this earth might as well be dead.*
> Priest: *No! I don't want to believe that!*
> Commoner: *No one will hear you, no matter how loud you shout. Just think. Which one of these stories do you believe?*
> Woodcutter: *None makes any sense.*
> Commoner: *Don't worry about it. It isn't as if men were reasonable.*

The bleak view of the world derived from Akutagawa's own experience; he killed himself at thirty-five for fear of going mad like his mother. But his nihilistic story was given a more hopeful ending by Kurosawa through the device of a baby abandoned at the gate. Though the commoner steals its clothes, claiming it will soon die, the woodcutter selflessly offers to take it home. This act helps to restore the priest's faith in mankind. The director was here pointing to the kind of thinking needed for Japan to overcome its post-war despair.

The film was made in the heat of a Kyoto summer, which fostered its suffocating character, and is notable for launching the career of Mifune Toshiro (1920-97). "I'm a person who is rarely impressed by actors, but in the case of Mifune I was completely overwhelmed," Kurosawa said. The pair went on to become one of cinema's greatest ever director-actor teams. Most of the film was shot on location in Kyoto (Honno-ji) and Nara. There was only one set: the crumbling Rashomon gate. It was intended to be a simple recreation, but it grew in the director's mind until, like Frankenstein's monster, it took on a life of its own. "What we built as a set was gigantic," said Kurosawa; "It was so immense that a complete roof would have buckled the support pillars... for the price of that one mammoth set they could have had over a hundred ordinary sets." The decaying structure dominates the scenes in which it appears, and for most people it presents the defining image of late Heian-kyo. Once again the city was trading on its past.

Mizoguchi's City

Kurosawa was part of a "holy trinity" of Japanese directors active during the post-war years. The others were Mizoguchi Kenji (1898-1956) and Ozu Yasujiro (1903-63). The latter, famous for *Tokyo Story* (1953), had an interest in fathers and families. Mizoguchi, by contrast, is associated with women and Kyoto. He not only spent his working life in the city, but used it as a setting for several of his award-winning films. Born in Tokyo, he had moved to Kyoto after the earthquake of 1923 destroyed the Nikkatsu studio for which he made his first film. He spent the rest of his life in the city and made over eighty films, although only half of these survive. He is remembered for his "feminist" subject-matter and his "one-scene, one-shot" technique: the former owes much to his family background, the latter to his training in Japanese art.

The son of a carpenter, Mizoguchi suffered misfortune at seven when his father bankrupted the family, with the result that they had to move to the poorest part of town. Desperate for money, his parents put up their fourteen-year-old daughter for adoption and she was sold to a geisha house. She found an aristocratic patron, whom she was able to marry following the death of his wife. The money from her patronage she used to fund her brother's studies in art and literature.

These events helped shape Mizoguchi's perception of life, and sympathy with the long-suffering mother was transmuted by the son into tragic and selfless heroines. At the same time, the blame Mizoguchi assigned his father found expression in deluded and oppressive male characters. He had a strong sense of class and injustice; he took part in Marxist demonstrations in his youth, and his early films were politically engaged. In the late 1930s, however, he was pressured into making patriotic films about samurai. After the war he returned to his theme of persecuted women, which fitted in with the anti-feudal tone of the occupation. Then, just when it seemed he had fallen out of favour, he found international acclaim with a trio of late masterpieces: *The Life of Oharu* (1952), *Ugetsu* (1953), and *Sansho the Bailiff* (1954).

The hallmark of Mizoguchi's films is the creation of atmosphere. Mood takes precedence over narrative as crafted vignettes fill the screen with a melancholic beauty in the tradition of *mono no aware*. In his desire not to disrupt the action, the director developed his "one-shot, one take" technique. It is as if the camera is rooted to the spot by the intensity of the moment. "He preferred long takes, and managed to squeeze into that one take all the trials and tribulations of life," observed Shindo Kaneto, a one-time collaborator. The director was a perfectionist and could be demanding, even irascible. It was hard for his staff perhaps, but the viewer reaps the benefit in knowing that all possible effort has been made to get the films right. Some have been mentioned in earlier chapters: *The New Tale of the Heike, Tale of an Amorous Man, Chushingura, Gion Sisters* and *Gion Bayashi*.

Personally, I find *The Life of Oharu (Koushoku Ichidai Onna)* to be the film that most haunts the imagination. Critics are divided over whether it outranks *Ugetsu* as Mizoguchi's masterpiece, but the director himself thought it to be his best. The film was a personal project into which Mizoguchi threw all his resources. According to screenwriter Yoda Yoshitaka, it was made in reaction to Kurosawa's triumph with *Rashomon*, which goaded the director into framing his own personal vision. Shot in Kyoto, it cost about six times the average for a film of the time. The story was taken from Saikaku's book *Tale of an Amorous Woman*. It combined the director's love of history with his theme of suffering women and starred his cinematic muse, Tanaka Kinuyo, with whom he was secretly in love. Perhaps this helped to enhance the tragic intensity of the film, whose epic scope makes it a female counterpart to *King Lear*. Consider what happens to the heroine, Oharu. She begins as an elegant lady-in-waiting, but loses her position at court after an affair with a man of lower rank, and then plunges from one disaster to another until she reaches rock bottom as an aging prostitute mocked for her looks. She ends up a penniless wandering nun.

For many, the film is unremittingly bleak. Yet it closes with a visionary moment. It was made after Mizoguchi came to believe in Nichiren Buddhism, and he gives the story a religious framework by starting and closing the film with temple settings. As Oharu goes begging from door to door in the final scene, she stops to pray, and the look on her face suggests she has come to terms with her life. Swelling religious music underlines the message: if Oharu can rise above her fate, then surely so can we.

The film brings together all the characteristics of late Mizoguchi: the evocation of time and place; the theme of suffering women; the attack on a feudal past; and a pictorialism that is steeped in the Japanese tradition. Among its most fervent fans was Jean-Luc Goddard, who saw the film more than twelve times. It brought Mizoguchi to world attention, and won him many admirers. Kurosawa was among them: "Of all Japanese directors, I like him the best. He creates a world which is purely Japanese," he said. But perhaps the most fulsome praise came from the respected film critic, Robin Wood. "If cinema has yet produced a Shakespeare," he wrote, "its Shakespeare is Mizoguchi."

Tanizaki's Key

Around the same time that Mizoguchi was portraying Kyoto on film, the three leading writers of the age turned their thoughts to the old capital. It was a curious coincidence, as if they sensed that in the forging of a new Japan time was running out for traditional ways. Within six years of each other Tanizaki, Mishima and Kawabata brought out *Kagi* (1956), *Kinkaku-ji* (1956), and *Koto* (1961-2). The novels all enjoyed success, and have been translated as *The Key*, *The Temple of the Golden Pavilion* and *The Old Capital* respectively. Their hold on the popular imagination has resulted in five different films, as the latter two were twice adapted for the big screen.

The authors had all started life with cosmopolitan tastes, yet each came to cherish their own version of "Japaneseness". Perhaps it was no coincidence, then, that they turned to Kyoto as a setting. At first glance, their stories have little in common: the sexual games of an aging professor; a disturbed youth's act of arson; and a young girl's search for her twin. Yet all are in a sense about obsession and beauty. It is as if the authors had steeped themselves in Kyoto's traditions in order to write of their own compulsions.

The first of the books to come out was by Tanizaki Junichiro (1886-1965), whose life illustrates the symbolic nature of Kyoto for his generation. Raised in Tokyo, he had cultivated Western tastes as a young man and held a strong bias towards anything foreign. "In spite of being Japanese, I hated Japan," he wrote:

> *Everything labelled as Western seemed beautiful and aroused my envy. I could not help looking at the West in some way that human beings look up to the gods... I made up my mind that the only way to develop my art fully was to come into ever closer contact with the West, if only by an inch closer than before, or even by assimilating myself into the West.*

The turning point for Tanizaki, as it was for Mizoguchi, was the Great Kanto Earthquake of 1923. Following this disaster, the author relocated to Kansai, where he discovered the appeal of traditional arts. "I loved the old Japan as a form of exoticism, in precisely the same way that a foreigner treasures the prints of Hiroshige," he wrote. In his novel *Some Prefer Nettles* (1928-9), Tanizaki writes of a Westernized man who is converted to Japanese ways through his father-in-law. The old man keeps a geisha mistress, and his attachment to the past is symbolized by the saké set he takes with him on outings:

> *The cup was one of three decorated in gold on vermilion with scenes from Hiroshige's prints, the old man having taken recently to insisting that saké must be drunk from wooden lacquerware. Everything—the saké, sweets, the cup, and boxes had been brought from Kyoto: with just such an assortment of gold-flecked lacquer, one could imagine, court maidens set out long ago to view the cherry blossoms.*

Five years later, Tanizaki brought out an essay on Japanese aesthetics that has won much attention. *In Praise of Shadows* (1933-4) was a follow-the-pen ramble which claimed that the climate had nurtured a tendency in Japanese architecture towards heavy roofs and dark interiors. From this had emerged an aesthetic of shadows. The use of gold leaf was a case in point, as it was intended for viewing in the dim half-light of temples. The theory, it followed, had implications for writing too. "In the mansion called literature," Tanizaki wrote, "I would have the eaves deep and the walls dark, I would push back into the shadows the things that come out too clearly, I would strip away the useless decoration."

Tanizaki's masterpiece, *The Makioka Sisters* (1943-8), is a case in point. Through the focus is on a family of four sisters from a traditional Osaka household, it describes a culture of hints and implication that flows with the rhythm of the seasons. The sisters are fond of trips to Kyoto (one feels they belong there), and one of the set-pieces is their trip to see the city's cherry-blossom. In Japanese fashion, this is turned into a seasonal rite:

> *The annual procedure was fixed; they arrived in Kyoto on Saturday afternoon, had an early dinner at the Hyotan Restaurant, and, after the spring dances, which they never missed, saw the Gion cherries by lantern light. On Sunday morning they went to the western suburbs. After lunch by the river at Arashiyama, they returned to the city in time to see the weeping cherries in the Heian Shrine; and with that, whether or not Teinosukue and Sachiko stayed on another night by themselves, the outing proper was finished.*

By the time Tanizaki came to write *The Key*, he was seventy. He already had a reputation for prurience, and the novel showed that his sexual interest remained as vigorous as ever. The protagonist, a fifty-five-year-old Kyoto professor with a waning sex drive, tries to manipulate his wife into an affair with their daughter's fiancé. Though the forty-four-year-old wife is a traditional Kyoto type, beneath her demure appearance there simmers a fiery passion. She would never admit to it, but one has the feeling that she is willingly playing along with her husband's schemes.

The titular "key" is that of the professor's diary, which he deliberately leaves in a place that he thinks his wife will find. Keys are a well-known phallic symbol (Shakespeare enjoyed playing with the word), but beyond that lies "the key" to human identity. By revealing his erotic thoughts, the professor lays bare his soul—or seems to, for he may be consciously shaping his writing for the eyes of his wife. If for some philosophers, you are what you think, for Tanizaki you are what you feel, and in his last novel, *Diary of a Mad Old Man* (1961), he wrote of a protagonist who "constantly needed to feel sexual desire, it helped him to keep alive."

Tanizaki's relationship with Kyoto was also a kind of love affair, and in a 1965 essay he wrote of how he had been "irresistibly lured from my native Tokyo by a sultry temptress in Western Japan." He lived for two periods in the city, once briefly in 1923, and then for a number of years after 1949. The food and women appealed to him, especially the latter. Kyoto women have long been famous for their beauty, and there is even a subgenre of painting dedicated to them called *Kyo bijinga*, or Kyoto Beauties. Saikaku ascribed their physical appeal to the quality of the water, but Tanizaki suggested it was rather the tradition of sending pretty girls to serve at court. Their offspring, trained in arts and graces, added elegance to their natural beauty.

Though the author moved away from Kyoto in later life, he returned every spring and autumn. He also arranged to have a grave at Honen-in, and his last novel suggests why. "I don't like the Tokyo of today," says the old man to his daughter: "I feel more nostalgic for Kyoto, which has a kind of charm that reminds me of what Tokyo used to be...":

> *"Then isn't Honen-in best?" said Itsuko, as we were going down the steps from Manjuin. "This temple is too out of the way, and even with Kurodani nobody would climb the hill unless they were making a special visit."*
>
> *"That's what I think too."*
>
> *"Honen-in is right in the city now, close to the streetcar line, and when the cherries are in bloom along the canal it's quite pretty; yet the moment you're in the hush of that temple compound you naturally feel calm. I'd say it's just the place for you."*

Given his love of Kyoto, it was perhaps only appropriate that the great literary passion of Tanizaki's life was *The Tale of Genji*. Such was his fascination that he translated it three different times into modern Japanese—no mean feat for such a huge novel. It combined several of his preoccupations: the oedipal pursuit of women, the delicate description of senses, the nature of beauty, and a poetic style of writing. "In his masterly storytelling and loving appreciation of traditional Japanese concepts of beauty, Tanizaki, more than any of his contemporaries, carried on the literary tradition of the Heian period," claimed the critic Takehiro Noguchi. Steeped in the culture of the city, Tanizaki is as close as Kyoto has come in modern times to producing a great writer.

Mishima's Golden Pavilion

The Temple of the Golden Pavilion came out in 1956, the same year as Tanizaki's novel. It was the time of the Suez crisis, when there were worldwide signs of change. In Britain the emergence of the Angry Young Man signalled dissatisfaction with the class system. In the US, Elvis Presley ripped open the generation gap with his first hit. And in Japan *Season of the Sun* by Ishihara Shintaro inaugurated a genre about dislocated youth raised on American values.

Mishima's novel also dealt with alienation, though his stuttering hero could hardly have anything less in common with the privileged figures of Ishihara's "sun tribe". It was based on a notorious case of arson that took place in 1950 when a young monk attached to the Golden Temple burned it down. The incident shocked the nation: a prized cultural treasure had survived the war only to be destroyed by one of its own. The arsonist was the son of a poor provincial priest who had been sent to train in Zen at the Golden Pavilion. Using this simple framework, Mishima Yukio (1925-70) created a psychological novel of stunning brilliance. In probing a psychotic mind, the author brought into play many of his favoured themes: child trauma, troubled sexuality, an obsession with beauty, and the purgative value of destruction.

Mishima's protagonist, named Mizoguchi, has a formative experience as a boy when he witnesses his mother's adultery. His father, covering his son's eyes, tells him of the Golden Temple whose beauty is such that it can dispel all sordid thoughts. Out of this childhood trauma is born a tormented mind that meshes beauty, sexuality, guilt and self-hate. Such is the potency of the writing that it weaves together a host of barely connected themes, one of which is oedipal. This is reinforced by the repeated imagery of breasts, and even the Golden Temple at one point assumes a breast-like shape as if to assert its role as substitute mother.

Throughout the book the beauty of the temple taunts the plain and stuttering Mizoguchi. His alienation is deepened by the corruption around him, and his destructive impulses are fed by social frustration and sexual impotence. Zen Koans vie within him with thoughts of destruction. As the troubled youth withdraws within himself, it seems that his only release is through violence and he sets fire to the building that so obsesses him; it is the only way to "liberation". When the temple goes up in flames, the phoenix that sits atop the roof speaks of the possibility of rebirth, and this is how the novel ends with Mizoguchi seated on a hill calmly watching his handiwork:

Then I noticed the pack of cigarettes in my other packet. I took one out and started smoking. I felt like a man who settled down for a smoke after finishing a job of work. I wanted to live.

The intensity of the writing owed itself no doubt to the way it fed off Mishima's own psychology. He had been brought up by a possessive and sickly grandmother, whose bed he shared until the age of twelve. It shaped his longing for escape, which took the form of story telling, a love of masks, and a yearning for death. Eros and Thanatos had bedded down within his soul, and from an early age he was fascinated with the imagery of swords penetrating flesh. His first orgasm took place on seeing a picture of St. Sebastian pierced by arrows, and during the war Mishima had been thrilled by the fiery apocalypse visited on Tokyo when the city burned "like a distant bonfire in a great banquet of extravagant death and destruction". A similar notion informs his novel, in which the temple seems consumed by the fires of Mizoguchi's desire.

Yet was it not natural that, when my will to live depended entirely on fire, my lust, too, should have turned in that direction? My desire molded the supple figure of the fire, and the flames, conscious that they were being seen by me through the shining black pillar, adorned themselves gracefully for the occasion.

Mishima's novel addressed a readership disoriented by defeat and occupation. As the young adopted the values of their conquerors, intellectuals became concerned about the spread of selfish materialism and the loss of traditional values. "We watched Japanese became drunk on prosperity and fall into an emptiness of spirit," said Mishima of his generation. It was this consciousness that lent the book a wider resonance. In the burning of the beauty by the beast, it seemed that Mishima had portrayed more than the tortured conflicts of a solitary soul; he had portrayed the turmoil of a nation.

It was precisely this resonance that appealed to the first of the novel's adapters, Ichikawa Kon (b. 1915). One of the top post-war directors, he enjoyed many successes (notably *Harp of Burma*, 1956), but said that *Enjo* (*Conflagration*, 1958) was his favourite. He saw in Mishima's novel an expression of the "pain of the age", and with the author's permission changed the emphasis to present the portrait of an alienated youth. Whereas Mishima's introverted hero is preoccupied with beauty, Ichikawa's troubled hero makes a stand against corruption. The altered emphasis was reflected in the altered title.

A later version, Takabayashi's *The Temple of the Golden Pavilion* (1976), took a more personal line and drew parallels between Mizoguchi and Mishima himself. It was made after the author's spectacular death by *hara-kiri* in 1970, which prompted the director to draw out the biographical aspects. This was the line taken, too, in the first "chapter" of the much praised bio-pic, *Mishima* (1985), by the Schrader brothers. The shy, budding homosexual with a speech impediment (Mishima in black and white) merges into the stuttering, impotent Zen acolyte (Mizoguchi in the colourful world of the imagination). The unattainable nature of beauty destroys both.

Kawabata's Old Capital

In *The Old Capital,* Kyoto is painted in nostalgic terms as a city in tune with the seasons, and the novel makes plain its elegiac nature in its very title. It was in keeping with the post-war declaration by its author, Kawabata Yasunari (1899-1972): "I have the strong, unavoidable feeling that my life is already at an end. For me there is only the solitary return to the mountains and rivers of the past. From this point on, as one already dead, I intend to write only of the poor beauty of Japan, not a line else."

At the heart of Kawabata's novel stands Chieko, the abandoned child of a poor woodcutter who has been brought up in the household of a Muromachi kimono designer. Her twin, Naoko, stayed in the family home and is a dark-skinned woodcutter who has been working since the age of seven. When the pair meet by chance during the Gion Festival, they recognize their likeness in each other. The social gap between them is vast, yet they share a desire to be together. At one point when they are caught in a storm they hug each other for protection, like babes in the womb. Yet the bond proves only temporary. Though Chieko invites Naoko to live with her, the woodcutter feels out of place in the well-to-do world and knows she would spoil her sister's wedding chances.

The theme of separation is one that resonates with Kawabata's own childhood. His earliest years brought one loss after another. His father died when he was two, his mother the following year. Separated from his sister, he was brought up by his grandparents. Then his grandmother died when he was seven, three years later his sister, and five years after that his grandfather. By the age of fifteen, all his closest family members had passed on, and he was known as "Master of Funerals" for his expertise.

The yearning for wholeness became his central theme and is found in most of his works. Here it takes the form of the light-skinned city-child and the dark-skinned child of nature, as if the yin and yang of life were in search of each other. Yet the point of the book hardly seems to lie in the story at all, but in the loving descriptions. At times it reads like a tour guide, at others like a lyrical evocation of place.

> *The groves of pines in Gosho and the imperial villa of Shugakuin and the trees in the expansive gardens of the old temples all catch the eye of the traveler, as do the rows of weeping willows in the centre of the city, along the banks of the Takase River. In Kiya, Gojo, and Horikawa, the willows truly weep, their branches drooping as if they would touch the ground. How gentle they are, these willows, and the red pines of Kitayama, whose branches sketch soft circles as they seem to join one to the next.*

The novel reverses normal fiction in which nature serves as background to human actions, as the city itself seems to act as the central character. It calls to mind Edward Seidensticker's comments about *Snow Country* (1935-48): "So fleeting and insubstantial is the affair that lyrical evocation of the mountain background almost seems to be Kawabata's principal concern."

Between the poetic lines one senses a city in flux, as if the book is mourning the passing of the old ways. Though Chieko's father is a lover of beauty in the old ways, he is going bankrupt and the future belongs to her fiancé, a charmless type who wants to introduce efficiency to the family business. It is as if the economic dynamic of modern life is forcing the city away from the seasonal round, separating it from nature, just as Chieko is separated from Naoko. Yet this is not a book of protest, but one of resigned acceptance. Kawabata's roots lay in

Buddhism, and his novel articulates the aesthetic of *mono no aware*. If all things must pass, then so, too, must the charms of the old ways. His book is a long melancholic sigh, a poetic rendition of what Donald Richie calls Japan's "national mantra": *shikata ga nai* (it can't be helped).

That the charms of old Kyoto are still there for those inclined to seek them is evident in Pico Iyer's *The Lady and the Monk* (1991). It is one of life's ironies that while outsiders like Iyer lovingly search out the "lost Japan", contemporary Japanese like the Kyoto-born Marukami Haruki write books that are almost exclusively Western-oriented. Read *Norwegian Wood* (1987) and you find a plethora of brand names and cultural references, not a single one of which is Japanese.

Iyer's Kyoto, like Kawabata's, is one of a delicate elegance that shields itself from the outside. Like a classical beauty, she protects herself with "cruel politenesses" from those who for centuries have been coming to ferret out her secrets. The author is a respected travel writer, and the sensitivity to place shows in his writing. Here are laid out all the city's finer aspects, from the intensity of the seasonal colours to the mysteries of Zen and the splendour of the festivals.

> *Here, after all, was a city built on an imperial grid, yet curlicued with scented gardens and pretty floral canals. Here was a city still inscribed with the bloody feuds conducted in its hooded temples and dark castles, yet a city that was now a repository of all that country's female arts. Kyoto today was the center of kimono and flower arrangement and geisha: of lacquerwork, paper umbrellas, and fans. Even the Kyoto dialect was famously a girls' tongue, best suited to a high, melodious delivery, in which* arigato *became* okini, *and* wakaranai, wakarahen. "Every city has its sex," *Kazantzakis had pronounced unequivocally. "This one is all female."*

It is here in "this most conservative of cities, in one of the most traditional of all societies" that Iyer finds the Heian lady of his dreams. Yes, it is a love story set in Kyoto, but more than that it is a story of love for what the city represents. In an age of "internationalization" it is perhaps only right that this graceful lady should be celebrated by a foreigner. "Four Seasons in Kyoto" runs the subtitle: one only wishes there were more.

The Modern Metropolis

When *gaijin* get together in Kyoto, they sometimes like to imagine the bemusement of tourists arriving in the city. "The soul of the nation"; "the heart of Japan"; "the home of traditional arts": such are the epithets that may have lured them. The first impressions can prove a shock. A railway station that looks like the inside of a giant spaceship. Roads that are clogged with traffic jams. A city of high-rises, neon lights, and overhead wires. "When you view Kyoto from any point of vantage, such as the elevated platform where the Bullet Train deposits you, its ugliness can make you weep," wrote Alan Booth in *Looking for the Lost* (1995).

Oddly enough, it is foreigners who seem the most outraged about the perceived failure to preserve Kyoto. "The Americans spared the city in the war, but the Japanese destroyed it afterwards," runs a popular quip. People joke too about how a city that lent its name to the Kyoto Protocol, framed in 1997 to tackle global warming, is run by an assembly for whom environmentalism means adorning nature with the liberal use of concrete. Local commentator, Alex Kerr, has been one of the most outspoken: "Kyoto hates Kyoto," he says of the authorities. He sees the building of the Kyoto Tower in 1964, to coincide with the Tokyo Olympics, as the beginning of the end. It was intended to show off the city's modernity by thrusting gloriously upwards through the low canopy of the housing, like a giant candle. For Kerr, it is more like "a stake through the heart".

Yet this dismal view is at best no more than a partial truth, which ignores the modern city's many attractions. There is a vigorous dynamism in the ever-changing urban scene and within the fold of the major arteries are quiet side streets where people go about age-old practices. Along with the bland apartment blocks is some exciting modern architecture, such as the Kyoto Concert Hall in the north, and in the interstices of the city are areas that combine natural beauty with historical interest. You can walk virtually the length of Kyoto, from Kiyomizu to Ginkaku-ji, and find a photographer's paradise the whole way, and in spring there is cherry-blossom heaven along the many miles of riverside and canal. If urban blues begin to bite, there are any number of pleasant mountain trails on the green fringes, so close to hand that they actually start in city lanes.

For the authorities, keeping up with the Osakas and Nagoyas of the country is a major concern, and the city's official website stresses the need to avoid being "a living museum". Most of the Kyotoites I know share a similar attitude, believing that the gains of progress outweigh the losses. Take local guide "Johnny Hillwalker", for example, who sees the controversial Kyoto Station as a welcome asset to the city. "Change is good," he says, "even the geisha are changing. Those who want to keep things as they were are strange to me." His view echoes the Buddhist notion that life is in eternal flux. "The relationship between tradition and change in Japan has always been complicated by the fact that change is in itself a tradition," notes Edward Seidensticker.

Modern industries now complement Kyoto's traditional crafts, and visitors are often surprised to learn that video game giant Nintendo has its head office in Kyoto. Another flourishing company is Kyocera, which produces semi-conductors, mobile phones and ceramic goods. Nishijin, too, has gone high-tech, with state-of-the-art machinery for its textile business. Nonetheless, it is tourism and the service industries that continue to make up the bulk (65 per cent) of the workforce. It is also a city of education, with the highest ratio of students to citizens in Japan: over 135,000 are enrolled at twenty-two universities, with another 14,000 at junior colleges. In this way the legacy of the past is infused with the vitality of youth, and alongside the temples you can find hip-hop dives, experimental arts, and a vibrant music scene.

It has been claimed that after Mecca in Saudi Arabia, Kyoto is the second most visited place on earth. Some forty million people descend on the city each year, of whom only 800,000 are foreigners. A good proportion are Japanese schoolchildren bussed in to learn of a heritage which is increasingly alien to them. Then there are those coming for religious events at the head temples of Buddhist sects. The city is also home to several *iemoto*, the heads of Japanese traditional arts (such as tea, music and dance) who form the apex of vast "pyramids" which funnel their money upwards. The Ikenobo School of *ikebana* is an example, with a soaring modern building dwarfing the hexagonal temple next door where flower arranging first began in Muromachi times.

For tourists, the number one destination is Kiyomizu Temple on the eastern hills. Founded in 798, it is famed for its views and surrounded by green woods. Among the attractions is a three-layered pagoda, a shrine noted for bringing luck in love, and a spring with healing properties. But its most famous feature is the fifty-foot platform supported by 139 pillars which projects out from the main hall over a precipice. The drop is terrifying, and you can see why "leaping from the Kiyomizu platform" should have come to mean taking a bold step.

There are many other sights in the city, but it is not just for these that visitors come, for nearly every day there is a special event of some kind taking place. Can anywhere compare with Kyoto in this respect? The major affairs attract hundreds of thousands, with the big three being the Aoi Festival (May), Gion Festival (July), and the Festival of Ages (Jidai Matsuri, in October). Other events also enjoy a wider fame: the January gathering of *kyudo* (Japanese archery) at Sanjusangendo; the springtime geisha dances; Mifune Boat Festival in May, with its Heian-era flotilla; the Kurama Fire Festival in October, when enormous torches shed sparks over participants; and the autumn "light-ups" at temples when buildings and maple trees are illuminated to spectacular effect.

Some of the best experiences, however, are to be had at the lesser-known events: the re-enactments of Heian poetry competitions, for example, or the full moon ceremony at Kurama with its Himalayan rites. Then there are the sprawling monthly flea markets, Kobo-san at To-ji and Tenjin-san at Kitano Tenmangu, to which bargain-hunters flock in pursuit of unexpected "treasures". And alongside these are the innumerable religious oddities. Priests who imitate the cawing of crows, cucumbers rubbed over the body to prevent illness, a memorial service for sewing needles, the ceremonial burning of old dolls, or a festival to pacify the spirit of falling blossoms. And if all that is not enough, there are the 8000 Daruma dolls at Horin-ji, the 8,000 statues of Adashino Nembutsu-ji, or the bell-crickets of Kegon-ji which chirp the whole year round.

Kyoto's backstreets have their attractions too, and exploring them can be something of an adventure in itself. Walk ten minutes away from the bustling streets, and you can find yourself in a backwater of old shrines and quiet housing. It is here that one gets a feel for the city of wood that Kyoto once was. Diane Durston's *Old Kyoto* (1986) is a litany of love to the old ways: "The famous temples and manicured villas may define the rarefied soul of feudal Japan," she writes, "but the old noodle shops and inns, the teahouses and bucket makers, are the marrow of its bones."

Twenty per cent of Japan's traditional craftsmen live in Kyoto, and this is the home of potters and weavers, doll-makers and Noh actors, teachers of dance and teachers of tea. It is here one finds the *machiya*, of which 27,000 remain in downtown Kyoto alone. Many of these shop-residences still contain crafts or kimono businesses, as they have done for generations. Recent years have seen a "*machiya* boom" as a new generation has come to appreciate them, and several have now been converted into trendy restaurants. These include Asian "ethnic fusion", as well as authentic European cuisine.

Culinary Capital

Few places in the world can claim as sophisticated a food culture as Japan. The traditional cuisine is nutritious as well as tasty, which helps explain why the Japanese are the longest-living people on earth. I have heard Tokyoites complain of not being able to find Japanese food among the plethora of foreign restaurants. Not so in Kyoto, which offers a rich variety of Japanese fare. It is said that as you move northwards in Japan, the soya sauce gets saltier and the saké gets sweeter. For connoisseurs, the Kyoto balance is just right, and the city's food has been claimed as the best in the country.

Kyoryori (Kyoto food) is known in particular for the quality of its vegetables and soybean products, thanks to the fertile soil and free-flowing waters. The city's "famous products" of tofu (soya bean curd) and *yuba* (skimmed tofu) originated in China and were introduced following the adoption of Buddhism. Rich in protein and low in calories, they suit the Japanese inclination towards light and healthy food. *Yudofu* (boiled tofu) is a Kyoto speciality, though I find it hardly compares with the creamy *oboro tofu* (literally "hazy tofu") which is so delicious that it makes ordinary tofu seem tasteless.

The soybean products play an important part in *shojin ryori*, which originated in Buddhist monasteries. It makes no use of meat, fish or eggs, out of compassion for animals. The food is associated with the city's large Zen temples, and in keeping with the tradition it is simple but pleasing. Care is taken not to waste anything, and boiled vegetables form the base together with rice, pickles, and soup. This is accompanied by dishes such as sesame tofu, *konnyaku* (rum root), edible wild plants like fern, and a Kyoto speciality called *fu* (wheat gluten). The latter has a chewy texture and can be prepared in a number of ways, with millet or mugwort added. A popular way of serving it is with *miso* (soya bean paste), so healthy and tasty that ancient Japanese considered it "a gift of the gods".

After the Middle Ages, *shojin ryori* spread from temple kitchens into ordinary Kyoto households, where it was augmented by other food such as eel pudding and shrimp balls. The result was *obanzai*, small dishes of food put together to make a balanced meal. A pattern emerged in Edo times of eating certain dishes on set days. The first of the month was for *kombumaki* (fish rolled in kelp and cooked in broth). On days with the number eight in the date *arame* seaweed was eaten with fried tofu, and the end of the month meant *okara* (bean curd lees cooked with vegetables).

In Maruyama Park restaurants cater to tourists wishing to sample Kyoto food, and one popular item is a kind of dried cod stew, known as *imobo*. The dish dates back to the late seventeenth century, when cod from Hokkaido was brought to Kyoto for the emperor. One of the chefs thought the preserved fish would go well with a type of potato (*ebiimo*) which originated from Kyushu. The dish thus united the two ends of the realm. It is prepared by soaking the dried cod till soft, then stewing it for a day with seasoning. When the twentieth-century novelist Yoshikawa Eiji came to try it, he praised it for having "a taste enriched by centuries".

A particularly eye-catching item in the local cuisine is *wagashi* (Japanese confectionary), in which Kyoto excels. The tradition stretches back to the Nara Era, and covers a variety of subtypes with their own distinctive style and ingredients. Some are little works of art and are sold in shops which may themselves have a long history (at least forty of them have been in business for over a hundred years). Many of the confectionaries are made with *anko*, a paste of azuki bean and sugar. Over this is stretched a dough of flour and starch, which is shaped, coloured and textured to reflect seasonal images. Some bear lyrical names, with literary or artistic references. They are not as sweet as Western cakes, nor do they contain animal fat, while the fresh ingredients lend them a delicate fragrance. *Matsu no yuki* (Pine Snow) has crushed white sugary pieces over a green base to represent snow on pine trees. *Sakuramochi*, my own favourite, is a spring creation wrapped in an edible pickled cherry leaf.

But of all the food associated with Kyoto, the most celebrated is called *kaiseki*. A typical meal consists of eleven courses of small but exquisite dishes, designed to delight the eye as well as the taste buds. The food developed out of gatherings of aristocrats, who wished for a more lavish banquet than that offered by the tea ceremony. It thus combines traditional aesthetics with sumptuous excellence. Only the freshest of seasonal ingredients are used, with minimal use of seasoning. Colour harmony, contrasting shapes, and the use of empty space are important in the presentation. Crockery is carefully chosen for its visual appeal, with perhaps a leaf or flower as decoration.

The contents and order of the meal are part of the chef's art, though for the most part there is an appetizer, a clear soup, slices of raw fish, something to "clean the palate", something grilled, something boiled, something steamed, something in vinegar, and a final dish. This is rounded off with rice, soup and pickles. Food items are served in odd-numbered groups, and banquets comprise seven, nine, or eleven courses depending on the occasion. For those unable to cope with the volume or the price (meals can exceed $200 per person), there are mini-*kaiseki* courses costing around $40. Pay that, and you can savour dishes such as lily root with grated mountain potato, raw fish morsels set on a bamboo leaf, a spoonful of tofu wrapped in spinach, or fried vegetables dipped in salt mixed with ground tea leaf.

To enjoy *kaiseki* food in this way in a traditional dining room is to experience Kyoto at its very best. Seated on *tatami* overlooking an enclosed garden, you have the sense of enjoying something much more than just a meal. The result is not just a satisfied stomach, but an appreciation of the aesthetic heritage of a remarkable city. It may well prompt a toast to what Donald Keene has called "the magic of Kyoto". Over 1200 years have gone into the preparation, and it is worth savouring every mouthful.

Further Reading

Guides

Clancy, Judith, *Exploring Kyoto: On Foot through the Ancient Capital.* New York: Weatherhill, 1997.

Durston, Diana, *Old Kyoto, A Guide to Traditional Shops and Inns.* Tokyo: Kodansha, 1986.

Einarsen, John, *Zen and Kyoto.* Japan: Uniplan, 2004.

JTB, *Must-See in Kyoto.* Japan: JTB, 1985.

Lonely Planet, *Kyoto.* Australia: Lonely Planet, 1999.

Martin, John H. and Phyllis G., *Kyoto, A Cultural Guide to Japan's Ancient Imperial City.* Tokyo: Tuttle, 1994.

Mosher, Gouveneur, *Kyoto: A Contemplative Guide.* Tokyo: Tuttle, 1964.

Plutschow, Herbert E., *Introducing Kyoto.* Tokyo: Kodansha, 1979.

Treib, Marc and Ron Herman, *A Guide to the Gardens of Kyoto.* Japan: Shufunotomo, 1980.

Others

Addis, Stephen, *How to Look at Japanese Art.* New York: Abrams, 1996.

Delay, Nelly, *The Art and Culture of Japan.* New York: Abrams, 1999.

Golden, Arthur, *Memoirs of a Geisha.* New York: Vintage, 1997.

Hirshfield, Jane, *The Ink Dark Moon: Love Poems by Ono no Komachi and Izumi Shikibu.* New York: Vintage, 1990.

Iwasaki, Mineko, *Geisha, A Life.* London: Simon and Schuster, 2002.

Iyer, Pico, *The Lady and the Monk: Four Seasons in Kyoto.* London: Black Swan, 1991.

Kamo-no-Chomei, *Hojoki, Visions of a Torn World.* New York: Stone Bridge, 1996.

Kawabata, Yasunari, *The Old Capital.* New York: North Point, 1962.

Kawashiwahara, Yusen and Koyu Sonoda, *Shapers of Japanese Buddhism.* Tokyo: Kosei, 1994.

Keane, Marc, *Japanese Garden Design.* Tokyo: Tuttle, 1996.

Keene, Donald, ed., *Anthology of Japanese Literature.* New York: Grove Press, 1955.

Kerr, Alex, *Lost Japan.* Australia: Lonely Planet, 1996.

McCullough, Helen, *The Tale of the Heike*. Palo Alto CA: Stanford University Press, 1988.

Mishima, Yukio, *The Temple of the Golden Pavilion*. New York: Knopf, 1959.

Morris, Ivan, *The World of the Shining Prince: Court Life in Ancient Japan*. Tokyo: Kodansha, 1994.

Murasaki Shikibu, *The Tale of Genji*. Mineola NY: Dover, 2000.

Okakura, Kakuzo, *The Book of Tea*. Tokyo: Tuttle, 2000.

Richie, Donald, *A Hundred Years of Japanese Film*. Tokyo: Kodansha, 2001.

Saikaku, Ihara, *The Life of an Amorous Man*. North Clarendon VT: Tuttle, 1963

Shonagon, Sei, *The Pillow Book of Sei Shonagon*. Harmondsworth: Penguin, 1971.

Suzuki, D. T., *Zen and Japanese Culture*. Tokyo: Tuttle, 1998.

Tanizaki, Junichiro, *In Praise of Shadows*. Trans. Thomas J. Harper and Edward G. Seidensticker. London: Jonathan Cape, 1999.

Tanizaki, Junichiro, *The Key*. New York: Knopf, 1960/Tuttle, 1971.

Tyler, Royall, *Japanese Noh Plays*. Harmondsworth: Penguin, 1992

Stanley-Baker, Joan, *Japanese Art*. London: Thames and Hudson, 1974.

Varley, Paul, *Japanese Culture*. Honolulu: University of Hawaii Press, 2000.

Yoshida, Kenko, *Essays in Idleness*. London: Wordsworth, 1998.

Yusa, Michiko, *Japanese Religions*. London: Routledge, 2002.

GLOSSARY

ajari	Tendai title awarded to those who complete the background scenery integrated into garden composition 1000 Day Austerity Course
Aoi festival	Parade in May, dating back to eighth century
Biwako	Large lake to the north-east of Kyoto, forty miles long borrowed scenery
chaji	Formal tea ceremony with banquet lasting about four hours
chakai	A gathering to partake of green tea served by a host
Confucianism	A code of conduct emphasizing social virtue introduced in the sixth century
daimyo	A title given to lords governing large territories
Daruma	Japanese name for Bodhidharma, the founder of Zen
dengaku	Dances and shows to entertain the kami, considered the predecessor of Noh
Esotericism	Teaching to reveal hidden truths to the initiated
fusuma	Sliding partition between rooms, made of wood and paper
gagaku	Serene music imported in the ninth century, played at court and for Shinto
gaijin	Japanese word for foreigner, applied to Westerners
Gion festival	Month-long series of events in July
haibun	A type of essay woven around haiku
haiga	Artwork accompanying a haiku
haiku	A short poem of seventeen syllables arranged in a five-seven-five pattern
hakama	Outer garment with skirt-like pants worn by both sexes
hara-kiri	ritual disembowelment (usually called *seppuku*)
ikebana	Japanese style of flower-arranging
Ikenobo	Oldest ikebana school, founded by Ikenobo Senke
Jidai Matsuri	Parade on October 22 to celebrate the city's foundation
Jodo Shinshu	True Pure Land Sect founded by Shinran (1173-1263)
Jodo-shu	Pure Land Sect founded by Honen (1133-1212)
Kabuki	A form of drama with elaborate costumes begun in 1603
kaiseki	Banquet of small dishes originally for the tea ceremony
kami	Shinto spirits or deities
kana	Japanese phonetic writing, namely hiragana and katakana
Kano	Family school of artists between the fifteenth and nineteenth centuries
Kansai	Area in western Honshu including Osaka, Nara and Kyoto

Kanto	Area in eastern Honshu around present-day Tokyo
karesansui	Dry landscape gardening, in which water is represented by pebbles and rocks
koan	Zen riddle designed to further spiritual development
Kodo	The Way of Incense, intended to further self-perfection
kyoyaki	Pottery made in Kyoto, beginning in the 1650s
literati	Those who devote themselves to literature and the arts
maccha	Green tea powder used for the tea ceremony
machiya	Wooden shop-residence with latticed windows and narrow frontage
maiko	A trainee geisha, usually a teenager
mandala	Symbolic representation of the universe used in Buddhism
manga	Illustrated comics intended for adults as well as children
mappo	Buddhist period of degeneration thought to begin in 1052
miyabi	An aesthetic of refined beauty, in taste as in manners
miyako	A word meaning "capital" used to refer to Kyoto
mono no aware	A sense of pathos about life's inherent sadness
mujokan	A sense of the transient nature of worldly things
nembutsu	A mantra calling on Amida—*Namu Amida Butsu*
Noh	Drama form with masks originating in 1374
nyorai	Supreme Buddhas who have attained nirvana
Obaku	A Zen sect brought from China in the seventeenth century
ochaya	Teahouse where geisha entertain guests
okiya	Boarding house for geisha where *maiko* are trained
Onmyodo	The Way of Yin-Yang, derived from Taoist divination
onnagata	Female impersonators in Kabuki
raigo	Descent of Amida from the Western Pure Land
Raku	Type of pottery developed in late sixteenth century by Chojiro and Rikyu
renga	Poetic form of linked verse
Rimpa	School of decorative art in the seventeenth century
Rinzai	Zen sect founded by Linji (d.867) and introduced by Eisai
ronin/roshi	Masterless samurai who rented out their services
sanmon	Main gate of a Buddhist temple, often found inside the entrance gate
sarugaku	Ancient dance to entertain the kami
seiza	Way of sitting with legs folded under the bottom
seppuku	Ritual disembowelment (known more vulgarly as hara-kiri)
Shakasama	The historical Buddha (also known as Shakyamuni)
shamisen	three-stringed lute imported from China
shikibu	Rank of office in Heian administration

shinden zukuri	Architectural style used in palaces with raised buildings linked by corridors
Shingon	Sect introduced from China by Kukai in early Heian period
shite	Lead role in Noh around whom the play revolves
shoin zukuri	Domestic style of architecture with square pillars, alcove, *tatami* and *fusuma*
shoji	Paper window screens
Soto	Zen sect based on Ts'ao-tung school introduced by Dogen
suiboku-ga	Pictures done in China ink, sometimes with inscription
sumi-e	Chinese ink painting, usually monochrome
tabi	Type of Japanese white sock with split toe
Taoism	Doctrine of Lao-Tse about the great force (*tao*) flowing through life
tatami	Rectangular straw matting, usually six foot by three
tayu	Shimabara courtesan (equivalent of Edo's "oiran")
Tendai	Buddhist sect introduced by Saicho in early Heian era
tengu	Imaginary creature with red face and long nose
tokonoma	An alcove for wall-hanging often containing a vase
Uji	City to the south-east of Kyoto, famous for tea production
ukiyo-e	Literally, "pictures of the floating world": woodblock prints of the Edo era
wabi-sabi	An aesthetic of refined austerity which treasures naturalness
waka	Japanese verse, divided into *choka* (long) and *tanka* (short)
waki	The role of "side man" in Noh, who introduces the play
Way of Yin-Yang	A Taoist form of divination popular in the Heian era
yamabushi	A mountain ascetic who strives to develop spiritual powers
yamato-e	A native form of painting with strong colours
yugen	An aesthetic suggesting mystery, elegance and sadness
zuihitsu	A genre of writing that "follows the pen" by free association of ideas

KEY HISTORICAL DATES

Before 600   Kyoto area known as Yamashiro. The Kamo clan lived in the north. The Hata clan settled in the west and carried out flood control

538   Buddhism introduced to Japan

544   First Aoi Festival held; Kamigamo Shrine predates this

603   Koryu-ji founded

711   Fushimi Inari Shrine founded

Nara Era

711   Japan's first permanent capital established at Nara

784   Capital transferred to Nagaoka-kyo

788   Saicho erects a temple on Mount Hiei, afterwards head of the Tendai Sect

Heian Era

794   Heian-kyo founded by Emperor Kammu

798   Kiyomizu Temple founded

823   Kukai makes To-ji into a Shingon seminary

ninth century Court poems by Ono no Komachi and Ariwara no Narihira, etc.

876   Gion Festival first held

894   Chinese missions abolished on advice of Sugawara no Michizane

905   Ki no Tsurayuki compiles *Kokinwakashu*

947   Kitano Shrine built to honour Michizane

c. 1000   Golden Age of Fujiwara no Michinaga, *Genji Monogatari* and *The Pillow Book*

1053   Byodoin established by the son of Michinaga

1156   The Hogen Revolt shows the power of samurai

1159   The Heiji Revolt brings Taira no Kiyomori to power

1162   Sanjusangendo built for Go-Shirakawa

c. 1174   Yoshitsune fights Benkei on Gojo Bridge

1175   Honen breaks from Tendai to start the Pure Land Sect

1185   Battle of Dan no Ura, in which the Genji defeat the Heike

Kamakura Era

1192   Minamoto no Yoritomo establishes power at Kamakura

1201   Shinran becomes a disciple of Honen

1202	Eisai founds a Zen community at Kennin-ji
1205	Imperial anthology *Shinkokinshu* compiled
1212	Kamo no Chomei writes *Hojoki* (Account of a Ten-Foot Square Hut)
c. 1215	*The Tale of the Heike* formulated and handed down
1331	Yoshida Kenko writes *Tsurezuregusa* (Essays in Idleness)
1333	Ashikaga Takauji returns power to Kyoto

Muromachi Era

1339	Godaigo sets up "the Southern Court" at Yoshino
1342	Tenryu-ji completed by Ashikaga Takauji and Muso Soseki
1374	Noh initiated by Kan'ami's performance for Yoshimitsu
1397	Yoshimitsu builds Kinkaku-ji (Temple of the Golden Pavilion)
1467-77	Onin War devastates Kyoto
1481	Ikkyu dies after having helped restore Daitoku-ji
1482	Ashikaga Yoshimasa establishes Ginkaku-ji (Silver Pavilion)
1551	Francis Xavier becomes the first foreigner to visit Kyoto
1571	Nobunaga razes Mount Hiei
1573	Nobunaga seizes power from Ashikaga Yoshiaki

Azuchi-Momoyama

1579	Raku pottery started by Chojiro under guidance of Rikyu
1582	Nobunaga killed at Honno-ji; Hideyoshi assumes power
1587	Great Kitano Tea Party
1585-91	Remodelling of Kyoto
1591	Sen no Rikyu commits suicide
1594	Construction of Fushimi Castle
1600	Battle of Sekigahara. Tokugawa Ieyasu removes power to Edo

Edo Era

1603	Izumo no Okuni starts Kabuki on the Kamo riverbed
c. 1603	Rimpa School started by Koetsu and Sotatsu
1603	Nijo Castle founded
1611	Suminokura Ryoi builds Takase Canal
1620	Katsura Imperial Villa started
1626	Nijo Castle garden by Kobori Enshu, palace painted by Kano Tanyu
1639	Beginning of Japan's isolationism
1640	Shimabara pleasure quarters established
1641	Shisendo built by Ishikawa Jozan

1646	Ura Senke and Omote Senke founded
1650s	First guidebooks of Kyoto
1659	Shugakuin Villa built by Go-Mizunoo
1680s	Yuzen dyeing invented; Ogata brothers active in the arts
1682	Saikaku Iharu's *Life of an Amorous Man*
1686	Basho writes *Saga Diary* in Rakushisha
1700-02	Oishi Kuranosuke plots revenge of the 47 Ronin
1750s	Geisha profession first mentioned
1760s	Buson and Ike no Taiga active in the arts
1864	Ikedeya Incident involving the Shinsengumi
1867	Tokugawa Yoshinobu resigns in Nijo Castle
1867	Ryoma Sakamoto assassinated in merchant's shop

Mejii Era

1868	Emperor Meiji moves residence from Kyoto to Tokyo
1869	First primary school in Japan opened
1872	Start of geisha spectacles, Miyako and Kamogawa Odori
1877	Kyoto linked by rail to Kobe
1890	Lake Biwa canal completed
1894-95	1100th anniversary; Heian Shrine built and Jidai Matsuri

Taisho Era

1923	Great Kanto Earthquake and relocation of film studios to Kyoto

Showa Era

1928	Start of city's bus service
1950	Golden Pavilion burnt down
1951-54	Kurosawa and Mizoguchi produce film masterpieces
1956	Tanizaki's *The Key* and Mishima's *Kinkaku-ji* (Temple of the Golden Pavilion)
1961-62	Kawabata's *The Old Capital*
1964	Kyoto Tower built to coincide with the Tokyo Olympics
1981	Opening of subway line

Heisei Era

1994	1200th anniversary; construction of 17-floor Kyoto Hotel
1997	Kyoto Protocol proposed at forum meeting
1997	Construction of 230-foot high railway station

INDEX OF CULTURAL & HISTORICAL NAMES

Abe no Seimei 18-19
ajari 43-45
Akechi Mitshuhide 111
Akutagawa Ryunosuke 207
Amida 39, 40, 48-59
Anraku 55
Aoi Festival 29
Ariwara no Narihira 14, 15-17
Asai Ryoi 154
Ashikaga shoguns 75, 81-85, 129, 167
Ashikaga Yoshimasa 82, 83-85
Ashikiga Yoshimitsu 82, 86, 97, 98, 99

Basho, Matsuo 69, 152, 156-60
Benkei 64, 65
Boshin War 170
Buson, Yosa 159-60, 179
chojugiga (Animal Caricatures) 38
Confucianism 3, 8, 143, 154, 160, 167

Daigo, Emperor 9
Daruma 89
Dogen 41
Dokyo 2

Eikan 52
Eisai 41, 77, 128, 142
Essays in Idleness 73-75
Esoteric Buddhism 40, 46

Forty-Seven Ronin 180-81, 186
Fujiwara family 9, 11, 63, 71
Fujiwara no Michinaga 11, 29, 31, 49, 51

Furuta Oribe 139

Genji clan 60-67, 69
Genji, Hikaru 7, 22, 25, 31-35
Genroku 152-53, 155, 162
Genshin 49, 50
Gion Festival 123, 216, 221
Go-Daigo, Emperor 81-82
Gofukakusa, Emperor 36
Go-Komatsu, Emperor 86
Golden, Arthur 191, 193
Go-Mizunoo, Emperor 149-50, 160
Go-Shirakawa, Emperor 52, 64, 66-67
Gossamer Years 25
Gozan temples 81
Great Kanto Earthquake 203, 208, 211

haiku 13, 156-59
hara-kiri (see also *seppuku*) 168, 193, 216
Hasegawa Tohoku 121
Hashimoto Kansetsu 201
Hata clan 2
Hearn, Lafcadio 59
Heike clan 60-67, 69, 73
Hideyoshi (see Toyotomi Hideyoshi)
Hijikata Toshizo 168, 70, 171
Hiroshige 144, 157, 211
Honami Koetsu 151, 179
Honen 41, 54-57

Ichiji, Emperor 20
Ichikawa Kon 215-16

Ieyasu (see Tokugawa Ieyasu)
ikebana 5, 74, 221
Ike no Taiga 161
Ikkyu Sojun 85-88, 128
Ikumatsu 181
Inabata Katsutaro 204
Ingen Ryuki 78, 161
Inoue Yachiyo 185
Ishikawa Jozan 160
Iwasaki Mineko 184, 189, 193-94
Iyer, Pico 218
Izumi Shikibu 22, 24, 28-30, 31
Izumo no Okuni 153-54

Jidai Matsuri (Festival of Ages) 200, 221
Jien 41
Jizo 39
Jocho 50, 53
Josetsu 90
Juko (see Murata Shuko)

Kabuki 153-54, 181, 205
Kaempfer, Engelbert 162
Kaiho Yusho 121
kaiseki 130, 152, 224
kami 11, 37
Kammu 1-5, 40, 41, 200
Kamo clan 2
Kamo no Chomei 70, 71-73
Kan'ami 97
Kannon 39, 40, 50, 52-53
Kano Eitoku 119-20
Kano Masanobu 91, 119
Kano Motonobu 91
Kano School 91, 119-120, 122, 152
Kano Tanyu 120, 145
Kawabata Yasunari 7, 31, 210, 216-18
Kawai Kanjiro 201-202

Kenreimon'in 66-67
Kenzan (see Ogata Kenzan)
Ki no Tsurayuki 12, 13, 20, 30, 149
Kiso no Yoshinaka 64, 159
Kobori Enshu 138, 149
Koetsu (see Honami Koetsu)
Kokinshu 12-14
Komachi (see Ono no Komachi)
Komei, Emperor 168, 200
Kondo Isami 168, 170, 171
Korin (see Ogata Korin)
Kukai 46-47
Kurosawa Akira 4, 205, 206-208, 209, 210
Kuya 49, 54
Kyogen 105-108
Kyo-yaki 141-2

Literati 160

machiya 164-65, 222
Makino Shozo 204-205
manga 11
mappo 49
Maruyama Okyo 179
Meiji, Emperor 171, 197
Michinaga (see Fujiwara no Michinaga)
Michizane (see Sugawara no Michizane)
Minamoto no Yoritomo 61, 64, 65, 70, 71, 77
Minamoto no Yoshitsune 61, 63-66
Miroku 39
Mitsui Takatoshi 166
miyabi 21
Mishima, Yukio 82, 210, 214-16
Miyamoto Musashi 146-47, 179
Mizoguchi, Kenji 42, 192, 208-10

mono no aware 33, 209, 218
Motoori Norinaga 33, 167
mujokan 14
Murasaki Shikibu 22-23, 30-36,
    49, 200
Murata Shuko 128-129
Mushanokoji 132, 136
Muso Soseki 81, 92

nembutsu 49, 51, 54, 55-57, 66,
    78
Nichiren 41, 42, 209
Niijima Jo 199
Nijo, Lady 36
Nikkatsu studios 205, 208
Noami 128
Nobunaga (see Oda Nobunaga)
Noh 14, 15, 16, 18, 30, 34, 60,
    65, 66, 83, 96-108, 116, 185

Obaku sect 77
Oda Nobunaga 42, 109-112
Ogata Kenzan 151-53
Ogata Korin 151-52
Ogawa Jihei 200-201
Oishi Kuranosuke 180
Okita Soji 169, 170, 171
Okochi Denjiro 206
Okuni (see Izumo no Okuni)
Omotesenke 132, 136
Onin War 83, 88, 91, 92, 109,
    122
Onmyodo 18
Onoe Matsunosuke 204
Ono no Komachi 14-15, 30, 194
Oshima Nagisa 171
Ozu Yasujiro 208

Perry, Commodore 167
Pillow Book 6, 26-28,
Pure Land Sect (Jodo Shu) 54-57

raigo 51-52
Raijin and Fujin 53, 151
Rai Sanyo 5, 167
Rakuchu rakugai zu 122
Raku pottery 141, 165
Rashomon 4, 207-08
Rikyu (see Sen no Rikyu)
Rimpa School 150-53
Rinzai Zen 77
Ryoma (see Sakamoto Ryoma)

sabi 68
Saga, Emperor 20
Saicho 41, 46
Saigyo 67-69, 70, 157
Saikaku Iharu 152, 155-56, 177,
    178, 209, 213
Sakamoto Ryoma 169-71, 179
Sarashina Diary 34
Sei Shonagon 6, 20, 23, 24, 26-28,
    74
Sen no Rikyu 129-33, 134, 135,
    140, 155
seppuku (ritual suicide) 65, 111,
    132
Serizawa Kamo 168, 179
Sesshu Toyo 90-91, 155
Shiba Ryotaro 170, 171
shinden zukuri 26
Shindo Kaneto 192
Shingon 40, 46-48, 56, 68
Shinkokinshu 70
Shinran 41, 57-59
Shinsengumi 168-69, 170-71
Shinto 26, 37, 38, 39, 40, 42, 48,
    99, 134, 188, 199
Shirakawa, Emperor 41
Shotoku, Prince 13, 37, 39
Shubun 90
Soami 93, 128
Sotatsu (see Tawaraya Sotatsu)

Soto Zen 78, 99
Stimson, Henry 202
Sugawara no Michizane 9-11
Suminokura Ryoi 162
Suzuki, D. T. 76, 78

Taira no Kiyomori 61-63, 64
Takauji, Ashikaga 82
Takayama Hikokuro 166
Takeno Joo 129
Tale of Genji 7, 22, 25, 26, 30-36,
    151, 155, 213
Tale of the Heike 60-67, 100
Tales of Ise 15, 16, 151, 152
Tanabe Sakuro 198
Tanizaki Junichiro 5, 189, 190,
    210-213
Tankei 53, 54
Taoism 19, 77, 79, 92, 94, 126
Tawaraya Sotatsu 151
tayu 177-179
Teika, Fujiwara no 70
Tendai 40-45, 46, 54-6
tengu 64
Tenjin 10, 19
Toei Movie Land 206
Tokaido 144
Tokugawa Ieyasu 109, 117, 144,
    177
Tokugawa shogunate 143, 145,
    149, 155, 161, 167-72
Tokugawa Yoshinobu 169-70
Tosa Diary 20
Tosa School 120-21, 152
Toyotomi Hideyoshi 104, 111,
    112-117, 129-132, 177

Toyotomi Hideyori 116
True Pure Land Sect (Jodo
    Shinshu) 57-59

ukiyo-e 123, 143, 152, 163, 178,
    186, 200
Ungoku Togan 121
Unkei 53, 54
Urasenke 132, 136, 165

wabi 83, 129, 131
wabi-sabi 130
waka 13, 28
Waley, Arthur 31, 35

Xavier, Francis 109

yamato-e 120, 121, 151
yin-yang 18, 126, 217
Yoritomo (see Minamoto no
    Yoritomo)
Yoshida Kenko 73-75
Yoshimasa (see Ashikaga
    Yoshimasa)
Yoshimitsu (see Ashikiga
    Yoshimitsu)
Yoshitsune (see Minamoto no
    Yoshitsune)
yugen 70
Yuzen 162

Zeami 16, 66, 68, 98-100
Zen 56, 59, 76-95, 99, 100, 127,
    129, 199, 214

INDEX OF PLACES AND LANDMARKS

Adashino Nembutsu-ji 22
Atago, Mount 7, 40
Arashiyama 81, 212

Biwako Canal 198, 201
Biwa, Lake 3, 7, 86, 156, 157, 198
Byodo-in 50-51, 53
Chion-in 51, 56
China 3, 9, 10, 14, 18, 41, 46, 49, 78, 91, 93, 112, 128, 140, 179, 197, 223
Chishaku-in 47, 121

Daigo-ji 115
Daikaku-ji 78, 79, 87, 88, 93, 129, 132, 135, 146
Daimonji 7, 38
Daishogun-hachi Shrine 19
Dan-no-ura 64, 66
Doshisha University 199

Edo (now Tokyo) 143-44, 153, 156, 161, 166, 176, 180
Eikando 52
Enryaku-ji 41, 42-43, 64
Former Imperial Palace (see Gosho)
Fushimi Inari 2
Fushimi Momoyama 114, 120

Ginkaku-ji (see Silver Pavilion)
Gion 181, 183, 184, 185, 186-190, 192, 194, 217
Golden Pavilion, or Temple 82-84, 98, 214
Gosho (Former Imperial Palace) 8, 148, 168, 198, 217

Hakusanso 201
Heian Shrine 1, 8, 9, 96, 136, 200, 212
Hiei, Mount 3, 7, 40, 41, 42-45, 49, 54, 77, 110, 157
Higashi Hongan-ji 58, 59
Hoko-ji 114, 116
Hokoku Shrine 116
Honen-in 213
Honno-ji 111

Ichiriki 181, 187
Ikedeya 168-69, 181

Jakko-in 66-67
Jingo-ji 71
Josho-ji 179
Jurin-ji 17

Kamakura 64, 81
Kamishichiken 183
Kamo River 42, 58, 83, 162, 167, 183
Katsura 2, 67, 137, 148-49
Kegon-ji 222
Kenkun Shrine 111
Kennin-ji 77, 81, 86, 190
Kinkaku-ji (see Golden Pavilion)
Kitano Tenmangu Shrine 10-11, 19, 38, 131, 154, 183, 222
Kodai-ji 137, 163
Kompuku-ji 159
Konchi-in 121, 138
Korea 1, 2, 37, 39, 112, 115, 197
Koryu-ji 2, 39
Koya, Mount 46, 68
Kozan-ji 129
Kurama 40, 63-64, 222

Kyoto National Museum 199
Kyoto Tower 219

Manpaku-ji 78, 161
Maruyama Park 69, 201, 224
Matsuo Shrine 2, 7
Mibu Temple 107, 168
Miyagawa-cho 183
Murin-an 201
Myoshin-ji 78. 79. 160

Nagaoka 2
Nanzen-ji 78. 81, 89, 198
Nara 1, 2, 4, 42
Narabigaoka 73, 75
Nijo Castle 144-46, 148
Nijo Jinya, or Inn 147
Ninna-ji 74
Nishi Hongan-ji 58, 118, 177
Nishijin 165-66, 183, 192, 196,
    204, 220

Ohara 66
Osaka 5, 7, 8, 87, 113, 155, 158,
    159, 176, 203

Philosopher's Walk 199
Pontocho 181, 183

Rokkaku-do 57
Rokuharamitsu-ji 54
Ryoan-ji 93

Saiho-ji 92
Sai-ji 4
Sanjusangendo 52, 222

Sanzen-in 50, 51
Seiryo-ji 108
Sekizan Zenin 38
Sennyu-ji 52
Shimabara 176-80, 181
Shimogamo 2, 71
Shinsen-en 4
Shisendo 160
Shoji-ji 67-68, 69
Shokoku-ji 78, 79. 81, 82, 90, 199
Shugakuin Villa 149-50, 217
Silver Pavilion, or Temple 83-85,
    129
Suzaku-oji 34

Takase Canal 162, 217
Tenryu-ji 78, 81, 92
Teradaya 169
Tofuku-ji 78, 79, 81, 89
To-ji 4, 46, 47, 147, 155, 222
Toji-in 81, 167
Tokyo (see also Edo) 62, 173, 182,
    193, 197, 199, 203, 204, 205,
    213, 215, 223

Uji 31, 35, 50, 51, 78, 144, 178
Uzumasa 2, 205

Yasaka Shrine 123, 183, 184
Yoshida Shrine 75
Yoshino 82

Zuishin-in 15